FOLLOWING

THE

MONEY

U.S. Finance in the World Economy

ANNE Y. KESTER

and

PANEL ON INTERNATIONAL CAPITAL TRANSACTIONS

Committee on National Statistics
Commission on Behavioral and Social Sciences and Education
National Research Council

NATIONAL ACADEMY PRESS
Washington, D.C.   1995

National Academy Press • 2101 Constitution Avenue, NW • Washington, DC 20418

NOTICE: The project that is the subject of this report was approved by the Governing Board of the National Research Council, whose members are drawn from the councils of the National Academy of Sciences, the National Academy of Engineering, and the Institute of Medicine. The members of the committee responsible for the report were chosen for their special competences and with regard for appropriate balance.

This report has been reviewed by a group other than the authors according to procedures approved by a Report Review Committee consisting of members of the National Academy of Sciences, the National Academy of Engineering, and the Institute of Medicine.

This project was supported by funds from the Bureau of Economic Analysis of the U.S. Department of Commerce, the Federal Reserve Board, and the U.S. Department of State.

Library of Congress Cataloging-in-Publication Data

Kester, Annie Y.
    Following the money : U.S. finance in the world economy / Anne Y.
Kester and Panel on International Capital Transactions, Committee on
National Statistics, Commission on Behavioral and Social Sciences
and Education, National Research Council.
       p. cm.
    Includes bibliographical references and index.
    ISBN 0-309-04883-4
    1. Financial services industry—United States. 2. Capital
movements—Data processing. 3. Automatic data collection systems.
I. National Research Council (U.S.). Panel on International Capital
Transactions. II. Title.
HG181.K42 1994
332.1'0973—dc20   95-32043
                                                            CIP

PANEL ON INTERNATIONAL CAPITAL TRANSACTIONS

SAM Y. CROSS *(Chair)*, School of International and Public
Affairs, Columbia University, New York
STEPHEN H. AXILROD, Nikko Securities International, Inc.,
New York
RICHARD N. COOPER, Department of Economics, Harvard
University
DAVID T. DEVLIN, Citibank, New York
RIMMER DE VRIES, Morgan Guaranty Trust Co., New York
JEFFREY A. FRANKEL, Department of Economics, University of
California, Berkeley
EDWARD I. GEORGE, Department of Management Science and
Information Systems, University of Texas, Austin
JOHN G. HEIMANN, Merrill Lynch and Co., New York
PETER B. KENEN, Department of Economics, Princeton
University
LAWRENCE R. KLEIN, Department of Economics, University of
Pennsylvania, Philadelphia
SAMUEL PIZER, Consultant, Washington, D.C.
ROBERT SOLOMON, Brookings Institution, Washington, D.C.
J. MICHAEL STEELE, Statistics Department, University of
Pennsylvania
NANCY H. TEETERS, IBM Corporation, Armonk, New York
(retired)
LAWRENCE A. THIBODEAU, Price Waterhouse, Washington,
D.C.
H. DAVID WILLEY, Morgan Stanley & Co., New York

ANNE Y. KESTER, *Study Director*
COURTENAY SLATER, *Consultant*
ROBERT F. GEMMILL, *Technical Adviser*
ROBERT L. SAMMONS, *Technical Adviser*
CANDICE S. EVANS, *Project Assistant*
ELIZABETH M. HUFFMAN, *Project Assistant*

Contents

Preface

This report on international capital transactions is the second from the Committee on National Statistics that considers issues of the U.S. economy in a global context. The first report, *Behind the Numbers: U.S. Trade in the World Economy* (Kester, 1992) resulted from a study undertaken in response to a recommendation by the Working Group on the Quality of Economic Statistics of the President's Economy Policy Council. That report assessed the adequacy of and recommended improvements for data on U.S. merchandise trade and international transactions in services. The report also noted the lack of information about international capital transactions and stressed that a fuller understanding of the U.S. position in the world economy could not be obtained without that information.

In response to that finding and with funds provided by the Bureau of Economic Analysis of the U.S. Department of Commerce, the committee in 1992 convened the Panel on International Capital Transactions to analyze what data are available and recommend improvements. Subsequent grants were received from the Federal Reserve Board and the U.S. Department of State.

Many people contributed to this report. First and foremost, of course, are the members of the panel. They worked hard to come to agreement on a wide-ranging set of recommendations to improve the nation's data on international capital transactions, although individual panel members may not necessarily agree with all of the analyses or discussions in the report.

The study would not have been possible without the unstinting efforts of Dr. Anne Y. Kester. Dr. Kester served as study director for the first panel on U.S. merchandise trade and international services and in a similar capacity for the Panel on International Capital Transactions. Dr. Kester deserves special recognition for developing the study, drafting the report, and contributing many of its original ideas. The committee joins the panel in expressing gratitude and appreciation for her outstanding work.

As time went on, the report had to be revised in order to incorporate many sets of new figures from BEA, acknowledge changes in some agency programs, and otherwise bring the report up to date. We asked Courtenay Slater, former chief economist in the Department of Commerce and a former member of the Committee on National Statistics, to help us. Thanks to her extensive assistance and hard work, the report has remained current. Additionally, John Kambhu, a research officer and senior economist at the Federal Reserve Bank of New York, provided much needed assistance in revising and strengthening our chapter on financial derivatives. We are indebted to him for his careful work.

In addition to the panel, staff, and consultants, many people contributed to the study by providing the panel with information and insights. We thank Robert Gemmill and Robert Sammons, who served as technical advisers; Christopher Bach, Betty Barker, Carol Carson, Anthony Dillulo, Steven Landefeld, Ann Lawson, Bill McCormick, Louis Moczar, and Allan Young of the Bureau of Economic Analysis; Douglas Carpenter, Peter Hooper, Russell Krueger, Lawrence Promisel, Gail Smith, Lois Stekler, Guy V.G. Stevens, and Edwin Truman of the Federal Reserve Board; Michael C. Egan of the U.S. Department of State; Akbar Akhtar, Terry Melford, Susan Moore, Beth Schwartzberg, and Monica Szemple of the Federal Reserve Bank of New York; Bill Griever, Sidney Jones, Gary Lee, and Ashby McCown of the U.S. Department of the Treasury; Gail Haas, John Lee, and Norman Nelson of the New York Clearing House; P. A. Bull, Phil Davis, Charles Enoch, Robert Heath, David I. W. Locke, D. M. H. Pennington, Colin Pettigrew, and Chris Taylor of the Bank of England; Bruce Buckingham of the Central Statistical Office of the United Kingdom; Rudolf Seiler of the Deutsche Bundesbank; Shinichi Yoshikuni of the Bank of Japan; Jack Bame, John McLenaghan, Michael Mussa, and John Wilson of the International Monetary Fund; and many others including Linda Bergen, Derek Hargreaves, and Peter Hancock of J.P. Morgan, Edward Bernstein, and Ralph C. Bryant of the Brookings Institution, Michael Boskin of the Council of Economic Advisors,

Jeffrey Carliner of the National Bureau of Economic Research, Robert DiClementi of Salomon Brothers, Inc., Bill Dobb of the International Swap Dealers Association, Ray Fitzgerald of Citicorp, Charles Taylor of the Group of Thirty, and the staff of the Financial Accounting Standards Board. We are also grateful to the many data users, filers, and compilers who responded to the panel's invitation for written comments.

The committee and panel also express their appreciation to Elizabeth M. Huffman for assisting the panel in so many ways, especially in the preparation of the manuscript for publication; to Candice S. Evans, who also assisted with the manuscript; and to Eugenia Grohman for editing and guiding the report through review and publication.

The committee thanks all of these people for what we believe is a major contribution to the statistical and policy issues in the rapidly evolving area of international capital transactions.

Burton H. Singer, *Chair*
Committee on National Statistics (1987-1993)

The National Academy of Sciences is a private, nonprofit, self-per-petuating society of distinguished scholars engaged in scientific and engi-neering research, dedicated to the furtherance of science and technology and to their use for the general welfare. Upon the authority of the charter granted to it by the Congress in 1863, the Academy has a man-date that requires it to advise the federal government on scientific and technical matters. Dr. Bruce Alberts is president of the National Acad-emy of Sciences.

The National Academy of Engineering was established in 1964, under the charter of the National Academy of Sciences, as a parallel organiza-tion of outstanding engineers. It is autonomous in its administration and in the selection of its members, sharing with the National Academy of Sciences the responsibility for advising the federal government. The National Academy of Engineering also sponsors engineering programs aimed at meeting national needs, encourages education and research, and recognizes the superior achievements of engineers. Dr. Harold Liebowitz is president of the National Academy of Engineering.

The Institute of Medicine was established in 1970 by the National Academy of Sciences to secure the services of eminent members of ap-propriate professions in the examination of policy matters pertaining to the health of the public. The Institute acts under the responsibility given to the National Academy of Sciences by its congressional charter to be an adviser to the federal government and, upon its own initiative, to identify issues of medical care, research, and education. Dr. Kenneth I. Shine is president of the Institute of Medicine.

The National Research Council was organized by the National Acad-emy of Sciences in 1916 to associate the broad community of science and technology with the Academy's purposes of furthering knowledge and advising the federal government. Functioning in accordance with general policies determined by the Academy, the Council has become the princi-pal operating agency of both the National Academy of Sciences and the National Academy of Engineering in providing services to the govern-ment, the public, and the scientific and engineering communities. The Council is administered jointly by both Academies and the Institute of Medicine. Dr. Bruce Alberts and Dr. Harold Liebowitz are chairman and vice chairman, respectively, of the National Research Council.

Summary

Over the past two decades, one of the most significant developments affecting the U.S. economy has been the enormous growth in international capital transactions—an increase that has far surpassed the increase in trade (goods and services) flows. This growth has resulted from liberalization and deregulation of world financial markets and technological innovations in telecommunications, as well as from revolutionary changes in the form and character of international financial transactions.

No longer are financial instruments confined to bank loans and deposits, stocks and bonds, and other traditional forms. Numerous financial products have emerged to meet new needs and preferences of individuals and institutions. At the same time, operations of major financial institutions increasingly have extended beyond national borders and are now carried out on a worldwide basis. Such changes in capital mobility, product innovation, and industry structure have transformed world financial markets and hastened the internationalization of the U.S. financial system.

In this new economic environment, public and private decision makers need relevant, accurate, and timely information on international capital transactions to analyze financial developments in the U.S. economy and to formulate policies arising from them. For example: How does capital mobility affect the functioning of U.S. monetary and fiscal policies? What is the effect on exchange

1

rates? What is the impact of the increased volume and complexity of financial transactions on the safety and soundness of the U.S. financial system? What is the extent of foreign ownership of U.S. industries, real estate, and other assets? How are the U.S. current account imbalances financed and how are they linked to the nation's savings and investment patterns? Is the external financing sustainable?

At a time when reliable data on U.S. international capital transactions have become more important, the developments in international financial markets have made it a more formidable task to collect such data. Although the United States produces as much detailed data on its capital flows as any country in the world, the explosion in such transactions since the early 1980s has outpaced improvements in the statistical systems that monitor them. The existing system for reporting U.S. capital transactions was originally designed some 50 years ago; it collects data primarily from large domestic financial intermediaries and other corporations, missing many new participants and new modes of transactions. There are both data gaps and major obstacles to tracking the many kinds of increasingly complex transactions that now occur.

With a recognition of these difficulties, as well as the budgetary constraints faced by statistical agencies in the public sector, the Panel on International Capital Transactions of the National Research Council convened in April 1992 to examine the new global financial environment, assess public and private needs for data on U.S. international capital transactions, review the adequacy of existing data, and explore alternative methods of data collection. The panel's goal has been to help ensure that the data collected are accurate, timely, relevant, cost-effective, and useful.

FINDINGS

Increased international capital mobility not only has led to growing linkages of world financial markets, but also has allowed the macroeconomic policies and market conditions of one country to significantly affect those of others. As world financial markets have become more closely linked, U.S. domestic financial conditions have increasingly become subject to external shocks and market pressures from other countries, and the liquidity and solvency of participants in one market have come at times to affect those in other markets. Meanwhile, the securitization of transactions and growth in derivative financial instruments have added new dimensions to the traditional process of intermediation, making international financial flows more complex and more difficult to characterize. These developments have complicated the formulation of U.S. monetary and fiscal policies and made it increasingly difficult to assess the stability and soundness of the U.S. financial system.

The unprecedented changes in world financial markets have also reduced the effectiveness of the traditional data collection methods and the adequacy of the data. The conceptual framework under which the existing data on U.S. international capital transactions are collected is that of the balance of payments, which defines international economic transactions as those between residents of the United States and nonresidents (foreigners), those outside U.S. boundaries. Under this framework, data are collected on economic exchanges that cross national borders between the United States and the rest of the world. These data provide vital information on the external sector of the economy and how it affects economic activity within the United States. International transactions, defined in this way, are a component of the national accounts (which include the national income and product accounts, the flow-of-funds accounts, and the balance sheets of the U.S. economy). However, as U.S. financial activities have become global in nature, cross-border financial exchanges increasingly represent capital transfers among worldwide offices and branches of U.S. financial institutions, not transactions between U.S. firms and foreign firms. There is also a growing presence of foreign-owned firms in U.S. domestic markets and of U.S.-owned firms in markets abroad. These developments have complicated identification of resident versus nonresident transactions. More important, internationalization of U.S. financial transactions has given rise to policy concerns about the liquidity, solvency, and stability of the U.S. financial system insofar as it is affected by foreign markets. These are issues that the balance-of-payments framework was not designed to treat. There is need to supplement the existing balance-of-payments data with other information on the international financial activities of U.S. and foreign institutions.

Existing international transactions data are also marred by measurement and collection problems and significant gaps. For example, the rise in nonbank market participants (in particular, institutional investors like pension funds, mutual funds, insurance companies, and other professional money managers), the surge in international financial flows and their diversification across currencies, the increase in offshore financial activities, and the burgeoning of international trading in derivative financial instruments (such as options, swaps, forwards, and futures on interest rates, foreign currencies, stocks, bonds, and commodities) have outstripped the coverage of the U.S. data system. The increased ability of domestic institutions to deal directly with their foreign counterparts through computer and telecommunications networks has put many of these transactions beyond the reach of the existing reporting system. Wide fluctuations in exchange rates and asset prices have also compounded the difficulty of determining the value of U.S. holdings of foreign assets and liabilities.

Existing U.S. international transactions data need both to be improved and to be supplemented with other information. Yet efforts intended to yield comprehensive information on the warp and woof of the full fabric of U.S. international capital transactions would be prohibitively costly both for the statistical agencies and for those who would have to supply the raw data. Thus, key recommendations in this report focus on streamlining existing statistical and regulatory reporting and using alternative financial databases to enhance the cost-effectiveness of the existing data collection system.

PUBLIC POLICY ISSUES ARISING FROM GLOBALIZATION

Increasingly, U.S. monetary and fiscal policy must take account of international financial developments. U.S. interest rates are influenced not just by the monetary policy decisions of the U.S. Federal Reserve system and domestic economic events. Official decisions made by monetary authorities abroad, as well as developments in international securities and foreign exchange markets, increasingly have an impact on U.S. interest rates. Meanwhile, it has become more difficult for the Federal Reserve to use monetary aggregates to monitor the relative tightness or slack in the U.S. monetary condition partly because substantial amounts of U.S. currency are held in Latin America, Asia, the Middle East, Africa, Europe, and, more recently, in the states of the former Soviet Union. There is now no accurate recording of international shipments of U.S. currency.

On issues of fiscal policy, the ability of institutional investors to move large pools of savings overseas in search of higher returns increases the uncertainty that tax and other measures will have their intended effects. Efforts to use tax incentives (such as, for example, more generous individual retirement account provisions) to boost domestic savings and generate increased capital for domestic investment may be seriously diluted by movement of funds abroad.

Similarly, the stability of the U.S. financial system cannot be adequately assessed solely on the basis of the activities of domestic U.S. financial institutions when growing linkages of world financial markets have rendered financial institutions of virtually every country sensitive to shocks and market pressures elsewhere. The 1987 stock market crash, for example, demonstrated how financial shocks can reverberate across international markets.

The role of foreign producers in U.S. markets cannot be determined just by considering imports and exports of goods and services that cross U.S. borders. It must be assessed in conjunction with foreign investment activities that build production and marketing bases in the United States. Also, nonresidents' acquisitions of U.S. assets can be financed through domestic or foreign sources: whether such investments result in an infusion of foreign capital into the U.S. economy cannot be determined without information on foreign investors' sources of funds. Likewise, the competitiveness of U.S. firms and the influence of U.S. investments abroad on the U.S. economy and the economies of the host countries have to be assessed in a similarly broad context.

As the U.S. economy becomes increasingly internationalized, there is a blurring of the traditional distinction between domestic and international economic activities. To address economic policy issues that transcend national geographical boundaries, there is need for data that adequately reflect the globalized financial activities of the U.S. economy.

SIGNIFICANT DATA GAPS

The altered conditions of world financial markets have implications for U.S. efforts to monitor its international capital transactions. Official statistics on the net U.S. international investment position show that at the end of 1991 the value of U.S. assets held by nonresidents was $368 billion more than the value of foreign assets held by U.S. residents. Statistics such as these have led to extensive media characterization of the United States as the largest debtor nation in the world. One cannot be certain that this characterization is correct, however, because there are serious deficiencies in these numbers (see Kester, 1992). More important, the existing data system tends to collect more complete data on foreign capital flowing into the United States than on U.S. capital flowing out of the country. Another major concern relates to the valuation and coverage of U.S. holdings of foreign securities. Although the Treasury Department has undertaken regular, periodic surveys to measure nonresidents' holdings of U.S. securities since the mid-1970s, there had not been a comprehensive survey of U.S. residents' holdings of foreign securities since World War II until one was undertaken in 1994. In addition, despite the recorded "net indebtedness," official data show that earnings (interest and profits) of U.S. residents on their investments abroad continue to exceed those received by foreigners on their U.S. investments; the excess reached $21 billion in 1990, although it had dropped to $4 billion by 1993. Furthermore, persistently large errors and omissions in the U.S. international transaction accounts in the late 1970s and the 1980s have undermined confidence in the accuracy of the measurement of the net U.S. international investment position and affected the interpretation of such data.

The foreign acquisition of Rockefeller Center in New York City and of the Seattle Mariners baseball team attracted a lot of attention. So did the auto plants that foreign firms have established in this country. Yet the extent of foreign (nonresident) ownership of U.S. business and, particularly, real estate is unclear. Nonresidents' purchases of U.S. real estate (including residential real estate) for commercial purposes are now covered in the survey of foreign direct investment done by the Bureau of Economic Analysis (BEA). However, because of the difficulties of identifying smaller transactions and of distinguishing between residential real estate purchased for commercial purposes and that purchased for personal use, survey coverage is undoubtedly incomplete. BEA's legal authority for conducting the direct investment survey does not extend to real estate held exclusively for personal use. Purchases by limited partnerships are considered portfolio investment and are covered in Treasury Department surveys rather than in the BEA direct investment survey. Obtaining complete coverage is difficult.

There is also limited information about the sources and uses of funds of foreign investors in the United States. Some foreign firms issue commercial paper—short-term, unsecured promissory notes, issued mostly by corporations—in the United States to secure funds for their operations both here and abroad. Yet the coverage of such activities and other financing mechanisms used in this country by nonresidents is extremely limited. Similarly, there is incomplete information on the sources and uses of funds by U.S. firms abroad. The existing data on foreign direct investment in this country can give a misleading impression of the extent of foreign ownership in the U.S. economy. If a foreign investor owns as much as a 10 percent interest in a U.S. enterprise, the entire enterprise will be classified as a U.S. affiliate of a foreign company.

The explosive growth in innovative derivative instruments has transformed world financial markets since the 1980s. One key feature of these instruments is that they allow borrowers and investors to hedge against the risks of fluctuating interest and exchange rates and of equity and commodity prices. Commercial and investment banks, along with large securities firms and other corporations, have become dominant players in these financial derivatives markets, which are largely international in nature. The risk exposures of U.S. participants in these volatile markets are a concern of the Federal Reserve and other federal regulatory bodies that oversee the U.S. financial system, but official data on transactions in financial derivatives are scanty.

Partly as a result of the surge in derivatives transactions, the capital flow data in the U.S. international transaction accounts no longer serve as adequate indicators of international sources of exchange market and interest rate pressures. One reason is that the balance-of-payments framework does not register the full dimension of derivatives activities. To assess potential exchange market pressures in this globalized market, one needs to know whether U.S. liabilities to and claims on foreigners are denominated in dollars or foreign currencies. When a foreigner borrows dollars in the United States and invests them in this country, there is no additional net dollar exposure, and the U.S. international investment position will not show a net change. However, when a foreigner invests foreign funds in the United States but fully hedges the investment in the derivatives market (for example, through a currency swap), the U.S. international investment position will show a net increase in U.S. obligations to foreigners, and it will not indicate that the foreign claimant has taken no dollar risk. Nor can one readily determine whether the counterparty (buyer or seller) to the currency swap is a U.S. resident. Derivatives transactions, therefore, can have significant implications for foreign, and even domestic, assessments about possible future fluctuations in the value of the dollar and, consequently, for reactions to domestic macroeconomic policies.

SHORTCOMINGS OF THE EXISTING DATA SYSTEM

Information on U.S. international capital flows is reported on a quarterly basis in the U.S. balance-of-payments accounts, along with data on U.S. merchandise trade, international services transactions, investment incomes and payments, and unilateral transfers. Private capital flows include direct and portfolio investment (banking, securities, and other commercial and financial transactions). The Bureau of Economic Analysis of the U.S. Department of Commerce is responsible for compiling direct investment data, as well as data on international services, investment income, transfers and official government international capital transactions. The U.S. Department of the Treasury, using the Federal Reserve banks as agents, collects information on portfolio transactions under the Treasury International Capital (TIC) data system.

Despite improvements in recent years, there are many shortcomings to the current TIC collection methods. The system relies heavily on manually collecting information from large financial intermediaries located in the United States. The emphasis has been on traditional banking business, largely in the form of loans and deposits. The system does not adequately capture the numerous transactions that bypass traditional financial intermediaries and channels, particularly those involving securities and new derivative financial products and those undertaken by nonbank participants in foreign financial centers.

One indication of the errors and gaps in the data on U.S. international capital transactions is the statistical discrepancy (representing net errors and omissions) in the U.S. balance-of-payments accounts. The discrepancy grew significantly during the 1980s, reaching $53 billion in 1989. It also increased as a percentage of exports of goods and services and investment incomes. Another indication is found by comparing TIC data on U.S. nonbanks' foreign claims and liabilities with data compiled by the Bank for International Settlements (BIS) on foreign banks' liabilities and claims on U.S. nonbanks. From 1986 to 1989, the TIC flow data averaged $20-25 billion less per year than data from the BIS. If, as is generally thought, banking data are more complete than data filed by nonbanks, the TIC data almost certainly have understated U.S. nonbanks' claims and liabilities.

The Treasury Department conducted a small survey of international transactions by U.S. pension funds in 1991. It indicated that a large part of U.S. pension fund transactions in foreign securities had been carried out by offshore (nonresident) money managers and that there had been significant underreporting of these transactions in the TIC data. The inclusion of these respondents resulted in an increase of nearly $170 billion in reported gross trading activities for the 17 months ending in May 1993.

As a result of a 3-year effort to incorporate information from foreign central banks and the BIS, BEA recently published dramatic upward revisions in its estimates of U.S. nonbank financial claims on foreigners. These claims were estimated at $254.5 billion in 1993; without the incorporation of these new data sources, the estimate would have been only $42.6 billion. In 1992 and 1993 the statistical discrepancy in the balance-of-payments accounts dropped to between 2 and 3 percent of exports of goods and services and investment income, reflecting in part the introduction of these improved data sources.

Timely and accurate reporting of portfolio transactions by data filers has been hampered by both the growing complexity of financial business and a lack of clear, consistent, and uniform guidance from the Treasury Department to data filers. Financial institutions now engage in myriad complex transactions that may span several countries and occur around the clock. To report information on their multifaceted international transactions, data filers generally have to expend considerable effort to examine financial accounts from offices in different countries and in different currencies. Moreover, the data required may not be readily available in their accounting records because of differences in definitions and concepts between accounting principles and statistical reporting instructions. In addition to filing statistical reports on international transactions, many filers have to submit other financial reports to federal regulatory agencies: the total number of forms filed by an internationally active financial institution can be as many as 1,300 a year. Many TIC filers do not fully understand the purposes of the TIC forms, and filers concede that the quality of some of the data they provide is poor. Under these circumstances, it may not be surprising that all but 1 percent of the responses to the Treasury Department's comprehensive survey of foreign holdings of U.S. securities for 1989 required extensive follow-up inquiries.

The panel underscores that, as the international financial environment evolves, the existing data on U.S. international capital transactions will become more deficient if the data collection system continues to lag behind global financial developments. Major steps must be taken now.

The United States is not alone in facing problems of collecting and integrating data on international capital transactions. Other countries are confronted with similar problems and are working to improve their data. As indicated in the 1993 *Balance of Payments Statistics Yearbook* of the International Monetary Fund, the statistical discrepancy in the global capital account averaged nearly $120 billion a year during 1989-1992: that is, recorded capital inflows exceeded outflows by that amount on the average every year during that period. (In principle, global outflows should equal global inflows.) Given the internationalization of capital transactions, there will be a growing recognition that the present reporting systems of individual national governments cannot perform as well working alone as they can working together. The panel's recommendations urge that the United States and other countries exchange statistical information and collaborate closely with international organizations to develop common standards for such data collection.

RECOMMENDATIONS

The panel recommends several major steps to improve the usefulness of the existing data and the cost-effectiveness of their collection. The success of each step, in turn, will depend on the concerted efforts, not only of the federal statistical agencies currently responsible for the collection of the data, but also of financial regulatory bodies, the accounting profession, myriad financial institutions, and public and private data users. International coordination will also be vital to these efforts.

The panel's most important recommendations are included in this summary. They are listed in terms of their relative importance, with the most important ones listed first in each of five sections: closing data gaps, streamlining reporting requirements, improving coverage of financial derivatives, using alternative data sources and methods, and expanding international data exchange and coordination. The number in parentheses at the end of each recommendation refers to the chapter in which the recommendation is discussed.

CLOSING DATA GAPS

Among existing data on U.S. international capital transactions, direct investment data are generally adequate in coverage but require constant and careful attention; improvements are most needed in portfolio investment data.

- To better assess the debtor/creditor position of the United States in the world economy, the outbound benchmark survey by the Treasury Department of U.S. holdings of foreign securities should be conducted not only in 1994 but also periodically thereafter—at least once every 5 years—to avoid cumulative errors. It can and should be carried out more frequently if a system is developed for collecting data from global custodians and the system is shown to be cost-effective. (3-7)

- The Treasury Department and the Federal Reserve Bank of New York should expand the TIC forms to improve the coverage of short-term securities, such as commercial paper. (3-8)

- To improve estimates of U.S. monetary aggregates, the Treasury Department, working with the Federal Reserve, should develop ways to monitor shipments of U.S. currency abroad. (3-9)

- For its inbound benchmark survey on foreign holdings of U.S. securities, the Treasury Department should improve the number of usable initial filings by continued educational efforts and other means to obtain the cooperation of filers. (3-10)

- Substitution by the Bureau of Economic Analysis of data from the Bank for International Settlements for data from U.S. sources has produced major improvements in coverage of the international claims and liabilities of U.S. nonbank firms and of investment income flows. BEA should continue its process of working with the BIS, the Federal Reserve, and the statistical authorities of other countries to seek further improvements in BEA's coverage of international transactions through additional use of data collected by international organizations and foreign central banks. (3-13)

- If resources permit, BEA should either resume collection of more complete data on sources and uses of funds of multinational corporations, covering both outward and inward direct investment, or extract comparable information from the existing data. The results should be analyzed and published to inform the public about this essential operational aspect of multinational corporations. (3-1)

- The Treasury Department should continue its efforts to collect more complete data on nonresidents' holdings of U.S. real estate in the form of limited partnerships. (3-2)

- BEA should devote additional resources to analyzing the immense volume of data it collects on direct investment and examining the economic effects of the growth of multinational enterprises on domestic production, employment, and transfer of technology.

BEA is in the best position to exploit the detailed information it gathers regularly on the activities of these enterprises. (3-3)

• BEA should undertake further reviews, by industry, on the rates of return of foreign direct investment in the United States, with particular attention to any data or reporting problems that may contribute to measured differences between rates of return on U.S. investment abroad and foreign investment in the United States. (3-4)

STREAMLINING REPORTING REQUIREMENTS

Because the structure of financial markets and the nature of financial instruments have changed dramatically over the past decade and will continue to evolve, a vigorous review of all regulatory and statistical reporting forms is urgently needed to ensure that only relevant data useful for public policy making are collected. Such a review is critical to enhance the cost-effectiveness of the existing data collection systems if they are to cover adequately the burgeoning volume of financial transactions in various forms and levels of complexity. Coordinated efforts by regulatory and statistical agencies to streamline reporting requirements, in consultation with filers, are likely to engender cooperation and compliance from them, yielding more accurate and timely data.

• The Treasury Department and the Federal Reserve Bank of New York should mount a vigorous publicity campaign to bring the existence of the reporting requirements to the attention of all parties active in the international trading of securities, including pension funds, mutual funds, insurance companies, and individuals or businesses that serve as money managers and investment advisers. Special attention should be directed to institutional investors that deal directly in foreign markets. (3-6)

• In response to the growing complexity of transactions and organizational structures of financial institutions, the Treasury Department and the Federal Reserve Bank of New York (FRBNY) should work together with data filers to streamline TIC reporting requirements (including level of details, frequency of reports, and exemption levels), clarify reporting instructions and guidelines, and determine how particular transactions should be reported. A major objective should be to eliminate unnecessary details, explore the feasibility of obtaining certain data on a quarterly instead of monthly basis (for example, data on country details), and simplify reporting forms. Periodic meetings between staff of the

Treasury Department and the FRBNY and filers should be held for these purposes. (3-18)

• The Treasury Department and the Federal Reserve Bank of New York should conduct an active educational campaign for data filers covering the purpose and use of the required data. This would be especially helpful to foreign-owned financial intermediaries operating in the United States. (3-19)

• The Treasury Department and Federal Reserve Bank of New York should formalize their consultation processes with filers. A manual of instructions and administrative guidance should be distributed to filers. The manual could be in the form of diskettes or a loose-leaf binder, in which updated instructions would replace old ones. (3-20)

IMPROVING COVERAGE OF FINANCIAL DERIVATIVES

• An interagency group led by the Federal Reserve and including the Federal Reserve Bank of New York, the Treasury Department, the Bureau of Economic Analysis, the Securities and Exchange Commission, the Commodity Futures Trading Commission, and other financial regulatory bodies, should be established to undertake several tasks. Specifically, the interagency group should identify the major participants in financial derivatives markets, the intermediaries involved, and the various forms of transactions. It should also examine the coverage, quality, and consistency of the limited data on financial derivatives currently collected by the Federal Financial Institutions Examination Council, the Commodity Futures Trading Commission, the Securities and Exchange Commission, and private institutions and determine ways to expand coverage, eliminate duplication, standardize definitions, and, whenever appropriate, integrate the data. The group should work closely with market participants, industry groups, and the accounting profession to ensure harmonization of accounting, regulatory, and statistical reporting practices, especially for classifying derivatives transactions and recognizing their market values, income flows, and gains and losses. It is important that the group secure the cooperation of filers and that filers have an appreciation of the purpose and significance of the transactions they are required to report. Because many of the fastest growing derivatives transactions are international in nature, consideration should be given to collecting data on such activities from large financial institutions and multinational corporations, and to classifying the data by major financial instruments and in key currencies. Over the long term, harmonization of international reporting standards for derivatives is desirable. (4-1)

USING ALTERNATIVE DATA SOURCES AND METHODS

In view of the global nature of transactions and their rapid expansion, improvements in the medium term in coverage and accuracy of data (in particular, those on portfolio transactions that bypass traditional financial intermediaries and those that are conducted directly through computer and telecommunications networks), without entailing substantial increases in resources, lie in drawing on information from existing custodians of financial assets, as well as large payment, clearance, and settlement systems. Over the long term, as rising numbers of multinational corporations and financial institutions commit large sums to developing in-house international information and communications systems to meet their operational needs, the possibility of collecting balance-of-payments data electronically will increase. The potential use of EDIFACT (Electronic Data Interchange for Administration, Commerce, and Trade) for balance-of-payments reporting has recently been analyzed by a task force of the Statistical Office of the European Community (EUROSTAT).

Global custodians are institutions that manage the custody of financial assets in multiple markets for clients who are largely institutional investors. Their main role is that of master recordkeeper and reporter. Clients are provided monthly or quarterly reports detailing information on assets held, including value and transaction date. Information on the nationality of the clients is also available. Data from global custodians should be developed to improve information, particularly on U.S. holdings of foreign securities. The Treasury Department targeted global custodians as its main source of data in its 1994 outbound portfolio investment survey of U.S. holdings of foreign securities because of this potential for improved coverage.

• The potential for using global custodians as a new source of data appears promising. In addition to information on securities holdings, the Treasury Department and the Federal Reserve Bank of New York should actively explore the feasibility of gathering flow data on securities transactions from global custodians and assess its cost-effectiveness. (5-1)

Payment, clearance, and settlement organizations are institutions that process financial transactions. In the United States, Fedwire and the ClearingHouse Interbank Payments Systems (CHIPS) are the two large-value payment and clearance networks. Fedwire is the Federal Reserve's wire transfer network. CHIPS is a private electronic payment system owned and operated by the New York Clearing House Association. The two systems together process enormous quantities of electronic payments each day.

• On the basis of the information currently available on Fedwire and CHIPS, it appears that it would be possible to secure statistical data on U.S. international capital transactions from the two systems. The Treasury Department and the Bureau of Economic Analysis should conduct a rigorous study to explore such feasibility by undertaking an in-depth analysis of a sample of transactions that pass through Fedwire and CHIPS. They should also determine whether cost savings would result from using data from Fedwire and CHIPS. If data for analysis cannot be released by CHIPS or Fedwire to outsiders due to privacy concerns, the Treasury Department and BEA could request the staffs of Fedwire and CHIPS to devise ways of providing the data without violating individuals' privacy. (5-2)

A EUROSTAT statistical task force is currently working to develop EDIFACT electronic messages for the collection of balance-of-payments data. Three factors have provided impetus for this initiative. First, the use of EDIFACT is spreading in Europe, and merchandise exporters and importers and the banking community are showing interest in pilot projects both nationally and internationally. Second, the compilers anticipate that paper recording of individual transactions may cease as customs barriers are removed within the unified Europe and as firms become increasingly automated. Third, savings will accrue to both customers and firms when they no longer have to file reports to their national statistical compilers.

An important aspect of this electronic approach is the development of standardized information codes and statistical systems for information extraction. Compilers of national statistics will need to be involved in the development of the coding systems, which should be designed to minimize retrieval costs. With regard to extraction systems, a crucial issue is the determination of how and when to aggregate information. This will affect costs because of the huge volume of information available.

• In the United States, the Federal Reserve, the Treasury Department, and the Bureau of Economic Analysis should allocate resources to study the systems architecture of information technology adopted by financial institutions and multinational corporations and to investigate ways to facilitate the development of these automated data collection systems to prepare for the emerging electronic global trading environment. (5-3)

EXPANDING INTERNATIONAL DATA EXCHANGE AND COORDINATION

Because of the internationalization of financial markets, data compilers can no longer rely largely on domestic data sources. Greater coordination and cooperation among countries are needed to exchange data and thereby improve data coverage. BEA has recently increased its utilization of data obtained by the BIS from central banks, and it also uses data obtained directly from authorities in other countries.

• Data exchanges and the use of the databases of international organizations require that the data of different countries be comparable in coverage, definitions, and concepts. Despite recent efforts of various countries to bring about greater convergence, significant conceptual differences and data inconsistencies among countries remain. This circumstance points to the need for careful and systematic comparisons of bilateral data, as well as for comparisons between national data and information contained in international databases, before substituting or making adjustments to national databases. This process is inevitably labor intensive and time consuming. One approach would be to focus on the countries of greatest quantitative importance and data that offer the most possibilities for improvement. Another promising approach is for U.S. statistical officials to consult closely with statistical experts in countries with which the United States is engaged in data exchanges. The aim would be to enhance understanding of how the bilateral statistical systems, definitions, and concepts can be modified to make the systems more consistent. (5-4)

• An essential step toward harmonizing data on international transactions of various countries is to encourage national compilers to adhere to standards currently being developed by international organizations, such as the International Monetary Fund, the Bank for International Settlements, the United Nations, the Organization of Economic Cooperation and Development, and other international securities and financial groups. In addition, different international organizations need to establish guidelines showing how their different databases can be reconciled. (5-5)

CONCLUDING OBSERVATION

For fiscal 1992, BEA's budget for the collection of all U.S. international transactions was about $12 million. The Treasury Department does not have a separate budget for its role in the TIC data system, and the costs to the Federal Reserve banks of collecting the TIC data for the Treasury Department are borne from their own budgets. According to the Federal Reserve Bank of New York, Federal Reserve banks expended about $2 million for this purpose in 1992. In view of the importance of capital flows in the increasingly internationalized U.S. economy, the panel believes that higher priority should be accorded to the collection of accurate, timely, and comprehensive data on such activities, particularly on U.S. holdings of foreign securities and U.S. nonbank financial transactions.

This report contains a number of recommendations for cost-effective approaches to obtaining needed statistical information. In particular, data can be improved and costs contained through sharing of information among national statistical authorities and international data-gathering institutions and through effective use of the data becoming available from the sophisticated electronic recording systems being adopted for international transactions clearing. Capitalizing on these opportunities requires immediate investment of the resources necessary to bring about change. The panel is conscious of the many competing demands on federal resources and of the need to restrain federal spending. We stress, however, that the current opportunities for longer run efficiencies through actions taken now and the urgency of better information about international capital transactions argue for immediate investment of the resources needed to bring about change. The funds required are minuscule relative either to the size of the federal budget or to the importance of a better understanding of international financial flows, but adequate funding is crucial to the ability of U.S. statistical agencies to accomplish the work that is needed.

The challenge facing data compilers is how to improve the data collection systems to reflect today's needs and to do so in an environment of the growing number and diversity of institutional and private players engaging in international capital transactions, the changing roles of intermediaries and financial instruments, and the complexity of modern financial transactions. Only when this challenge is met will U.S. analysts, business people, and policy makers be in a position to adequately understand the impact of international financial activity on the U.S. economy and the role of U.S. financial activity in the world economy.

1

Globalization of Financial Markets

Even the most cursory review of major international economic trends over the past several decades shows there have been revolutionary changes in world financial markets. During the 1950s and 1960s, financial institutions and their regulatory structures in major industrial countries evolved in relative isolation from external developments. During those years, most countries, including the United States, imposed restrictions on international capital movements. Major international institutional agreements after World War II, such as the Bretton Woods agreement and the General Agreement on Tariffs and Trade, liberalized world trade but did little to free the movement of international capital. After the financial disruptions of the 1930s, many had questioned whether free capital flows and liberalized capital markets were even desirable. In the International Monetary Fund, the basic obligation of member nations—their code of good behavior—was framed exclusively in terms of avoiding restrictions on current account payments: that is, payments for merchandise trade, international services, investment incomes and payments, remittances, and official government transfers. Meanwhile, the rules and the philosophy with respect to capital transactions were far different: many countries restricted outward capital transfers either because they preferred their capital to be invested within their domestic economies or because they wished to prevent downward pressure on their exchange rates.

That situation and those views changed dramatically in the 1970s, and the pace of change accelerated in the 1980s.[1] The interaction of several powerful forces has produced massive capital flows across national boundaries. At the same time, the structure and operation of world financial markets have been transformed. Today, world financial markets are highly integrated, and transactions have become increasingly complex. These phenomena are reflected in cross-listing of securities in several countries, cross-country hedging and portfolio diversification, and 24-hour trading in financial instruments at exchanges around the world.

Many of the channels used for financial transactions have also changed. There has been a major shift, relatively, from banks to nonbank financial intermediaries, such as brokerage houses, securities firms, insurance companies, and pension funds. There has also been a shift from loans to securities and a rise in the use of foreign financial centers. In addition, there has been a surge in the use of new financial instruments and, in particular, of derivative products (such as financial options, futures, and swaps on interest rates, foreign currencies, stocks, bonds, and commodities). These instruments have been developed to meet the needs and preferences of different customers, including their desire to hedge risks in an environment of fluctuating exchange rates, interest rates, stock prices, and commodity prices.

The unprecedented changes in world financial markets have had significant implications for public policy and data collection. Because of international capital movements, policies and developments in other countries increasingly influence domestic economic performance. As a consequence, there is a need for information about the new and emerging global financial environment. Yet changes that have taken place in world financial markets themselves compound the difficulty of acquiring the information.

Given the difficulties involved and the budgetary constraints faced by statistical agencies in the public sector, several questions arise: What is the current need for data on international capital transactions? In what ways are current U.S. collection systems adequate or inadequate? Are there conceptual flaws or data defi-

---

[1]A number of significant international financial developments have occurred over the past half century, including the emergence of the Euromarkets in the early 1960s, which circumvented domestic financial regulations. This report focuses on changes in world capital markets associated with financial deregulations in major industrial countries since the late 1970s.

ciencies that should be corrected? Are there alternative ways to gather the data that would be more accurate, more useful, more timely, more technologically advanced, or less burdensome and costly?

THE STUDY AND THE REPORT

With the support of the Bureau of Economic Analysis (BEA) of the U.S. Department of Commerce, the Panel on International Capital Transactions was convened to examine the changes in the global financial environment, assess public and private needs for data on international capital transactions, review the adequacy of existing data, and consider alternative collection methods. Subsequent research grants from the Federal Reserve Board and the U.S. Department of State also supported the study. The panel's goal has been to develop recommendations for the collection of data on U.S. international capital transactions to help ensure that the data are accurate, timely, relevant, cost-effective, and useful for decision making in the years to come.

This study is a follow-on to the one completed by a previous panel of the Committee on National Statistics. That report, *Behind the Numbers: U.S. Trade in the World Economy* (Kester, 1992), reviewed the adequacy of data on U.S. merchandise trade and international services transactions. It recommended steps to correct the problems of underreporting of U.S. merchandise exports and inadequate coverage of U.S. international services transactions. It also proposed measures to improve monitoring of sales and purchases by U.S. firms at home and abroad, as well as those by foreign firms in the United States. It pointed out that, of all U.S. international transactions (in goods, services, and capital flows), transactions representing capital flows are the least adequately documented. That report concluded that improving the data on U.S. international capital transactions would yield high payoffs, and this report addresses that issue.

Although the changing global trade and financial environment has led several international organizations to undertake initiatives to improve the concepts and methods of compiling international economic statistics, none of the resulting studies focuses specifically on data on U.S. international capital transactions. Nevertheless, improving the quality of U.S. data would have major implications for international financial statistics. Better U.S. data would greatly enhance the usefulness of information on global capital flows because the United States accounts for a large part of all international transactions. Other countries would also benefit if improved U.S. statistics were available, since U.S. transactions involve many other developed and developing countries, and the statistical problems of the U.S. data are not unique. Refining U.S. data concepts, definitions, and methodologies and harmonizing them with international ones would promote international data comparability. This improvement in comparability, of course, would apply to the data of other countries as well. Data comparability is important not only for international economic policy coordination, but also for data exchanges between the United States and other countries. The panel believes this report will contribute to a better understanding of the global financial flows that have come to characterize the rapidly evolving global economy.

In conducting this study, the panel extensively reviewed existing literature, including recent studies by the International Monetary Fund (1987, 1992b), the Federal Reserve Board (Stekler, 1991; Stekler and Truman, 1992), and the Bank for International Settlements (1986, 1992a, 1992b). It examined the concepts, methods, and procedures that U.S. federal agencies use to collect data on international capital transactions, as well as those used by other industrial countries. It drew on the insights and expertise of many individuals in federal agencies, international organizations, foreign government agencies, businesses, trade associations, and research organizations, including those from the U.S. Department of Commerce, the U.S. Department of the Treasury, and the U.S. Federal Reserve system, as well as the International Monetary Fund, the Bank for International Settlements, the Bank of England, the Bank of Japan, and the Deutsche Bundesbank. It consulted experts in the accounting profession and other expert groups currently examining the changes in global financial markets and the treatment of complex financial transactions. The panel heard expert testimony and reviewed written comments from numerous government, academic, and industry users on the adequacy of the existing data. The panel also canvassed data filers from commercial and investment banks, securities firms, brokerage houses, and multinational corporations to learn their views on data reporting requirements.

In developing its recommendations, the panel took into account the current budgetary constraints that face statistical agencies, as well as the rapidly evolving world financial environment and the advent of innovative information and telecommunications technologies. Recommendations in this report are ranked in terms of their relative importance; the most important are listed first in each section.

The rest of this chapter reviews the forces that have dramatically transformed world financial markets over the last decade or so and their implications for U.S. economic and financial policies. Chapter 2 describes the existing system for compiling data on U.S. international capital transactions, noting its concept, coverage, and methods of collection. Chapter 3 examines the adequacy of the existing system, taking into account the views of data collection agencies, data filers, and data users, and makes recommendations for improvements. Chapter 4 reviews the surge of transactions in financial derivatives and discusses their implications for the coverage and the interpretation of existing data on U.S. international capital transactions. Chapter 5 explores the feasibility of using alternative data sources and collection methods to improve the coverage and accuracy of existing data, including automation, the use of global custodians, exchanges, settlement and clearinghouses, and databases of international organizations.

Appendix A highlights key features of the data collection systems of the United Kingdom, Germany, and Japan and discusses actions being taken by these countries to improve information on their international capital transactions. Appendix B summarizes the results of the panel's canvass of data compilers, filers, and users on the adequacy of the existing data system.

Throughout this report, following the balance-of-payments framework for current U.S. data, "foreign" means non-U.S. resident, and international capital transactions are those between residents and nonresidents (foreigners). Other terms commonly used in the field, and in this report, are "offshore," "abroad," and "overseas," all of which are the same as foreign for purposes of international capital transactions, which are also sometimes called cross-border transactions.

FACTORS CONTRIBUTING TO GLOBALIZATION

The rapid expansion and integration of world financial markets since the late 1970s can be attributed to several factors. They include a worldwide move toward deregulation of financial institutions and transactions; macroeconomic imbalances among countries, which have induced capital flows; improved knowledge about market and economic conditions around the world; and breakthroughs in information and communications technology that have increased exponentially the capacity for handling large volumes

of financial transactions while significantly reducing unit transaction costs and making possible the use of new financial instruments. In addition, competition has grown among financial institutions of various types and in various countries, whose portfolio
management strategies in volatile markets have resulted in new
products and new modes of operation. The development of world
financial markets in response to these forces and the U.S. experience can be traced back about two decades.

DEREGULATION AND LIBERALIZATION OF FINANCIAL ACTIVITIES

The trend toward financial deregulation accelerated in the early
1970s, when the government controls on financial activities that
had been established in the 1950s and 1960s and earlier were
proving ineffective and causing serious inefficiencies in the allocation of capital and the operation of monetary policy. The United
States removed its last capital controls in 1973; Germany significantly reduced its restrictions on capital movements in the 1970s;
and the United Kingdom dismantled its exchange controls in 1979,
Japan in the early 1980s, and France and Italy in the late 1980s.
Countries embraced deregulation because it was thought that free
flows of capital would open up both saving and investment opportunities for firms and individuals and better match the changing
needs of suppliers and users of funds, thereby facilitating the efficient allocation of capital and promoting growth in income and
output.

In the United States, the liberalization of domestic financial
markets since the late 1970s has further facilitated international
capital flows. The phaseout of interest rate ceilings (Regulation
Q),[2] the easing of portfolio restrictions on pension funds and insurance companies, and the removal of a variety of restrictions on
the permissible activities of banks[3] have facilitated large transfers
of money, both within national borders and across them. The
lowering of institutional barriers was intended to allow firms and
individuals to adjust their claims and liabilities with greater ease
in order to improve the liquidity of their portfolios and diversify

---

[2]Regulation Q set the maximum level of interest rates that banks and savings
and loan companies could pay on deposits.

[3]Banks are still limited in the extent to which they can diversify into insurance,
investment, and underwriting services. As of mid-1994, banks, unlike enterprises
in other industries, were prohibited from branching freely across state lines.
However, under recently enacted legislation, this prohibition will be removed
over the next few years.

their risks. The drive toward international diversification by U.S. institutional investors (especially pension funds, insurance companies, and mutual funds) has been a major force behind the internationalization and integration of U.S. financial markets.

The process of integration has also intensified as foreign investors and financial institutions have been allowed relatively freely to enter domestic markets in different parts of the world. Between 1978 and 1991, for example, the number of foreign banks in the United States rose from about 122 to 280. Branches and agencies of foreign banks held aggregate assets of $626 billion in 1991, up from $90 billion in 1978. In 1991 foreign banks accounted for 18 percent of total banking assets in this country and operated 565 offices (Federal Reserve Board of Governors, 1993:1).[4] Meanwhile, at the time of the "big bang" of 1986—the deregulation of securities markets in the United Kingdom—many U.S. securities firms and banks expanded their presence in London through acquisitions and other means. There are other measures of increased integration of financial markets: over the same 1978-1991 period, the value of U.S. assets abroad rose more than three-fold while the value of foreign assets in the United States showed an even more dramatic six-fold increase. (Bureau of Economic Analysis, 1993a; 1994a).

MACROECONOMIC CONDITIONS

In an environment of deregulated and liberalized financial markets, international capital movements have been driven mainly by economic fundamentals. The macroeconomic conditions of various countries and their trade and tax policies, for example, affect the expected rates of return on various investments in different markets. In the mid- to late 1970s, large capital flows resulted from the recycling of the oil export surpluses of the Organization of Petroleum Exporting Countries, many of them through international banks to sovereign borrowers in the developing countries. During the late 1970s and early 1980s, there was considerable capital flight from many developing countries as uncompetitive interest rates and exchange rates, large fiscal deficits, and high

---

[4]Foreign banks with U.S. branches and agencies first became subject to federal regulation with the adoption of the International Banking Act of 1978. Additional regulatory authority was provided by the Foreign Bank Supervision Enhancement Act in 1991.

external debt burdens took a toll in those countries. Beginning in the early 1980s, large capital inflows into the United States were an important source of financing for the sizable federal budget deficits being incurred.

Differences in the mix of fiscal and monetary policies between the United States and other industrial countries over the past decade have directly affected exchange rates for the dollar. The large movements of the dollar against other major currencies since the 1980s, in turn, have contributed to increases in sales and purchases of dollar-denominated securities and the expansion of foreign-currency trading.

In 1992, differentials approaching 6 percentage points or more in interest rates between the United States and Germany attracted capital to Germany from the United States (and other countries). Following unification, Germany relied on high interest rates to dampen inflationary pressures arising from the huge costs of revitalizing the economy of the former East Germany. Also in the early 1990s, rapid economic growth in East Asian countries and large export surpluses in those countries have generated pools of savings that flow into the global economy to finance the investments that offer the highest rates of return.

TECHNOLOGICAL INNOVATIONS

Technology is another force that has changed the operation and structure of international financial markets. Information and telecommunications technologies have greatly increased the speed with which information is processed and disseminated. Around the world, market participants are bombarded with a plethora of information and a cacophony of opinions, reports, and rumors, much of which is communicated by computers.

In addition, electronic trading has allowed orders to move across continents, directly from customers to brokers and dealers. Automated trade execution and international clearing and settlement have also encouraged cross-listing of securities and further integrated world financial markets. Today, traders have access to instruments and overseas markets after U.S. trading hours have ended. If they choose to, they can also "pass the book" to their affiliates in foreign markets, who can continue trading in daylight hours overseas.

Automated trading execution systems provide a 24-hour trading market, allowing traders to enter buy and sell orders that are automatically matched according to price and time preferences.

One example of such systems is GLOBEX, an electronic trading system launched by the Chicago Mercantile Exchange and the Chicago Board of Trade in conjunction with Reuter, the British information services firm. Key U.S. government securities and foreign exchange are traded in global markets. Round-the-clock trading is expanding because increases in speed and control over the direction of information flows can result in large profits or reduced losses in financial markets. The greater ease with which financial traders can gain access to different markets and their reduced costs have enabled them to take advantage of even small profit margins around the world.

Furthermore, interactions among markets, which have been facilitated by technological innovations, have provided market participants with opportunities to diversify, hedge, and increase profits on their investments, thereby promoting the use of new financial products and instruments. Over the past several years, there has been rapid growth in financial derivatives, such as forwards, futures, options, swaps, and sophisticated combinations of them on interest rates, exchange rates, stocks, and bonds. A primary purpose of these instruments is to hedge exposure against risk, and many are traded across borders. Accompanying this rise in derivatives has been the rapid expansion of over-the-counter markets that involve trading over computer networks in securities tailored to the specific needs of individual investors, borrowers, and intermediaries. (A detailed discussion of financial derivatives is presented in Chapter 4.)

COMPETITION AMONG FINANCIAL AND NONFINANCIAL INSTITUTIONS

The easing of capital controls, the liberalization of financial markets, and technological innovations have stimulated competition among financial and nonfinancial institutions in various countries. This, in turn, has further transformed the structure of world financial markets.

Over the past 25 years, a notable development in international finance has been the growth of *securitization*—a process of converting assets that would normally serve as collateral for a bank loan into securities that are more liquid and can be traded at a lower cost than the underlying asset. This process has been fostered, among other things, by technological innovations. With computers and electronic record-keeping, financial institutions can cheaply bundle together a portfolio of loans (originally, mortgage loans) with small denominations, collect the interest and principal payments, and sell the claims to these payments to a third party as a security. This process of pooling loans and selling securities backed by the loans has been found by financial institutions to be more efficient than traditional financing through financial intermediaries in certain situations, and it has been used, for example, for auto loans and credit card obligations.

In an environment of deregulation, nonbank financial companies have devised new and different ways to move money from savers to borrowers. In recent years in the United States, for example, pension funds, money market funds, and insurance companies, among others, have increasingly lured savings away from bank deposits. In turn, these institutional investors, which are better able than individuals to acquire the needed information for foreign investment, have heavily invested in foreign securities, fostering the rapid expansion of international bond and equity markets.[5] Under these circumstances, there now are diverse institutions competing to provide financial services; securities have become an increasingly important element in international capital flows.

Meanwhile, multinational corporations that produce and sell goods and services on a global scale seek worldwide sources for their financing and investment needs. To serve these clients, financial institutions have diversified the services they offer, among which are transactions in foreign exchange, money market instruments, and derivative products, all on a worldwide scale. These sophisticated financial instruments allow investors an array of alternatives for hedging and shifting risks, which, at a cost, can provide greater certainty of international receipts and payments, or, in some cases, for taking on exposure with a highly leveraged position. There is a large market for such instruments in today's environment, as international businesses, speculators, and investors are faced with volatile exchange rates, interest rates, and commodity prices.

The rise in new financial instruments has added flexibility to

---

[5]A 1993 study by a private financial consulting firm estimated that holdings of foreign stocks by U.S. public pension funds rose from $28.9 billion in 1991 to $48.1 billion in 1992; those of corporate pension funds rose from $59.3 billion to $70.7 billion during the same period. In 1992, foreign stocks accounted for almost 8 percent of assets of corporate pension funds and about 5.6 percent of assets of public pension funds. A survey of pension funds reported in the study showed that public and corporate pension funds expected to increase their holdings of foreign stocks to $100 billion and $116 billion, respectively, by 1995 (Greenwich Associates, 1993).

portfolio management operations. As a result, more and more debt and equity products now originate and are traded in several world financial centers and in different currencies. For example, hedging and other position taking can be carried out with financial and commodity futures and options; they can also be undertaken with interest rate swaps and forward agreements for major exchange rates and commodity prices. Hedging operations can also be combined with other lending arrangements (for example, in a commodity swap) to secure—at a cost—both access to additional funds and greater protection from changing international interest rates and commodity prices. In addition, some multinational corporations act, in effect, as their own in-house financial intermediaries, raising funds wherever they are cheapest and moving them through diverse channels (including offshore—foreign—holding companies) to where they are needed. To some extent, these organizations can be thought of as arbitraging national financial markets. Overall, these private firms, both financial and nonfinancial, now rely heavily for their funding on marketable instruments; the use of commercial paper,[6] floating rate notes, bonds, convertible bonds, shares, and related instruments has grown rapidly in recent years at the expense of traditional bank deposits and loans in financing big businesses.

According to a recent Federal Reserve study (Post, 1992), the U.S. commercial paper market since the early 1980s has become an important source of short-term funds for manufacturers, commercial concerns, and utilities to finance increased production, new inventories, or new receivables. Business enterprises turned to commercial paper to avoid high interest rates on long-term funds and bank loans in an expanding economy. Two other developments in the late 1980s also increased the issuance of commercial paper: the numerous mergers and acquisitions and the expansion of the swaps market, as borrowers combined commercial paper with swaps to create liabilities in other currencies. Asset-backed commercial paper also came into use, providing off-balance-sheet financing for trade and credit card receivables.[7] Money market

---

[6]Commercial paper consists of short-term unsecured promissory notes, which are issued mostly by corporations.

[7]Off-balance-sheet activities are business transactions that do not generally involve recording assets or liabilities in the balance sheet: examples include trades in swaps, options, futures, and foreign exchange forwards and the granting of standby commitments and letters of credit.

mutual funds provided the largest source of funds to this market in the 1980s.

Over the past decade, commercial paper outstanding grew at an average annual rate of about 17 percent. In 1988 the size of the commercial paper market even temporarily surpassed that of the market in U.S. Treasury bills. The issuers of commercial paper in the United States have included foreign corporations and foreign financial institutions. According to the Federal Reserve study (Post, 1992), commercial paper will remain a major source of short-term funds for corporations in the 1990s. High-rated foreign corporations in the United States, attracted by the liquidity and the low cost of the market, are likely to be among the new issuers.

While foreign corporations have been raising capital in the United States, the use of foreign financial centers by U.S. businesses has also been extensive. The Federal Reserve Bank of New York (1992a) estimates that loans to U.S. commercial and industrial companies that originated offshore rose from $37 billion in 1983 to $174 billion by the end of 1991. Offshore bank loans to U.S. businesses surged in the 1980s as foreign banks availed themselves of the opportunity to avoid the reserve cost of making loans in the United States.[8] The fastest growth in these offshore loans to U.S. commercial and industrial businesses has occurred in the Cayman Islands and in industrial countries, such as Japan.

In this competitive environment, banking activities have also significantly changed. During the late 1970s and the early 1980s, large commercial banks in many countries, including those in the United States, sought to boost their profits by lending large sums to developing countries. Since then, although deposit-taking and lending have remained the core business of commercial banks, an increasing portion of their income has come from sources other than the differentials between the interest they pay on deposits and the interest they charge on loans. To improve profit margins, in addition to offering fee-paying business advisory services, banks have increasingly packaged assets not traditionally traded (such as mortgage loans, car loans, corporate receivables, and credit card receivables) into tradable securities. They also have turned to derivative instruments as opportunities have declined in traditional interbank deposit markets.[9] Banks have also pursued off-

---

[8]The growth of offshore loans declined after the Federal Reserve removed the relevant reserve requirements in 1990.

[9]The sharp cutback in interbank business has been attributed to the low returns and potentially large counterparty risks related to this type of business (Bank for International Settlements, 1992a).

balance-sheet activities to shift assets off their balance sheets and thereby improve their capital ratios. Currently, an increasing proportion of banks' credit and liquidity exposures has been incurred off their balance sheets (see Chapter 4). With the growth of nonbank financial institutions, banks have also offered backup lines of credit or guarantees to these institutions, such as the backing of commercial paper issues. Under the 1988 Basle Capital Accord, banks' recommended capital requirements for these activities are much lower than for regular loans.[10] One major role that large commercial banks have retained is to provide payments and clearing mechanisms for most financial transactions.

Yet another development in the structure of world financial markets is that, with the rise in the use of derivative instruments by both bank and nonbank financial institutions, securities, forwards, futures, and options markets have become increasingly linked. Advances in telecommunications technologies have facilitated interactions among these markets.

POLICY ISSUES ARISING FROM GLOBALIZATION

Several benefits have been cited as a result of the changes in the structure and operation of international financial markets. Capital mobility and financial innovations are credited with having provided savers and borrowers with a wider range of investment alternatives and easier and cheaper access to external financing. They are also believed to have facilitated greater diversification of portfolios and increased the size of markets. Internationalization of capital markets is said to have facilitated the financing of global payments imbalances and encouraged more efficient allocation of global resources.

Nonetheless, there has also been a widespread perception that deregulation, globalization, and financial innovations have complicated the formulation and the implementation of monetary and fiscal policies, led to greater volatility in financial markets, and introduced new and highly complex elements of risk that can

---

[10]The Basle Capital Accord refers to the minimum capital standards agreed to by the Basle Committee on Banking Supervision for the supervision of international banking groups and their cross-border establishments. The Basle Committee is made up of the banking supervisors of the Group of Ten industrial countries and Luxembourg. The 1988 accord called for a minimum 8-percent ratio of a bank's capital to its risk-weighted exposure to credit risk, which was to be attained by the end of 1992. Proposals for capital standards covering market risks are under discussion.

cause major disruptions in international financial systems. International capital mobility not only has led to growing linkages of world financial markets, but also has increased the extent to which macroeconomic policies and market conditions of one country can significantly affect those of others. Meanwhile, the securitization of transactions and growth in the use of financial derivative instruments have made international financial flows more complex and less transparent, complicating supervision of financial institutions. This section discusses several aspects of the effect of new global realities in financial markets on a nation's economic policies and financial oversight.

MACROECONOMIC POLICIES

Interest rates and the availability of capital in an industrial country are now much more influenced than in the past by interest rates and credit availability in other countries. A corollary is that monetary (and fiscal) developments in a major industrial country have larger macroeconomic effects on other countries than they did when capital was less mobile internationally. A vivid example was the effect in 1992 of high interest rates in Germany on other members of the European Monetary System, as well as on other industrial countries, including the United States. The freer flow of funds among countries does not necessarily bring their interest rates into line with one another. Interest rates can differ among countries when there exists an expectation that exchange rates will change or when there is a premium related to other types of risk. Nonetheless, a change in interest rates in a major industrial country can strongly affect both interest rates and exchange rates in other countries.

The growth in cross-border deposits also has implications for monetary policies. When cross-border deposits were small and relatively stable, they could be ignored when examining the behavior of domestic monetary aggregates. In recent years, however, the growth in these deposits has added to questions about the usefulness of monetary aggregates as indicators of the tightness or slack of U.S. monetary conditions, in part because measures of U.S. monetary aggregates do not fully capture deposits held by U.S. residents in banks located in foreign countries.[11] In

---

[11]The three major measures are M1, M2, and M3. M1 includes currency outside the Treasury Department, Federal Reserve banks, and the vaults of depository institutions; traveler's checks of nonbank issuers; demand deposits at all commercial

addition, because of foreign offerings of dollar-denominated obligations, net U.S. international capital flows do not fully indicate exchange market pressures on the dollar (Cooper, 1986).

Furthermore, it is argued that under floating exchange rates, increased international capital mobility can quicken the speed with which tight monetary policies slow inflation, since currencies tend to appreciate in response to higher interest rates. The unusual speed of the U.S. disinflation in the early 1980s is an example (Willett and Wihlborg, 1990).

Enhanced capital mobility also affects fiscal policy. In the past, when a country's fiscal policy led to a large budget deficit, the effect was primarily domestic, in the form of more rapid expansion of national income and output and possibly also in some crowding out of private investment as the government borrowed more and interest rates rose. Now a significant result may be a large trade deficit, if high interest rates attract funds from abroad and the exchange rate appreciates. This phenomenon was evident in the United States in the 1980s, when large federal budget deficits were accompanied by large trade deficits.

Today, external imbalances are in many cases more easily financed than in the past by movements of foreign capital. As a result, large trade surpluses and deficits may cause less concern to market participants and to policy makers. From another perspective, the more ready availability of international capital may provide domestic officials with more time to undertake the adjustments needed to correct domestic and external imbalances. Changes in current account balances do, of course, affect domestic income and employment. And sustained imbalances can lead to the buildup of large international debtor and creditor positions that affect the real incomes and debt burdens of future generations.

Yet another effect of capital mobility on domestic macroeconomic policies is that tax incentives to boost domestic savings (for example, through increased tax deductions for individual retirement accounts) may be less likely than in the past to generate a rise in capital for domestic investment. Uncertainty about effects has

---

banks other than those due to depository institutions, the U.S. government, and foreign banks and official institutions; and other checkable deposits including share draft accounts in credit unions and demand deposits at thrift institutions. Overnight Eurodollar deposits of U.S. residents at foreign branches of U.S. banks are included in M2. Term Eurodollar deposits held by U.S. residents at foreign branches of U.S. banks and at all banking offices in the United Kingdom and Canada are included in M3.

risen because institutional investors and other professional money managers can move large pools of savings abroad. They increasingly do so when they calculate they can earn higher rates of return, after allowing for exchange risk.

ASSESSING THE STABILITY OF FINANCIAL MARKETS

As funds move more easily and more readily from one country to another, the prices of financial instruments (for example, securities and foreign exchange) may be subject to greater volatility. Increasingly, exchange rates (the prices of foreign exchange) are affected by "news"—the flow of new information—and by the expectations it engenders. The prices of bonds and stocks are similarly influenced. And exchange rates and securities prices interact with each other. Hence, securities prices in one country can now be affected by the behavior of foreign as well as domestic lenders and investors, although the degree of influence differs from one situation to another, depending on a variety of circumstances. Thus, when the U.S. stock market declined sharply in October 1987, there were worldwide effects, but the large drop in the prices of Japanese stocks in 1991-1992 had little discernible impact on stock markets in the United States and other countries.

In principle, enhanced capital mobility could lead to more stable markets rather than to greater volatility of securities prices and exchange rates, since it makes markets less "thin" in terms of numbers of participants and potential flows of funds. Nonetheless, the information revolution, which has increased familiarity with economic, financial, and political conditions around the world and thereby encouraged international lending and investing, also brings a constant flow of news that can cause lenders and investors to make abrupt changes in their holdings in their own and other countries. Thus, markets are vulnerable to larger swings—both in the short and medium term—in a world of integrated financial markets and enormous worldwide liquidity.[12]

---

[12]The price dynamics created by derivative instruments can also exacerbate this potential. In foreign exchange markets, such swings in prices have led at times to coordinated intervention by central banks aimed at dampening the short- and medium-term volatility of exchange rates. Since the February 1987 meeting of the Group of Seven finance ministers and central bank governors at the Louvre, the monetary authorities of those countries have attempted to maintain their exchange rates within broad ranges.

MONITORING THE SOLVENCY AND LIQUIDITY OF MARKET PARTICIPANTS

The enormous volume of funds flowing across national boundaries and from one currency to another creates a risk that a breakdown in one financial system could spread across the world. The U.S. stock market crash of October 1987 demonstrated the speed with which major financial shocks can reverberate across global markets, and it drew attention to the types of liquidity, settlement, and clearance problems that can arise in money and equity markets.[13] Many financial intermediaries receive and send extremely large sums, relative to their capital and liquid assets, through payments networks. To make the required payments, they are dependent on receipts from others. If one intermediary in the payments mechanism finds itself unable, for whatever reason, to make the payments for which it is liable and others will not lend to it, problems for other institutions and in other centers can develop quickly.

In the commercial banking system, central banks have long been prepared to act as lenders of last resort to enable banks to cope with liquidity problems. The bank examination process also aims to guard against insolvency in commercial banks, and there is close international cooperation among supervisors of commercial banks, who meet regularly at the Bank for International Settlements at Basle. But there are questions as to whether nonbank financial intermediaries—including brokers and dealers and investment banks—are equally well supervised and, if these nonbank institutions are adequately supervised, whether central banks should also act as their lenders of last resort.[14]

---

[13]There have been some initiatives in the United States and abroad to improve the clearing and settlement systems since then.

[14]The Technical Committee of the International Organization of Securities Commissions has been working toward international risk-based capital adequacy standards for securities firms. Efforts are being made to reconcile the differences between the capital requirements applicable to nonbank securities firms and those applicable to banks that engage in securities activities. In the United States, Congress recently provided authority to the Commodity Futures Trading Commission to more fully share information and cooperate with foreign regulators. In addition, the Securities and Exchange Commission is considering adjusting U.S. securities firms' capital standards to recognize more foreign markets and to collect data necessary to assess the need for additional regulation of the financial activities of U.S. securities firms' unregulated affiliates and broker-dealer holding companies.

Central banks and financial regulators have also become concerned about the risk exposure of participants engaging in derivatives transactions. Risks are posed in many ways, including by the volatility of the underlying markets. A market participant's exposure can change drastically with fluctuations in interest rates or equity prices: a small shift in share prices, for example, can result in a big change in the value of a stock-index option. Other risks pertain to the management of sizable positions by large financial institutions and the credit quality of these "wholesale" enterprises and their customers. Still another risk concerns illiquidity. Although derivatives traded on exchanges have many buyers and sellers, those tailored to specific customers' needs (such as those traded in the over-the-counter markets) are more difficult to liquidate since they are more difficult to value and to hedge against. In addition, the opaqueness of some of these transactions, especially over-the-counter contracts, compounds the difficulty for regulators of monitoring market participants in derivatives. Furthermore, as more and larger traders, driven by technical trading methods, seek to move increasingly large sums between markets, market volatility is likely to increase. The closer linkages among markets that are fostered by the growth of derivatives mean that financial shocks can be transmitted across markets quickly.

The growth in derivative instruments has created not only complex chains of counterparty (buyer or seller) exposures but also, in the case of exchange rate contracts, a significant expansion of international payment and settlement activities. To reduce risks and guard against payment "gridlock," the Federal Reserve and other central banks are closely monitoring their payment and settlement mechanisms. In addition, the Basle Committee has focused on ways of expanding the Basle Capital Accord to cover credit risk and various types of market risks, such as foreign exchange rate risk, interest rate risk, and position risks in traded equity securities. (For a discussion of the various types of risks arising from derivatives transactions, see Federal Reserve Board of Governors et al., 1993; Bank for International Settlements, 1992b; Group of Thirty, 1993.)

In sum, the interactions among countries' interest rates, exchange rates, and securities prices, hastened by the increase in capital mobility and the linkages of world financial markets, have major policy implications. The economic performance of one country—especially an industrial one with high capital mobility—will be affected by policies and market developments in other countries. There is a blurring of the traditional distinction between domestic and international economic policy. Policy makers in major industrial countries need to take account of policies and policy intentions elsewhere. In a world of growing interdependence among nations, enhanced capital mobility will, in some cases, help policy makers achieve their domestic macroeconomic objectives; in other cases, however, it may undercut the effect of national policies on domestic economic performance.

IMPLICATIONS OF GLOBALIZATION FOR DATA COLLECTION

In this new global economic environment, to better formulate U.S. macroeconomic policy, monitor financial market performance, and oversee the stability of the domestic financial system, comprehensive information on U.S. international capital transactions will be required. At the same time, the unprecedented changes in global financial markets have reduced the effectiveness of traditional data collection methods and the adequacy of the existing data. This section provides an overview and some examples of the deficiencies of the existing data. The rest of the report addresses the shortcomings in detail and presents the panel's recommendations for data improvement.

The present U.S. data collection system for international capital transactions originated some 50 years ago (see Chapter 2). At that time, portfolio investment was largely channeled through such traditional financial instruments as bank loans and deposits, denominated mostly in U.S. dollars, and handled by a relatively small number of large banks and financial institutions. The current system, as it has evolved, still emphasizes the collection of data on traditional international banking transactions. But the rise in nonbank market participants (in particular, institutional investors), the surge in international financial flows and their diversification across currencies, the increase in offshore financial activities, and the burgeoning international trade in derivative financial instruments have outstripped the coverage of the U.S. data system. Rapid technological innovations have also allowed numerous transactions to bypass domestic financial intermediaries, and such transactions are beyond the reach of the traditional reporting mechanisms, thus raising questions about the adequacy of relying largely on domestic data filers. Meanwhile, as U.S. international capital transactions have proliferated and become more complex, the work required to compile comprehensive information on them has greatly expanded and become much more costly for both statistical agencies and those who report the raw data.

The conceptual framework under which the existing data are collected, that of the balance of payments, defines U.S. international transactions as those between U.S. residents and those outside U.S. boundaries. (See Chapter 2 for a detailed discussion of the U.S. balance-of-payments accounts.) The purpose of this framework is to compile information on economic exchanges that cross the border between the United States and the rest of the world. These data provide vital information needed to understand the external sector of the economy and how it affects domestic economic activity. International transactions, defined in this way, are a component of the national accounts (which include the national income and product accounts, the flow-of-funds accounts, and the balance sheets of the U.S. economy). However, as financial activities have become global in nature, the resident-nonresident distinction has become inadequate to fully depict all facets of these activities. Increasingly, cross-border financial exchanges represent capital transfers among the worldwide offices and branches of U.S. financial institutions, rather than transactions largely between U.S. firms and foreign firms. There is also a growing presence of foreign-owned firms in the U.S. domestic markets and of U.S.-owned firms in markets abroad. These developments have complicated the identification of resident versus nonresident transactions. More important, as discussed above, internationalization of financial transactions has given rise to policy concerns about the liquidity, solvency, and stability of the U.S. financial system insofar as it is affected by foreign markets. These are issues the balance-of-payments framework was not designed to treat. There is need to supplement the existing balance-of-payments data with other information on U.S. financial activities to guide the decisions to be made on myriad emerging public policies.

In its report (Kester, 1992), the Panel on Foreign Trade Statistics recommended supplementing the existing trade statistics, collected under the balance-of-payments framework, with economic information collected outside it to better depict the globalized U.S. business activities in goods and services. Such a broader framework would greatly assist in addressing such issues as U.S. international competitiveness and the impact of foreign trade and direct investment on U.S. employment and production. This report makes recommendations to improve the coverage and accuracy of the existing data, but it also proposes ways to supplement them with data on the burgeoning financial derivatives transactions collected outside the traditional balance-of-payments framework.

The need for improved data is further evidenced by the incomplete accounting of the sizable U.S. international capital flows in recent years and the uncertainty associated with it about the U.S. financial position in the world economy and other economic and financial developments. A few examples follow.

- U.S. statistics for 1982 indicate that the rate at which nonresidents were acquiring assets in the United States was less than the rate at which U.S. residents were securing assets abroad. But the statistical discrepancy of the U.S. balance-of-payments accounts in that year was larger than the difference between these two totals: current account receipts or net inflows of capital of about $41 billion were not identified or recorded. Thus, the direction of the net capital flow could have been the opposite of that reported in the 1982 U.S. balance-of-payments accounts.

- When initially released, data for 1985 on the U.S. net international investment position showed that foreign assets of U.S. residents were less than their liabilities to foreigners. The press referred to the United States as being "a debtor nation" for the first time since before World War I. The cumulating liabilities, whose burden could fall on the next generation as well, were deemed to imply the obligation to pay future interest, dividends, profits, and amortization to foreign investors. However, the U.S. data on U.S. residents' direct investments and claims on foreigners was listed at book value, omitting any increase in market value of the investment over time. Some analysts believed that this source of understatement in the U.S. international investment position was so large that U.S. liabilities to foreigners for 1985 were, in fact, smaller than U.S. holdings of foreign assets. Yet others pointed out a measurement error in the other direction: the cumulative statistical discrepancy in the U.S. balance-of-payments accounts as reported at the same time totaled $117 billion for the years 1981-1985 alone, indicating possibly sizable unreported capital inflows.

These data have subsequently undergone several revisions, and BEA has also begun publishing market value as well as historical cost estimates of total asset values. According to recently published data (Bureau of Economic Analysis, 1994a:71), foreign assets owned by U.S. residents in 1985 *exceeded* foreigners' ownership of U.S. assets, measured either by historical cost or market value. Since 1989 however, foreigners' ownership of U.S. assets has exceeded the foreign holdings of U.S. residents', using either the historical cost or market value measures.

Even the revised data may tend to more closely track foreigners' investments in the United States than U.S. residents' investments abroad, however. Until 1994, U.S. holdings of foreign securities had not been comprehensively surveyed since World War II.[15] In addition, despite the recorded "net indebtedness," official statistics show that U.S. earnings (interest and profits) on investments abroad continue to be larger than the earnings paid by the United States to foreigners on their U.S. investments.

• Until the 1980s, as noted above, banks dominated the international financial system, but securitization has occurred rapidly since then. U.S. official statistics show foreign purchases of U.S. securities as exceeding bank-reported liabilities as the largest component of the capital inflow in 1985. But a recent study by the Federal Reserve Bank of New York (1992a) indicates that as much as $70 billion of foreign lending to U.S. business that took place offshore in the 1980s was not included in the official statistics of U.S. international capital transactions. This funding raises the question of whether official statistics have overstated securities as a source of financing and understated the major role still played by banks.[16]

• U.S. statistics show that 1985 sales of U.S. Treasury securities to foreigners, although many times greater than those in 1980, were still relatively small ($20.5 billion, of which 83 percent was sold to Japanese residents) (Frankel, 1988:592). Yet official Japanese statistics show that the value of U.S. Treasury securities bought by Japanese residents was much larger than was shown in the U.S. data. For 1986, the discrepancy between U.S.-reported sales of U.S. Treasury securities to Japan and Japanese-reported purchases of U.S. Treasury securities was $37 billion ($12.8 billion and $49.4 billion, respectively). Since U.S. Treasury securities are sold in global markets and the U.S. official data do not identify the ultimate owner of the securities, the holdings of U.S.

---

[15]The survey was conducted in 1994, but as of mid-1994 there was no firm schedule for data release.

[16]Recently published revised data (Bureau of Economic Analysis, 1994a) contain dramatic upward revisions in estimates of U.S. nonbanks liabilities to foreigners for the years 1983-1993. These revisions result largely from BEA's continuing program to use data reported by foreign banks. Much of the revision is based on data from the Bank for International Settlements (BIS) on bank claims reported in Caribbean and Asian banking centers.

Treasury securities held by particular countries remain unclear. In addition, U.S. data on capital transactions do not identify the extent to which U.S. assets held by foreigners are in practice hedged in foreign currencies. This deficiency has hampered the analysis of the vulnerability of the dollar to foreign portfolio shifts.

• The United States was able to continue financing large trade deficits in 1987 and thereafter without major depreciation of the dollar: one explanation is that foreign central banks stepped in to buy dollars when private investors had become wary of trading. Although official statistics on central bank transactions are believed to be better than those on private transactions, even the official statistics are problematic. When a foreign central bank acquires dollars and deposits them in a commercial bank abroad, the dollar holdings will not show up in the U.S. statistics as foreign *official* holdings of dollars. They will appear as U.S. liabilities to foreign commercial banks. The published figures of foreign official holdings of dollars, therefore, may understate the extent of foreign government intervention in foreign exchange markets; this happened in 1987. The Federal Reserve Bank of New York, using its own data and other sources, has estimated that foreign official purchases of dollars in 1987, including the private channeling of official capital, may have been almost three times higher than the $45 billion that was recorded in the U.S. balance-of-payments accounts.

• In the late 1980s, Americans became more concerned about another sizable component of the capital inflow: foreign direct investment in the United States. The news media carried stories that Japanese and other foreign investors were building factories and buying assets in the United States, including such national symbols as Rockefeller Center and the Seattle Mariners baseball team. How extensive is foreign direct investment in the United States and what is its economic impact? The availability of data bearing on these questions has expanded in the last few years, but gaps remain (see Chapter 3).

• In 1990 and 1991, with the American economy in recession, the question arose as to whether monetary policy had been too tight. During 1990, M1 grew at 4.0 percent, and it grew 8.7 percent in 1991. On the face of it, this might have appeared to be adequate money growth to finance the economy. In 1990, however, an increase in currency outstanding constituted three-quarters of the increase in M1 ($24.2 billion of $32.0 billion). Some estimates suggest that over half of U.S. dollar currency outstanding is held in Latin America and other foreign countries, where it is often a good shelter from local inflation and taxation. A Federal Reserve analysis suggests that there was a large unmeasured outflow of U.S. currency in 1990 (perhaps $15 billion of the $47.4 billion errors and omissions in the U.S. international transaction accounts[17]) and that, as a result, the observed M1 growth gave a misleadingly expansionary indication of monetary conditions (Stekler and Truman, 1992:5). In 1991, the increase in currency explains only 28 percent of the increase in M1 ($20.5 billion of $72.0 billion). Clearly, better data on international shipments of U.S. currency would help the Federal Reserve to design monetary policies for the goals it seeks.

In summary, U.S. financial activities are becoming increasingly globalized. The formulation of U.S. macroeconomic and financial supervisory policies and the public debate over U.S. external indebtedness depend on reliable statistics that accurately depict the nature and extent of U.S. international financial transactions. They are also needed to evaluate exchange market conditions and potential pressures, to examine the risk exposure of U.S. financial institutions, and to assess foreign ownership of U.S. business. Without such statistics, informed decisions will be difficult to make and sound policies will at times be lacking.

It should be noted here that the United States produces as much detailed data on its international capital transactions as any country in the world. The United States is not alone in facing problems of collecting and integrating data on such transactions. Other countries are confronted with similar problems and are working to improve their data (see Appendix A). In principle, global outflows should equal global inflows. However, as reported by the International Monetary Fund (1993b), the statistical discrepancy in the global capital account averaged nearly $120 billion a year during 1989-1992: that is, recorded capital inflows exceeded outflows by that amount, on average, for every year during that period.

---

[17]The errors and omissions for 1990 have since been revised downward to $40 billion (Bureau of Economic Analysis, 1994a:95).

2

Current U.S. Data Systems

Information on U.S. international capital flows is published on a quarterly basis in the U.S. international transaction accounts (commonly referred to as the U.S. balance-of-payments accounts), along with data on U.S. merchandise trade, international services transactions, investment incomes (and payments), and unilateral transfers.[1] The balance-of-payments accounts represent a summary statistical statement of transactions in goods, services, incomes, unilateral transfers, and capital flows between U.S. residents and nonresidents (foreigners) during a given period. Residents and nonresidents are distinguished by geographical boundaries.[2]

This chapter discusses concepts underlying the balance-of-payments accounts, describes the methods used to collect data on U.S. international capital transactions and the major sources of

---

[1]Unilateral transfers cover international transactions in which goods, services, or financial assets are transferred between U.S. residents and residents of other countries with no requirement for payment. U.S. government grants are examples of unilateral transfers. Also included are private remittances by individuals and institutions.

[2]Under the balance-of-payments framework, the terms *residents* and *nonresidents* are broadly defined to include individuals, business establishments, governments, and international organizations. A nonresident (foreign) business establishment is any plant, office, branch, or other entity that is physically located outside the geographic boundaries of the United States, irrespective of the nationality of its owners.

the published information. Its purpose is twofold: to set the stage for the analysis in Chapter 3 and to note the use of the information required of data filers and how it is compiled into national statistics. In its survey of filers and users of currently required data, the panel found that filers were not familiar with the purposes of the data required of them and that users were uncertain about the quality of the published data. In addition, data filers and, to a certain extent, data users were not fully aware of the various published sources of information on U.S. international capital transactions (see Appendix B). The panel believes that accurate knowledge of the system will encourage accurate and timely reporting by filers and will enhance users' knowledge of the availability of the data and an understanding of its limitations.

BALANCE-OF-PAYMENTS FRAMEWORK: CONCEPTS AND USES

The basic assumption underlying the balance-of-payments framework is that receipts equal payments. Just as, in business accounting, debits equal credits, the same principle applies to the transactions of a nation. By definition, total receipts on current account items are necessarily equal to current account payments plus the net increase in claims on foreigners. The current account of the U.S. balance of payments covers exports and imports of goods and services, unilateral transfers, and incomes on investment, while the capital account records financial transactions. Data for these accounts for 1990-1993 are shown in Table 2-1. The Bureau of Economic Analysis (BEA) of the Department of Commerce is responsible for the compilation of the U.S. balance-of-payments accounts.

In principle, the balance of the current account equals that of the capital account because the underlying framework is the double-entry accounting concept. Under this concept, it is assumed that when merchandise is exported (a credit), the exporter receives a payment either in a foreign bank (a capital outflow debit) or in a domestic bank (a debit as a foreign account is drawn down) or extends credit to the importer (a capital outflow debit). It is an accounting convention that an export is treated as a credit or a plus entry; an import, a debit, is represented by a minus entry. For financial transactions, decreases in an economy's foreign assets or increases in an economy's foreign liabilities are treated as credit entries. Conversely, debit entries reflect increases in for-

TABLE 2-1   U.S. International Transactions, Current and Capital Accounts, 1990-1993 (in millions of dollars)

Category	1990	1991	1992	1993
Current account				
Exports of goods, services,				
and income	696,841	717,041	731,373	755,533
Merchandise	389,303	416,913	440,361	456,866
Services	147,239	163,215	176,563	184,811
Income	160,300	136,914	114,449	113,856
Imports of goods, services,				
and income	−754,926	−730,680	−767,217	−827,312
Merchandise	−498,336	−490,981	−536,458	−589,441
Services	−117,016	−117,618	−120,850	−127,961
Income	−139,574	−122,081	−109,909	−109,910
Unilateral transfers				
(excluding military grants				
of goods and services, net)	−33,663	6,687	−32,042	−32,117
Current account balance	−91,748	−6,952	−67,886	−103,896
Capital account				
U.S. assets abroad, net	−70,363	−51,512	−61,510	−147,898
U.S. official reserve assets	−2,158	5,763	3,901	−1,379
U.S. government assets				
other than official				
reserve assets	2,307	2,900	−1,652	−306
U.S. private assets	−70,512	−60,175	−63,759	−146,213
Foreign assets in the U.S., net	122,192	98,134	146,504	230,698
Foreign official assets				
in the U.S.	33,910	17,199	40,858	71,681
Other foreign assets				
in the U.S.	88,282	80,935	105,646	159,017
Capital account balance	51,829	46,622	84,994	82,800
Statistical discrepancy	39,919	−39,670	−17,108	21,096

SOURCE: Data from Bureau of Economic Analysis (1994a:94-95).

eign assets or decreases in foreign liabilities. This concept is useful because people want to know both the size of the trade balance and how it is financed. Or they want to know why a country is gaining or losing official reserves.

Under the double-entry concept, the sum of all transactions should be zero: both sides of each transaction should offset one another and the balance of the current account should equal that of the capital account, with opposite signs. However, unlike the internal consistency of ordinary business accounts, the compilers of the balance-of-payment accounts must gather information from a variety of independent sources: merchandise trade is based on

customs data, and the entries in banking or other financial accounts are derived from a variety of sources. Since the data or
estimates used are from diverse sources, they usually cannot be
reconciled exactly, leading to a balancing item representing the
net errors or omissions, denoted as "statistical discrepancy" in
the accounts. The statistical discrepancy represents only the ar-
ithmetical difference between the balances of the current and the
capital accounts; it does not reflect the gross errors and omissions
of the different types of transactions, which may be larger than
the statistical discrepancy. Gross errors and omissions in different accounts may offset one another.

An important purpose of the balance-of-payments data is to
provide information needed to understand the impact of the external sector on the domestic economy. The balance-of-payments
data form a key component of the national accounts, which also
include the national income and product accounts (NIPA) compiled by BEA, and the flow-of-funds accounts and the balance
sheets of the U.S. economy, both prepared by the Federal Reserve.
The balance-of-payments data enter into these other components
of the accounts; Figure 2-1 shows the sources and uses of the
balance-of-payments data.

The NIPA measures the production, distribution, and use of
output in the United States by four economic groups: persons,
business, government, and "the rest of the world." It would be
impossible to have a complete set of NIPA for an open economy
without taking account of net exports and their composition. Exports of goods and services are part of the gross domestic product
(GDP). Imports are part of consumer expenditures, gross domestic investment, and the other components of gross national expenditure. The difference between a nation's saving and its investment has to include net foreign investment (positive or negative)
to be complete.[3] During the past decade, for example, the United
States financed an important part of its federal budget deficit by
incurring a current account deficit, which showed up, cumula-
tively, as a reduction in net foreign assets. This development is
reflected in the balance-of-payments accounts.[4]

---

[3]Consider the basic equation: $(I - S) + (G - T) + (X - M) = 0$, where I is gross
domestic investment, S is gross private saving, G is government spending, T is
tax revenue ($G - T$ is the budget deficit), X is exports of goods and services, and
M is imports of goods and services (so that $X - M$ is the current account position).
That is, if the federal deficit is not offset by net saving in the private sector, the
current account will be in deficit. This is a useful way of analyzing what is
happening in a country, and it involves the balance-of-payments data.

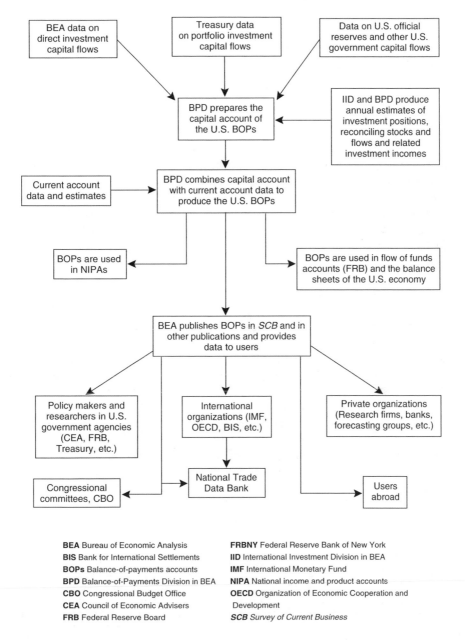

FIGURE 2-1   Sources and uses of U.S. balance-of-payments data on capital accounts.

The flow-of-funds accounts detail the sources and uses of savings in the U.S. economy by sector and by type of transaction. They are useful in assessing the effect of monetary policy and the general financial conditions of various domestic sectors. The balance sheets of the U.S. economy show the assets and liabilities of the country. These data, together with other information gathered for regulatory purposes, are used in monitoring the safety and soundness of U.S. financial systems.

Another use of the balance-of-payments data is to show the external financial position of the nation as reflected in its net foreign investment position and how this position is changing over time. If the United States is increasingly becoming a net debtor to the rest of the world, that has implications for the welfare of future generations. Similarly, the trends of trade and capital flows, as displayed by the current and the capital account data over time, are intended to guide assessments about the nation's foreign exchange rate, whether the rate is likely to change or should be changed, and whether the country's external trade imbalance can be sustained.

BEA publishes U.S. balance-of-payments data quarterly in its *Survey of Current Business*. Figure 2-2 (box) lists selected publications prepared by BEA on U.S. international transactions.

In addition to providing an important data source for the preparation of the national accounts, various components of the U.S. balance of payments are used by both the public and the private sectors, as well as by international organizations and abroad. Researchers and policy analysts extensively use the direct investment data collected by BEA, as well as other available data sources, in their analysis of the effects of foreign direct investment in the United States on U.S. production and employment and the competitiveness of U.S. firms in global markets. Data on international transactions in U.S. and foreign securities, as well as other

---

[4]Note that the identity, $S - I = X - M$, fundamental to the balance-of-payments framework, implies that to the extent domestic saving is not matched by an increase in domestic capital accumulation, there will be an increase in U.S. private or official claims on the rest of the world. By the same token, a deficit in the current account must be financed by some combination of a decrease in claims on nonresidents and an increase in liabilities to nonresidents so that the result is a decline in net foreign assets held by the domestic economy.

The identity defines the relationship among the variables. It does not, however, describe the behavior of economic agents. By itself, the equation cannot provide a comprehensive analysis of the forces behind the developments in the current account.

available data sources, inform market research. Data on short- and long-term international capital transactions, by country, are examined to assess market pressures and determine worldwide capital flows. Data on cross-border deposits are analyzed to determine their significance for implementation of monetary policy. The data are also reviewed to assess the long-term sustainability of the U.S. external imbalances and their relationship to domestic saving and investment. In short, the balance-of-payments data are used in both the public and private sectors to analyze the nation's short-term external payment imbalances, its longer term structural finance, exchange rate movements, and sources of credit and liquidity creation, among others.

The statistical discrepancy in the U.S. balance-of-payments accounts grew significantly during the 1970s and 1980s, both in absolute and relative terms. It was also marked by large fluctuations; see Figure 2-3: it surged from a cumulative total of –$5.5 billion for 1960-1969 to +$36.9 billion for 1970-1979 and to +$221.6 billion for 1980-1989. In 1989 alone, the statistical discrepancy was +53.1 billion, or more than 8 percent of exports plus investment income. In 1992 and 1993 however, the discrepancy dropped to between 2 and 3 percent of exports plus investment income.

The striking difference in the magnitudes, variations, and trends between the statistical discrepancy before and after the early 1970s suggests that the net errors and omissions in the U.S. balance-of-payments accounts since the early 1970s have not resulted largely from random events. In its report (Kester, 1992), the Panel on Foreign Trade Statistics found that U.S. exports of goods and services have been persistently underreported. Complex developments in U.S. international financial transactions since the 1970s, coupled with a data collection system that lagged behind those changes, also led to increasingly inaccurate valuations, growing inadequacies in coverage, and errors in estimation procedures of capital flows and investment incomes that affected the size of the statistical discrepancy (see also Stekler, 1991). To understand how the adequacy of the existing data on U.S. international capital transactions has been affected by changes in the world financial markets, the next section describes how these data are collected.

CAPITAL ACCOUNT DATA

Capital flows in U.S. balance-of-payments accounts refer to transactions in financial assets between U.S. residents and nonresidents (foreigners). Financial assets include loans, bank deposits,

GENERAL

The Balance of Payments of the United States: Concepts, Data Sources, and Estimating Procedures
Survey of Current Business (monthly)
  U.S. international transactions (March, June, September, and December)
  The international investment position of the United States (June)
  Foreign direct investment in the United States
    Direct investment position and related flows of capital, income, and
      royalties and license fees (June)
    Operations of U.S. affiliates of foreign companies (May)
    U.S. business enterprises acquired or established by foreign direct
      investors (May)
U.S. direct investment abroad
    Direct investment position and related
      flows of capital, income, and royalties and license fees (June)
    Operations of U.S. parent companies and their foreign affiliates (June)
    Capital expenditures by majority-owned foreign affiliates of U.S.
      companies (March and September)

U.S. DIRECT INVESTMENT ABROAD

Gross Product of U.S. Multinational Companies, 1977-91
U.S. Direct Investment Abroad: 1989 Benchmark Survey, Final Results
U.S. Direct Investment Abroad: Operations of U.S. Companies and Their Foreign Affiliates. Annually from 1990
U.S. Direct Investment Abroad: Balance of Payments and Direct Investment Position Estimates,1977-81
U.S. Direct Investment Abroad, Country by Industry Estimates. 1950-91 (only on computer tape)

FOREIGN DIRECT INVESTMENT IN THE UNITED STATES

A Guide to BEA Statistics on Foreign Direct Investment in the United States
Characteristics of Foreign-Owned U.S. Manufacturing Establishments
Foreign Direct Investment in the United States: Operations of U.S. Affiliates of Foreign Companies. Annually from 1989
Foreign Direct Investment in the United States. 1987 Benchmark Survey. Final Results; 1992 preliminary result
Foreign Direct Investment in the United States: Establishment Data for 1987 (also available on diskette). Establishment data for manufacturing available annually from 1988
Foreign Direct Investment in the United States: Balance of Payments and Direct Investment Position Estimates. 1980-86
Foreign Direct Investment in the United States: Direct Investment Position and Related Capital and Income Flows. Annually from 1980 (only on diskette)
1992 Benchmark Survey Results
U.S. Business Enterprises Acquired or Established by Foreign Direct Investors. Supplementary Tables

OTHER RECENT STUDIES

Gross product of U.S. affiliates of foreign direct investors, 1987-90, *Survey of Current Business*, November 1992 (updates data in June 1990 Lowe article, below)

Rates of return on direct investment, by J. Steven Landefeld, Ann M. Lawson, and Douglas Weinberg, *Survey of Current Business*, August 1992

U.S. direct investment abroad: 1989 benchmark survey results, by Jeffrey Lowe and Raymond Mataloni, *Survey of Current Business*, October 1991

Valuation of the U.S. net international investment position, by J. Steven Landefeld and Ann M. Lawson, *Survey of Current Business*, May 1991

Gross product of U.S. affiliates of foreign direct investors, 1977-87, by Jeffrey Lowe, *Survey of Current Business*, June 1990

FIGURE 2-2 Selected BEA publications and articles on balance-of-payments data by topic.

drafts, acceptances, notes, government and private debt, equity securities, trade finance, and direct investments. When U.S. residents increase their financial assets abroad or foreigners decrease their financial assets in the United States, a capital outflow takes place and should be recorded. The converse is true for capital inflows.

There are two major types of capital flow transactions: private and official. Private capital flows include direct investment and portfolio investment (banking, securities, and other commercial and financial transactions). U.S. official capital flows include changes in the reserves of U.S. monetary authorities—monetary gold, foreign exchange, special drawing rights at the International Monetary Fund (IMF)—and loans and credits to foreigners by U.S. government agencies. These capital flows are reported in the capital account of the balance of payments (see Table 2-2). Incomes (earnings and profits) on direct and portfolio investment are reported in the current account.[5]

Among private capital flows, portfolio investments have far exceeded direct investment in recent years; see Figures 2-4 and 2-5. For example, in 1993, net private capital flows pertaining to inward and outward direct investment activities totaled approximately $79 billion in absolute terms ($21.4 billion and $57.9 bil-

---

[5]Also included in the current account are government grants and private remittances, which are considered unilateral transfers.

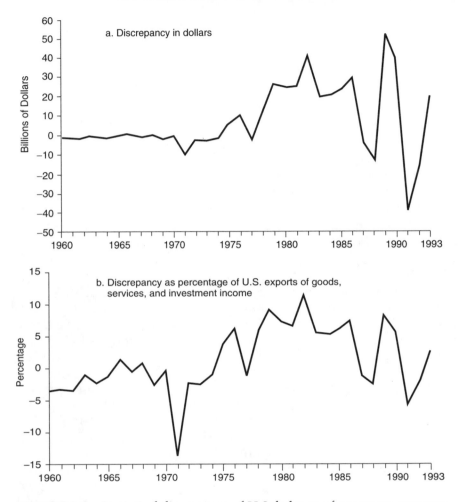

FIGURE 2-3 Statistical discrepancy of U.S. balance-of-payments accounts, 1960-1993.

lion, respectively); those that were induced by international port-folio transactions amounted to $226 billion in absolute terms (Table 2-2).

As noted above, the value of accumulated stocks of U.S. assets abroad and of foreign assets in the United States—resulting from capital flows in and out of this country over time (as adjusted for factors affecting their values)—is annually compiled and published in the statement of U.S. international investment position; see Table 2-3.

TABLE 2-2 U.S. Capital Account Transactions (in millions of dollars)

Transaction	1991	1992	1993
U.S. assets abroad, net	−51,512	−61,510	−147,898
U.S. official reserve assets, net	5,763	3,901	−1,379
Gold	0	0	0
Special drawing rights	−177	2,316	−537
Reserve position in the International Monetary Fund	−367	−2,692	−44
Foreign currencies	6,307	4,277	−797
U.S. government assets, other than official reserve assets, net	2,900	−1,652	−306
U.S. credits and other long-term assets	−12,874	−7,392	−6,024
Repayments on U.S. credits and other long-term assets	16,776	5,805	6,026
U.S. foreign currency holdings and U.S. short-term assets, net	−1,002	−65	−308
U.S. private assets, net	−60,175	−63,759	−146,213
Direct investment	−31,295	−41,004	−57,870
Foreign securities	−44,740	−45,114	−119,983
U.S. claims on unaffiliated foreigners reported by U.S. nonbanking concerns	11,097	45	−598
U.S. claims reported by U.S. banks, not included elsewhere	4,763	22,314	32,238
Foreign assets in the United States, net	98,134	146,504	230,698
Foreign official assets in the United States, net	17,199	40,858	71,681
U.S. government securities	16,147	22,403	52,764
U.S. Treasury securities	14,846	18,454	48,702
Other	1,301	3,949	4,062
Other U.S. government liabilities	1,177	2,572	1,666
U.S. liabilities reported by U.S. banks, not included elsewhere	−1,484	16,571	14,666
Other foreign official assets	1,359	−688	2,585
Other foreign assets in the United States, net	80,935	105,646	159,017
Direct investment	26,086	9,888	21,366
U.S. Treasury securities	18,826	36,857	24,849
U.S. securities other than U.S. Treasury securities	35,144	29,867	80,068
U.S. liabilities to unaffiliated foreigners reported by U.S. nonbanking concerns	−3,115	13,573	14,282
U.S. liabilities reported by U.S. banks, not included elsewhere	3,994	15,461	18,452

SOURCE: Data from Bureau of Economic Analysis (1994a:94–95).

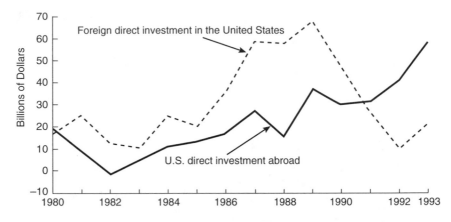

FIGURE 2-4   Direct investment flows, 1980-1993.

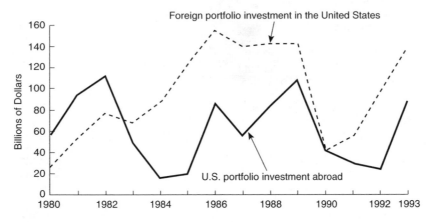

FIGURE 2-5   Private portfolio investment flows, 1980-1993.

DATA COLLECTION SYSTEM

With regard to capital flow data, there are three main elements in the present system (see Figure 2-1):

1.   BEA collects information on U.S. direct investment abroad and foreign direct investment in the United States using a series of questionnaires completed by the U.S. parent companies that invest abroad and the U.S. affiliates of foreign companies in the United States.

2.   The Treasury Department, using the Federal Reserve banks

TABLE 2-3   International Investment Position of the United States, December 31, 1993, preliminary figures (in billions of dollars)

Type of Investment	Position
Net international investment position of the United States	
With direct investment positions at current cost	–556
[With direct investment positions at market value]	[–508]
U.S. assets abroad	
With direct investment positions at current cost	2,370
[With direct investment positions at market value]	[2,647]
U.S. official reserve assets	165
Gold	103
Special drawing rights	9
Reserve position in the International Monetary Fund	12
Foreign currencies	42
U.S. government assets, other than official reserve assets	81
U.S. credits and other long-term assets[a]	79
Repayable in dollars	78
Other[b]	1
U.S. foreign currency holdings and U.S. short-term assets	2
U.S. private assets	
With direct investment at current cost	2,125
[With direct investment at market value]	[2,402]
Direct investment abroad	
At current cost	716
[At market value]	[993]
Foreign securities	518
Bonds	221
Corporate stocks	298
U.S. claims on unaffiliated foreigners reported by	
U.S. nonbanking concerns	255
U.S. claims reported by U.S. banks, not included elsewhere	635
Foreign assets in the United States	
With direct investment at current cost	2,926
[With direct investment at market value]	[3,155]
Foreign official assets in the United States	517
U.S. government securities	389
U.S. Treasury securities	371
Other	18
Other U.S. government liabilities[c]	23
U.S. liabilities reported by U.S. banks, not included elsewhere	70
Other foreign official assets	36

continued on next page

TABLE 2-3 Continued

Type of Investment	Position
Other foreign assets	
With direct investment at current cost	2,409
[With direct investment at market value]	[2,638]
Direct investment in the United States	
At current cost	517
[At market value]	[746]
U.S. Treasury securities	254
U.S. securities other than U.S. Treasury securities	733
Corporate and other bonds	393
Corporate stocks	340
U.S. liabilities to unaffiliated foreigners reported by	
U.S. nonbanking concerns	233
U.S. liabilities reported by U.S. banks, not included elsewhere	672

[a]Also includes paid-in capital subscriptions to international financial institutions and outstanding amounts of miscellaneous claims that have been settled through international agreements to be payable to the U.S. government over periods in excess of one year. Excludes World War I debts that are not being serviced.

[b]Includes indebtedness that the borrower may contractually, or at its option, repay with its currency, with a third country's currency, or by delivery of materials or transfer of services.

[c]Primarily U.S. government liabilities associated with military sales contracts and other transactions arranged with or through foreign official agencies.

SOURCE: Bureau of Economic Analysis (1994a:71).

as agents, collects data on portfolio investment, including international banking, securities, commercial, and miscellaneous capital flows and positions. These data are collected on a number of reporting forms called the TIC (Treasury International Capital) reports, and data aggregates are provided to BEA.

3. BEA obtains data from relevant U.S. government agencies on their international capital transactions. It also compiles data on the international official reserve assets and liabilities of the United States from the Treasury Department and the Federal Reserve system.

BEA is responsible for collating data from all these sources to construct the data for the U.S. balance of payments and U.S. international investment position. BEA's budget for these functions was about $12 million for fiscal 1992, of which about $8 million was allocated for the collection of data on foreign direct investment in the United States and U.S. direct investment abroad.[6] The Treasury Department has no separate budget for its TIC data program. The costs to the Federal Reserve banks of collecting the TIC data are borne by their own budgets. The Federal Reserve Bank of New York (FRBNY) estimated that for 1992 Federal Reserve banks expended approximately $2 million for this purpose. To put these budget figures in perspective, one needs to note that, in the same year, the Bureau of the Census expended approximately $20 million in compiling data on U.S. merchandise exports and imports. In that year, federal funding for major statistical programs was about $2.4 billion, of which $944 million was allocated to ten major statistical agencies.[7]

Much of the data collection system on U.S. international capital transactions, which has been developed and refined over the years, depends on collaboration between BEA, the Treasury Department, and the Federal Reserve system.[8] For instance, it is essential that all definitions used be consistent, that the coverage of respondents not be duplicated, that there not be major gaps due to missing potential respondents or to new or unusual types of international transactions or market participants, and that requirements of timeliness be met. Since June 1992 BEA has also moved to coordinate data on direct investments with data collected by the Bureau of the Census and the Bureau of Labor Statistics to develop more detailed information by industry and employment on foreign investment in the United States. Recently, BEA and

---

[6]BEA's fiscal 1993, 1994, and 1995 requests for additional funding for improving balance-of-payments and international investment data were not approved. Late in fiscal 1994, BEA found it necessary to shift $750,000 from its other work to the international area, in part to support processing of the Treasury Department's 1994 benchmark survey of U.S. holdings of foreign securities.

[7]The ten statistical agencies were the Bureau of the Census and the Bureau of Economic Analysis in the U.S. Department of Commerce; the Bureau of Labor Statistics of the U.S. Department of Labor; the Statistics of Income Office of the Internal Revenue Service of the U.S. Department of the Treasury; the National Agricultural Statistics Service and the Economic Research Service of the U.S. Department of Agriculture; the Energy Information Administration of the U.S. Department of Energy; the National Center for Health Statistics of the U.S. Department of Health and Human Services; the National Center for Education Statistics of the U.S. Department of Education; and the Bureau of Justice Statistics of the U.S. Department of Justice. Figures exclude Census Bureau periodic programs (U.S. Office of Management and Budget, 1994).

[8]A detailed description of the methods of collecting these data can be found in Bureau of Economic Analysis (1990). Recent revisions of the collection procedures are reported in Bureau of Economic Analysis (1992a; 1993a; 1994a).

the Treasury Department have embarked on a data-sharing program intended to improve capital flow data. In all these collaborative efforts, strict confidentiality of individual reports is preserved.

All of the direct and portfolio investment reports are mandatory, although some exemption levels are set to avoid unduly burdensome reporting of relatively insignificant amounts. Current legal authority for the collection of data on international capital flows and investment positions is provided by the International Investment and Trade in Services Survey Act of 1984. As stated in the act, direct investment is defined as "the ownership or control, directly or indirectly, by one person of 10 per centum or more of the voting securities of an incorporated business enterprise or an equivalent interest in an unincorporated business enterprise." Portfolio investment is defined as all investment that is not "direct investment." These definitions conform to the general guidelines provided by the International Monetary Fund (1993a).[9]

DIRECT INVESTMENTS

The BEA system for collecting data on direct investment, which has been developed since World War II, uses several sets of surveys to collect the data; see Table 2-4. Separate quarterly surveys are conducted to gather data on capital flows between U.S. parent companies and their foreign affiliates and between foreign companies and their U.S. affiliates. Data cover intracompany accounts, changes in holdings of equity or debt securities, and changes in capital employed out of undistributed profits (reinvested earnings). These data are tabulated in extensive geographic and industry detail. Data are collected from all known significant investors. For U.S. direct investment abroad, reports are required from U.S. companies that hold 10 percent or more of voting stock or equivalent interest in a foreign business enterprise (affiliate) when the affiliate's total assets, annual sales, or annual net income exceed $15 mil-

---

[9]This fifth edition of the *Manual* provided new guidelines for countries to reclassify transactions under the current account and the renamed "capital and financial account." The U.S. balance-of-payments accounts, like those of most other countries, are still prepared under the general guidelines of the fourth edition of the IMF *Manual*. U.S. conformance to the fifth edition guidelines is expected to take some time.

lion. For foreign direct investment in the United States, reports are required from U.S. business enterprises (affiliates) in which a foreign company holds 10 percent or more of voting stock or equivalent interest when the affiliate's assets, annual sales, or annual net income exceed $20 million. Annual reports are required from all significant direct investors to confirm the quarterly data and provide additional operating data. At approximately 5-year intervals, BEA conducts benchmark surveys (or censuses) of all outward and inward direct investments covering not only the data needed for the capital account, but also other economic data on each significant affiliate. These additional data are derived from the affiliates' balance sheets, profit and loss statements, and other operating accounts. They cover, for example, the book values of the enterprises, sales (local and exported), trade with the United States, wages paid and other operating expenses, taxes paid, and other information. With respect to inward direct investment, BEA also requires notification of any new acquisitions by foreigners (nonresidents) of direct investments in the United States.

Most U.S. outward and inward direct investments involve ownership of more than 50 percent, and certain types of data are required to be reported only when a majority ownership is held. When calculating the amount of earnings on direct investment in the international accounts, BEA makes allowance for the extent of partial ownerships. In addition, quarterly earnings data obtained by BEA are adjusted to allow for the relatively small amounts (below the exemption levels) not covered by the quarterly reporting system. Since 1992 BEA has made a similar adjustment to capital flow data to account for amounts below the exemption level and for delinquent reporters (see Bureau of Economic Analysis, 1992a:75). The process BEA uses in compiling direct investment data is illustrated in Figure 2-6.

By its nature, direct investment tends to be large, especially when the transaction involves the acquisition of an existing enterprise or the initiation of a new project. In order to maintain as complete coverage of each investment as possible, BEA actively seeks out all available sources of information—including the financial press and financial periodicals, among others—on new U.S. affiliates of foreign firms and new foreign affiliates of U.S. firms to identify new reporters.

According to BEA, reports by U.S. companies on their direct investment abroad in 1991 covered 9,200 affiliates in the quarterly reports (BE-577) and 10,800 in the annual reports. For the same year, 3,325 U.S. affiliates of foreign companies filed quar-

TABLE 2-4 Direct Investment Data Collected in BEA Surveys

Kind of Survey and Form Used	Who Reports	What Is Reported	Requirement Cutoff for Reporting[a]	Number of Reports Filed (year)
Direct transactions of U.S. reporter with foreign affiliate: BE-577	U.S. persons who hold 10 percent or more of voting stock or equivalent interest in a foreign business enterprise	Receipts of income on U.S. direct investment abroad; royalties and license fees; charges for services; U.S. direct investors' equity and debt position in their foreign affiliates	$15 million	9,200 (1991)
Transactions of U.S. affiliate, except an unincorporated bank, with foreign parent; transactions of U.S. banking branch or agency with foreign parent: BE-605 and BE-606B	U.S. business enterprises (affiliates) in which a foreign person holds 10 percent or more of voting stock or equivalent interest	Payments of income on foreign direct investment in the U.S.; royalties and license fees; charges for services; foreign direct investors equity and debt position in their U.S. affiliates	$20 million	3,325 (1991)

| Benchmark survey of U.S. direct investment abroad: BE-10, BE-10A Bank, BE-10B, and BE-10B Bank | U.S. persons who hold 10 percent or more of voting stock or equivalent interest in a foreign business enterprise and foreign affiliates of U.S. direct investors | Complete financial and operating data for U.S. persons who are direct investors abroad for each foreign affiliate; data on investment position and transactions between foreign affiliates and U.S. direct investors | $3 million | 18,800 (1987) |
| Benchmark survey of foreign direct investment in the United States: BE-12 | U.S. business enterprises (affiliates) in which one foreign person holds 10 percent or more of voting stock or equivalent interest | Complete financial and operating data for each U.S. affiliate of foreign direct investors; data on investment position and transactions between U.S. affiliates and foreign direct investors | $1 million | 10,500 (1989) |

NOTE: See Chapter 3 (Table 3-2) for details of all forms and their coverage.

Reporting is required when the affiliate's total assets, annual sales, or annual net income exceed the cutoff figure.

SOURCES: Data from Bureau of Economic Analysis (1990), and BEA staff.

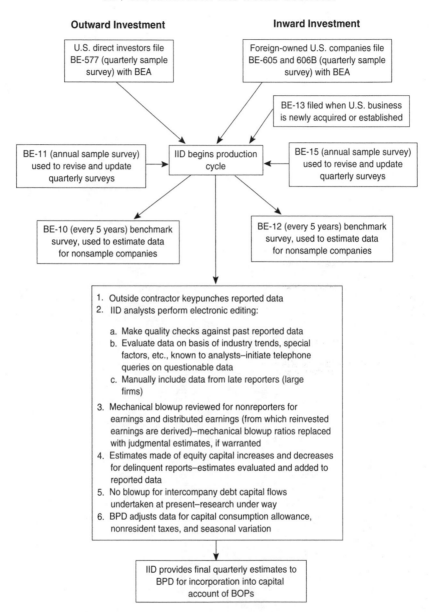

FIGURE 2-6 Direct investment data: sources and output.

terly reports (BE-605/606B), and 5,100 of them filed annual ones (BE-15).

The value of the U.S. direct investment position abroad at the end of 1993 (historical cost basis) was $549 billion. Of this amount, 36 percent was in manufacturing; 33 percent in banking and other finance, insurance and real estate; and the remainder spread over other industries. The foreign direct investment position in the United States was $445 billion, of which 37 percent was in manufacturing and 28 percent in finance (including banking), insurance and real estate (Bureau of Economic Analysis, 1994a).

PORTFOLIO INVESTMENTS

In principle, all international capital flows other than direct investment between private U.S. residents and nonresidents are covered by the Treasury Department's TIC reporting system. The TIC system also covers all foreign purchases or sales of U.S. government securities. The Treasury Department has been responsible for collecting data on capital movements between the United States and foreign countries in some form since 1935. The legal authority to collect these data is vested in the Treasury Department, which maintains an oversight of the system. Operationally, the 12 district Federal Reserve banks, principally the Federal Reserve Bank of New York, collect the data, maintain contact with respondents, and ensure the accuracy and integrity of the data. The Treasury Department also maintains contact with respondents and is responsible for resolving reporting issues, handling policy questions, and pursuing data enhancement efforts. The FRBNY consolidates the data from various Federal Reserve banks, but it does not tabulate the data for publication. The data remain in the FRBNY's computers in databases to which the Treasury Department has access. The Treasury Department publishes the aggregate data in its quarterly *Treasury Bulletin.* It also transmits the aggregate TIC data to BEA on a magnetic tape. In addition, the TIC data are provided to the Federal Reserve Board for internal use and for publication of selected aggregates in the monthly *Federal Reserve Bulletin.*[10]

---

[10]Specialized summaries of the data are sent to the IMF; to the Bank for International Settlements (BIS) for use in monthly meetings of central bank representatives and for their quarterly analysis of international banking developments; to the Organization for Economic Cooperation and Development (OECD); and to the Bank of England, the Bank of Canada, and the Bank of Mexico.

Under the TIC system, information on international portfolio transactions is collected from both financial and nonfinancial institutions; see Figure 2-7. There are three main elements in the system; see Table 2-5. First, U.S. banks, other depository institutions (including the U.S. branches and agencies of foreign banks), bank holding companies, and securities dealers located in the United States are required to file a combination of monthly, quarterly, and semiannual B-series reports (B forms) on U.S. claims on and liabilities to foreign residents. The amounts of claims and liabilities outstanding, including short-term instruments held in custody for domestic customers, are reported by major types of claims and liabilities (such as deposits, loans, and U.S. government short-term obligations), by major types of foreign residents (such as official institutions, unaffiliated foreign banks, own foreign offices, and other foreign parties as a group), and by an extensive list of partner countries. Reports are required from entities whose aggregate claims on or liabilities to foreigners amount to at least $15 million as of the end of the month. About 950 institutions report monthly. Claims and liabilities denominated in foreign currencies are shown in a separate category as aggregate amounts in dollar-equivalent values, but not in separate foreign currencies. At the end of 1993, aggregate claims and liabilities reported on the B forms totaled $587 billion and $992 billion, respectively.

FRBNY's task of validating the B form data is facilitated by the fact that the Federal Reserve system has a supervisory relationship with the banking industry: all banks are required to file with banking regulators the quarterly Consolidated Reports of Condition and Income (commonly known as the Call Reports). These reports provide FRBNY with data to assess banks' TIC reporting compliance.

A second part of the TIC system is designed to capture all significant transactions between U.S. residents and nonresidents in domestic and foreign long-term securities. All banks, securities dealers, investment firms, and, in principle, any person in the United States conducting such transactions above a certain minimum amount ($2 million or more in the aggregate during a reporting month) directly with foreigners are required to report such transactions monthly on the S form to the Federal Reserve. The gross (turnover) value of reported securities transactions on the S forms in 1993 was $8.6 trillion. As of 1993, there were about 475 S form respondents. The data are broken down into domestic and foreign securities and into equity and debt securities. Domestic debt securities are further differentiated by type, including gov-

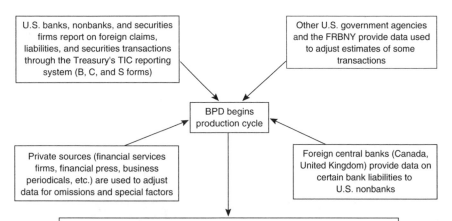

U.S. banks, nonbanks, and securities firms report on foreign claims, liabilities, and securities transactions through the Treasury's TIC reporting system (B, C, and S forms)

Other U.S. government agencies and the FRBNY provide data used to adjust estimates of some transactions

BPD begins production cycle

Private sources (financial services firms, financial press, business periodicals, etc.) are used to adjust data for omissions and special factors

Foreign central banks (Canada, United Kingdom) provide data on certain bank liabilities to U.S. nonbanks

1. TIC data are received by BEA electronically (magnetic tape, diskettes); other data arrive through electronic means, telephone, etc.
2. BPD analysts begin editing process:
   a. Develop flow data from stocks and gross trading of securities
   b. Classify data by BOP areas
   c. Identify and separate official from private transactions
   d. Examine large transactions to ensure proper recording of offsets
   e. Compare data with alternative data sources (e.g., FRB, bank reports, foreign governments)
3. Adjust TIC data to BOP concepts:
   a. Develop separate estimates for newly issued securities in U.S. and abroad; estimate securities redemptions
   b. Develop estimates for significant categories of assets not separately available, e.g., floating-rate notes, zero-coupon bonds, conversions, writeoffs, etc.
   c. Examine data for omissions and duplications with direct investment reporting
   d. Confirm and include special transactions not covered by TIC
4. For current account items:
   a. Prepare income estimates by applying appropriate yields to various categories of stocks and bonds
   b. Prepare estimates for financial services using stock data, transaction turnover, gross trading data
5. For annual investment position, prepare estimates involving valuation and other adjustments
6. Prepare bilateral presentations for reconciliation with Canada and selected comparisons with other countries
7. Analyze data and develop analytical tables for BOP presentation in *SCB*

Provide data on portfolio capital for incorporation into capital account of BOPs

BEA Bureau of Economic Analysis
BOP Balance of payments
BOPs Balance-of-payments accounts
BPD Balance of Payments Division in Bureau of Economic Analysis
FRB Federal Reserve Board
FRBNY Federal Reserve Bank of New York
SCB Survey of Current Business
TIC Treasury International Capital

FIGURE 2-7 Portfolio investment data: sources and output.

TABLE 2-5 Treasury International Capital Reports

Kind of Data and Form Used	Who Reports	What Is Reported	Requirement Cutoff for Reporting	Number of Respondents (1993)	Aggregate Claims and Liabilities (1993)
Banks' international positions: B forms	Banks, depository institutions, bank holding companies, securities dealers in the United States	U.S.-booked liabilities and claims positions, including custody items, with foreign residents, by major type of item (deposit, loan) and type of foreign resident (official institutions, unaffiliated foreign banks, own foreign offices, other foreign parties). Excludes positions in long-term securities	$15 million or more at the end of the month	950	Claims: $587 billion Liabilities: $992 billion
U.S. international long-term securities transactions: S forms	Banks, securities firms, investments intermediaries, other entities	Transactions with foreign residents in domestic and foreign long-term securities	$2 million or more in a reporting month	475	Gross value of reported transactions: $8.6 trillion
Positions of nonbanking firms with unaffiliated foreigners: C forms	Nonbanks in the United States (such as exporters, industrial and commercial firms)	Liabilities positions with unaffiliated foreigners. Excludes positions in long-term securities	$10 million in either claims or liabilities	400	Claims: $43 billion Liabilities: $50 billion

NOTE: See Chapter 3 (Table 3-1) for details of all forms and their coverage.

ernment obligations. The countries for which detail is provided are the same as for the banking data. Respondents do not report individual transactions; the monthly reports are a combination of all their transactions in the period.

Under the balance-of-payments framework, the geographic allocations of these data are based on the place of residence of the foreign transactor. A recorded transaction with Britain, for example, does not necessarily mean that the trade is in British securities, or that the ultimate buyer or seller is British. It can mean that a French broker, acting on behalf of a Japanese investor, carries out a transaction with a U.S. firm in London. This problem of geographic allocation applies to all balance-of-payments data compiled under the concept of residents and nonresidents as a basis of distinction between the United States and foreign countries. This distinction, however, is particularly problematic for securities transactions, as discussed in Chapter 3.[11]

This part of the TIC system currently covers only long-term securities (those with original maturities of longer than 1 year). For domestic securities, these include Treasury bonds and notes, federal agency issues, corporate bonds, and corporate stocks. For foreign long-term issues, the major categories are foreign bonds and foreign stocks. Warrants and options are covered only when the underlying security is a stock or long-term bond; the sales and purchases of such derivative instruments are not separately reported from purchases and sales of the underlying securities. Short-term securities (maturity of 1 year or less) are reported on either the B form or the C form, depending on type.

Unlike the B form data, which provide positions of claims and liabilities, S form data are flows, covering transactions each month. They do not provide information directly on U.S. holdings of foreign securities or foreign holdings of U.S. securities. Estimates for holdings (or investment positions) are derived by aggregating the annual flow data over time and adjusting for changes in securities prices. For foreign holdings of U.S. securities, the Treasury Department also conducts periodic benchmark surveys. As noted above, however, for U.S. holdings of foreign securities, there were no surveys between 1943 and 1994.

---

[11]For foreign holdings of U.S. securities, the Treasury Department conducts periodic benchmark surveys (described below) that gather information on the ultimate holders of U.S. securities. This information, while imperfect, does permit construction of estimates of the country distribution of the ultimate holders of U.S. securities for the years between benchmark surveys.

To validate the completeness and accuracy of the S reports, the FRBNY regularly compares the reported data with available information on international securities offerings, purchases, and redemptions. Since borrowers and lenders now have ready direct access to foreign markets and can easily bypass domestic financial intermediaries, it has become increasingly difficult for the FRBNY to ensure complete coverage and accuracy of the S form data.

The third major element in the TIC system covers the foreign claims and liabilities of U.S. nonbanks (other than those classified as direct investment or securities). Nonbanking enterprises in the United States include importers, exporters, industrial and commercial firms, and financial entities other than depository institutions and securities firms. A monthly report (CM) is required for dollar denominated deposits abroad (such as Eurodollar deposits and certificates of deposit), and quarterly reports (CQ-1 and CQ-2) are required, respectively, for financial claims and liabilities (deposits, loans, and borrowings abroad) and for commercial or trade-related claims and liabilities (such as international trade receivables and payables). The reporting threshold for these C forms is $10 million with respect to claims or liabilities on the bases of closing balances. In principle, all U.S. residents with foreign claims and liabilities that exceed the exemption level are required to report. The reports contain a limited amount of detail on the types of claims and liabilities. The geographic information is the same as in the other TIC reports; financial claims and liabilities denominated in foreign currencies are shown separately.

At the end of 1993, aggregate claims and liabilities shown on the C forms totaled $43 billion and $50 billion, respectively (see Table 2-5). In that year, about 400 nonbanking entities in the United States filed C forms. Since the universe of potential reporters of the C form is large and diverse, data validation for these forms is particularly difficult for the FRBNY. The possibility of missing some relevant potential reporters is high (see Chapter 3). Comparisons of the TIC data with data from other countries indicate that substantial amounts of foreign claims and liabilities by U.S. nonbanks are not reported in the TIC system.

On receipt of the TIC data from the Treasury Department, BEA collates the data with all other available information. It checks for internal consistency and consistency with other elements of the balance-of-payments accounts, makes adjustments, whenever necessary, to comply with the balance-of-payments definitions and concepts, and enters the data into the accounts; see Figure 2-8.

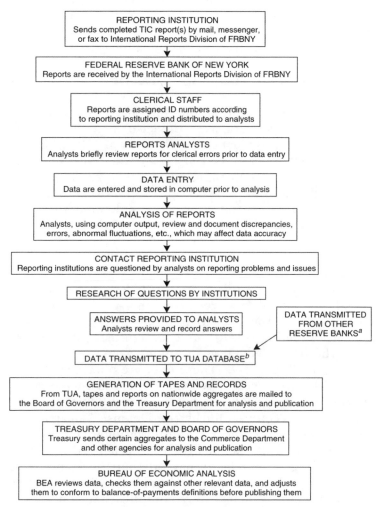

FIGURE 2-8   Treasury International Capital (TIC) reports: data sources and output.

For example, for the B form banking data, BEA converts the position figures into flow data by "differencing" the positions reported between two consecutive months and by making adjustments for changes in coverage and in the dollar equivalents of claims and liabilities items denominated in foreign currencies. For the S form securities data, BEA makes an adjustment to exclude fees and other charges, which are included in the reported transactions to account for capital flows in securities transactions.[12] BEA also compares the TIC securities data with data on direct investment or any other information that might be available. With regard to the C form data, as in the case of the banking data, BEA converts the position data into flow data. BEA also compares these data with those received on direct investment flows. In view of the weakness in the C form coverage, BEA has begun to use banking data from the Bank for International Settlements and from some foreign central banks to supplement the C form data (see Bureau of Economic Analysis, 1994a:79ff).

U.S. GOVERNMENT CAPITAL FLOWS

The other major segment in the U.S. capital account is the financial activity of U.S. government agencies and the international reserves of the U.S. government. BEA compiles quarterly data on the lending activity and foreign asset and liability positions of the many federal government agencies involved in such activities; see Figure 2-9. These data are obtained through direct contact with the agencies involved. There is a wide range of such activities, which include the lending by the Export-Import Bank, military loans accounted for by the Defense Department, foreign currencies held by the Agency for International Development (AID), foreign Persian Gulf war pledges to the United States, and U.S. grants to foreign countries to pay off their outstanding debts. In addition to the data on loans and credits that BEA collects from U.S. government agencies, BEA compiles data on all other U.S. foreign grants and aid. BEA also includes in the balance-of-payments accounts the changes in U.S. international official reserves as reported by the Treasury Department, including changes in the gold stock, foreign currencies held, and special drawing rights and the reserve position with the IMF. As with other position data,

---

[12]Fees and other charges are reported as international financial services transactions in the current account of the balance of payments.

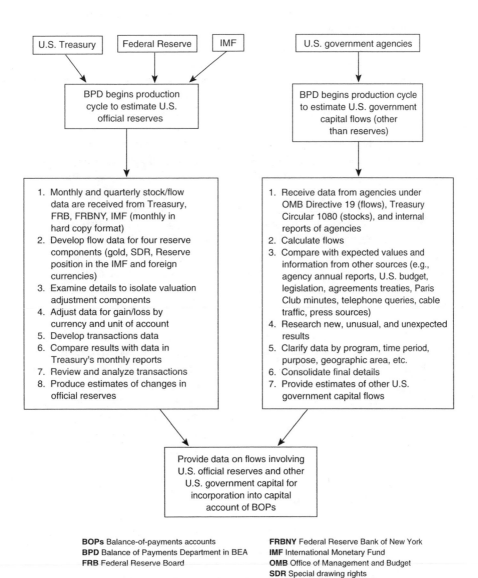

FIGURE 2-9 U.S. official reserves and other U.S. government capital flow data: sources and output.

BEA makes adjustments to derive the flow amounts. Statistical Directive 19, from the U.S. Office of Management and Budget (OMB), provides the authority for collecting this information.

The information collected by BEA from the various government agencies is primarily in the form of government records. The great majority of these records are the accounting records that must be maintained to accomplish the various agencies' missions, to report to Congress, or to report to OMB. Those uses are different from BEA's uses. An example is loans to developing countries. An agency making a loan has a function that directly parallels that of a commercial bank: there is a need to service the loan, and data must be maintained on payments and disbursements as well as on closing balances. In contrast, BEA is primarily concerned with the flows between two consecutive closing balances. BEA computes the flow for balance-of-payments purposes by looking at the difference between the balance of the loan reported for the current quarter and that reported for the previous quarter. (As noted above, grants are classified as unilateral transfers and shown in the current account of the balance of payments, not the capital account.)

Reporting on government international capital transactions is expected to be comprehensive and complete; the information is not collected using sample surveys. Data cover all programs and subprograms that involve sending dollars overseas or receiving them from abroad. All transactions are reported on a cash basis and are, at least in theory, reported when they occur. More than 150 agencies typically report on U.S. government international capital transactions. Among the largest are the Department of State, the Export-Import Bank, AID, and the Departments of Defense and Agriculture. The organizations report on a quarterly basis. Unlike data on private capital flows, these transactions are reported in almost any format convenient to the provider.

Data editing and verification are accomplished in a number of ways. Historical comparisons are frequently made to determine whether information from a particular agency is out of the usual pattern. BEA maintains reported data from as far back as 1945. In addition, BEA monitors legislation and tracks changes—for example, when new programs begin, when programs are merged, or when programs are discontinued. In addition, budget statements and reports to Congress by the various agencies are compared with what is reported to BEA.

INTERNATIONAL INVESTMENT POSITION

BEA prepares an annual statement on the international investment position (assets and liabilities) of the United States and reconciles the changes in the investment position with the flow data shown in the capital account of the U.S. balance of payments (see Table 2-3). There are several factors other than capital flows that affect the value of outstanding assets and liabilities. Changes in exchange rates, for example, have an impact on the value of assets overseas. Changes in market prices of assets and capital gains and losses (including writeoffs) can also influence the market value of assets. To take into account these and other relevant factors, BEA includes in the U.S. international investment position a number of elements excluded from the balance-of-payments data:

- for direct investment, capital gains and losses from exchange-rate translations or disposition of fixed assets;
- also for direct investment, estimates of changes in market value or replacement cost;
- for securities, estimates of changes in market value and exchange rates;
- for banking positions, allowances for writeoffs, breaks in series, or other factors affecting reported positions; and
- for U.S. government assets, any changes in reported amounts outstanding that do not result from actual transactions.

The basic data for the annual statement on U.S. international investment position are derived from the BEA and TIC systems described above. However, some flow data are supplemented by the collection of data on outstanding positions, as in the case of direct investment, and other banking and nonbank data are derived from original position statements as reported by banks and nonbanks. For securities, however, as indicated above, there are recent stock data, compiled from benchmark surveys, only for foreign holdings of U.S. securities. These data, which are collected on a 5-year schedule and are relatively comprehensive, provide a check at intervals on the accuracy of the flow data. Current position estimates for these holdings are essentially the summations of flow data and price and exchange rate changes over the years.

These data on the magnitude of U.S. international assets and liabilities are important in at least three respects: (1) they reflect the net external position of the United States (net debtor or net creditor) with the rest of the world economy; (2) they are used to calculate the investment income flows (earnings) on portfolio claims and liabilities, which are reported in the current account of the balance of payments; and (3) insofar as they are generated by separate benchmark surveys, they serve as one of the few available checks on the accuracy of the flow data shown in the U.S. balance-of-payments accounts.

Rapid changes in world financial markets have strained the coverage of the existing data system, rendering some of the data inaccurate and incomplete in depicting U.S. international capital transactions. Chapters 3 and 4 discuss these issues in detail.

3
Capital Account Data: Gaps and Needs

In response to changes in world financial markets, the Bureau of Economic Analysis (BEA) in the U.S. Department of Commerce, the U.S. Department of the Treasury, and the Federal Reserve Bank of New York (FRBNY) have made significant strides over the past several years to improve U.S. capital flow data. At the same time, the Federal Reserve Board has taken steps complementing their efforts. Nonetheless, existing data on U.S. international capital transactions remain of varying quality. For financial transactions that have changed most in form and character and for which adjustments in data collection systems have lagged behind, the quality of data have been adversely affected. The accuracy and coverage of some data can be improved with changes in current methods and procedures at minimal additional cost. For other data, new initiatives and development efforts are required, as well as international coordination.

This chapter examines in detail the adequacy of the capital account data in the U.S. balance of payments and addresses ways to improve them. The types of data are discussed in the same order as they are presented in Chapter 2.

DIRECT INVESTMENT AND RELATED DATA

As discussed in Chapter 2, BEA conducts separate outward and inward surveys on direct investment. Comprehensive benchmark surveys covering the universe of filers are undertaken every 5 years. In other years, samples of companies are surveyed on a quarterly and an annual basis to update the benchmark surveys. Compilers and users familiar with the direct investment data, including the related statistics on capital expenditure, production, and employment, appear generally satisfied with them (see Appendix B). BEA has addressed a problem frequently raised about these data in the past—the need to update asset values: beginning in 1991, BEA reported the value of direct investment positions using three alternative methods. In addition to the traditional historical-cost basis, two current-price bases were introduced: current cost and market value. Under the current-cost valuation, direct investment stock figures are adjusted to reflect changes in the average price of affiliates' tangible assets. Under the market-value basis, the adjustments reflect changes in estimated market prices of affiliates, based on changes in equity market indices (see Landefeld and Lawson, 1991).[1]

In addition, under the Foreign Direct Investment and International Financial Data Improvements Act of 1990, BEA has begun linking its direct investment database to the Bureau of the Census's establishment (plant) data to produce detailed industry data on foreign investment in the United States. For example, BEA recently produced detailed data covering the number, employment, payroll, and shipments or sales of the establishments (plants) of U.S. affiliates of foreign companies for 1987 (Bureau of Economic Analysis/Bureau of the Census, 1992). The data show the activities conducted by affiliates in over 800 industries. Foreign-owned establishments (excluding banks) accounted for 1 percent of U.S. business establishments and 4 percent of U.S. nonbank business employment. In manufacturing, the employment share of foreign-owned establishments was 8 percent.[2] Although foreign-owned companies accounted for a small share of the overall U.S. economy, they had significant shares of employment in a few industries: hydraulic cement manufacturing, 61 percent; polyester and nylon manufacturing, 60 percent. More than one-fourth of the employment of foreign-owned establishments was in California, New York,

---

[1]These alternative valuation methods are imprecise and cannot be applied to adjust data on individual countries and industries.

[2]Data from the 1992 benchmark survey show U.S. nonbank affiliates of foreign firms accounting for 5.1 percent of U.S. nonbank business employment and 11.6 percent of manufacturing employment in 1992 (Bureau of Economic Analysis, 1994b:161).

and Texas, but the share of total state employment was largest in Delaware (13 percent) and Hawaii (7 percent).

Foreign-owned establishments tended to be in capital-intensive industries, although foreign firms also own financial, insurance, and other business services establishments in the United States. BEA and the Census Bureau have also published expanded information for 1988 through 1991 on the manufacturing establishments of foreign-owned companies, including value added, capital expenditures, and other details (Bureau of Economic Analysis/Bureau of the Census, 1994). Under the same act, BEA is also authorized to give the Bureau of Labor Statistics (BLS) access to its foreign direct investment data so BLS can identify foreign-owned establishments in its database. BLS released data on the number, employment, and payroll of foreign-owned establishments in 1992 (Bureau of Labor Statistics, 1992). Additional BLS data on occupational structure in foreign-owned manufacturing establishments was released in 1993 (Bureau of Labor Statistics, 1993).

Despite these expansions in data and analysis, concerns have been expressed about the definition of direct investment and inadequate data in several major areas.

DEFINING DIRECT INVESTMENT

Investments by foreigners are treated as direct investments if 10 percent or more of the equity in a firm is owned by a single nonresident. In some instances, however, a single nonresident can hold 10 percent of the equity without exercising effective control. For example, Du Pont is treated as a U.S. subsidiary of a foreign firm because of the minority equity interest held by Seagrams (Canada), and some well-known financial institutions are treated as foreign-owned firms because of the minority equity interests held by Japanese institutions.

The 10 percent cutoff is an international standard adopted by the International Monetary Fund (IMF) and used by most countries. This dividing line is not intended to represent a controlling interest; it was adopted mainly to separate investments representing an active voice in the management of an enterprise from passive investments, for which the primary objective is capital gain or dividend income.

There is a question of whether the arbitrary statistical definition of direct investment (10 percent) causes problems with data collection and analysis. As the percentage of ownership declines, the ability of parent companies to comply with requests for detailed information on the operations of their minority-owned affiliates also may decline. In the United States, the capital flow data between a parent and its affiliate (essentially transactions in the debt or equity securities of the affiliate, together with intracompany accounts) are available to the creditor-entity at any level of ownership. The parent also has information on dividends received. At levels below 20 percent of ownership, however, the parent company may have difficulty in obtaining information on earnings and, therefore, reinvested earnings, because under U.S. accounting rules, if the reporting entity owns less than 20 percent of a foreign affiliate, it does not have to maintain detailed information on its investment. Also, the lesser detail available on U.S. minority-owned foreign affiliates reflects the difficulty U.S. parent companies face in obtaining detailed operational information from foreign affiliates over which they do not have majority control.

Certain distortions can arise due to the treatment of minority ownerships. For instance, when a foreign investor acquires as much as a 10 percent interest in a U.S. enterprise, BEA begins to include the entire operation of that enterprise as part of the aggregate of the foreign share of U.S. employment, production, exports, imports, etc. BEA also publishes limited data on majority-owned affiliates of foreign firms: that is, affiliates for which foreign direct investors own more than 50 percent. In 1992 majority-owned nonbank affiliates accounted for about four-fifths or more of the gross product, total assets, sales and employment of all nonbank U.S. affiliates (Bureau of Economic Analysis, 1994b). Thus, in the aggregate, the distortion introduced into the data by the inclusion of minority-owned affiliates is modest.

There are some industries in which minority-owned affiliates represent an important share of total direct foreign investment. In 1992 minority-owned affiliates accounted for more than one-half of the gross product of all foreign affiliates in three industries: primary ferrous metals, transportation, and communication and public utilities. In the latter two of these industries, however, employment by all foreign affiliates accounted for only 5.1 and 2.2 percent of total employment, respectively (Bureau of Economic Analysis, 1994b).

BEA's ability to publish detailed data about minority-owned U.S. affiliates of foreign firms is to some degree restricted by the need to preserve the confidentiality of individual respondents. Publication of separate information about majority- and minority-owned affiliates, to the extent that confidentiality requirements permit, is helpful in better understanding the role of foreign ownership in the U.S. economy.

Data Gaps and Problems

Income Reported by U.S. Affiliates of Foreign Firms

The rates of return on investments earned by foreign direct investors in the United States are markedly lower than those earned by U.S. investors on direct investments abroad. At one time, this gap was commonly ascribed to the undervaluation of U.S. assets abroad, which are older on average than foreigners' assets in the United States. But the difference has persisted, although it is reduced when assets are revalued by BEA under the current-cost and market-value bases. Moreover, the difference is pervasive, showing up in bilateral comparisons as well as in the global data. The difference in rates of return is frequently cited to support the assertion that foreign firms are evading U.S. taxes by manipulating transfer prices to minimize the amounts of income attributable to their U.S. operations. That allegation has spawned proposals to impose higher taxes on those firms.

Several explanations have been offered for the difference in rates of return (see Landefeld et al., 1992; KPMG Peat Marwick, 1992; Grubert et al., 1991; Graham and Krugman, 1991). It has been suggested, for example, that many foreign investments in the United States are still relatively new, so that earnings are reduced by start-up costs, and that the United States is a safe place in which to invest, so that earnings on foreign investments in the United States do not have to earn as large a risk premium as U.S. investments in many other countries. The first explanation may apply when a foreign investment in the United States represents construction of a completely new industrial facility. The second hypothesis is called into question by the pervasive character of the difference in rates of return, which holds in cases of both safe and risky foreign locations. Another possibility relates to exchange rates. When the dollar is depreciating, charges billed (including goods imported by affiliates from parent firms) by foreign parent companies to their U.S. affiliates in appreciating currencies can reduce the affiliates' rate of return.

BEA recently examined why the rates of return on foreign direct investment in the United States are so low relative to the rates of return on comparable U.S. domestic investment. The study provided interesting insights, but the findings were inconclusive. BEA observed that the low returns on foreign direct investment in the United States appear to reflect certain long-term factors associated with the operations of multinational companies and the effect of a number of transitional factors that led to a surge of foreign direct investment in the United States in the 1980s. Multinational corporations may accept low returns in the United States in order to take advantage of economies of scale, gain access to a large U.S. market, or secure raw materials. The study also noted that current account surpluses in Japan and several other countries in the 1980s generated excess funds available for investment. Funds were attracted to the United States by average yields on U.S. investments that were higher than those on home-country investments. This spread allowed foreign investors to accept yields below the average yield on U.S. investments. Nonetheless, BEA cautioned, underlying economic conditions and motivations for direct investment vary markedly among countries, and it is difficult to generalize about the factors leading to low returns of foreign direct investment in the United States (Landefeld et al., 1992).

Late Reporting

Late filings by U.S. affiliates of foreign firms affect data on foreign direct investment in the United States. Late reporting imparts a bias to the direct investment data. The first figures released for any quarter, for example, can show that direct investment flows are falling, or rising less rapidly, because coverage is incomplete. The impression is corrected by subsequent revisions, but it is a source of concern. While knowledgeable users understand the limitations of the preliminary numbers, unsuspecting users can be misled by them.

Until recently BEA did not estimate capital flows of late filers in the quarterly surveys, which resulted in large annual revisions for foreign direct investment in the United States and for U.S. direct investment abroad. In June 1992 BEA introduced a methodology that uses matched sample data from filers on changes in direct investment equity positions to estimate equity capital flows for late filers. Nonetheless, direct investment flows can be lumpy, and there may thus be no stable relationship between the figures of firms that report promptly and those that do not. BEA has been regularly monitoring the results of its estimates of equity capital flows for delinquent reporters and will continue to do so and adjust estimating procedures if experience shows adjustment to be desirable.

Financing of Multinationals

One aspect of the activities of multinationals that is not presently contained in BEA's published data is a presentation of sources and uses of funds. Information about sources and uses was collected for several years during the 1970s in an annual BEA survey, using a simple reporting form, but that survey was eliminated in the late 1970s.

Since 1982 BEA has instead conducted regular annual surveys of foreign direct investment in the United States and U.S. direct investment abroad. Data collected in these surveys includes items such as retained earnings, depreciation, capital expenditure, inventories, receivables and other assets. The data are published in balance sheet and income statement formats (see, for example, Bureau of Economic Analysis, 1994c). These data could be used to present information on sources and uses of funds, and it would be useful for BEA to do so. Data on sources and uses of funds of multinational enterprises would shed light on the extent to which they are financed by the local economy, as well as their contributions to the domestic sector. Such information is needed for analyzing the effect of foreign direct investment on the financial sector of the U.S. economy and that of U.S. direct investment abroad in host countries.

Real Estate Transactions

It is likely that foreign (nonresident) investment in U.S. real estate is not fully captured in the U.S. balance of payments. First, many of these transactions are in the form of limited partnerships.[3] Limited partnerships are considered portfolio investment, not direct investment, and should be captured under the Treasury International Capital (TIC) system. Presently, however, they are covered only if they are listed on organized stock exchanges. Thus, large transactions representing the bulk of foreign investment in limited partnerships are covered, but smaller transactions may not be. Second, data on purchases of U.S. residential real estate by nonresidents for their personal use are not collected. Because

---

[3]Non-U.S. citizens are prohibited by law from investing in certain types of limited partnerships (such as oil and gas exploration partnerships).

of the large number and the difficulty in identifying and locating potential respondents, it appears that it is impractical to obtain such information as a part of BEA's data collection system on foreign direct investment in the United States. Nor does BEA's present legal authority cover such transactions. Nonresident purchases of residential real estate for personal use are thought to be a relatively small component of foreign investment in the United States as a whole, but are of interest to some states, such as Hawaii. Efforts to date to collect such information at the state level have encountered difficulties in separating resident from nonresident transactions.

RECOMMENDATIONS

• If resources permit, BEA should either resume collection of more complete data on sources and uses of funds of multinational corporations, covering both outward and inward direct investment, or extract comparable information from the existing data. The results should be analyzed and published to inform the public about this essential operational aspect of multinational corporations. (3-1)

• The Treasury Department should continue its efforts to collect more complete data on nonresidents' holdings of U.S. real estate in the form of limited partnerships. (3-2)

• BEA should devote additional resources to analyzing the immense volume of data it collects on direct investment and examining the economic effects of the growth of multinational enterprises on domestic production, employment, and transfer of technology. BEA is in the best position to exploit the detailed information it gathers regularly on the activities of these enterprises. (3-3)

• BEA should undertake further reviews, by industry, on the rates of return of foreign direct investment in the United States, with particular attention to any data or reporting problems that may contribute to measured differences between rates of return on U.S. investment abroad and foreign investment in the United States. (3-4)

• BEA should continue to regularly review its new estimation procedure for late reporting in its direct investment surveys to ensure its reliability and cost-effectiveness. (3-5)

TRANSACTIONS IN SECURITIES

CURRENT PRACTICES

Banks, brokers, and dealers in the United States (and, in principle, other U.S. transactors) make monthly reports on U.S. securities bought and sold by foreigners (nonresidents) and on foreign securities bought and sold by U.S. residents. The transactions are classified geographically by the country of residence of the foreign party, although that party is often a financial intermediary rather than the ultimate owner or issuer. These flow data are reported in the balance of payments. In addition, they are used in conjunction with separate benchmark survey data to estimate holdings of securities, which, in turn, are used to estimate investment income flows.

This methodology produces three problems. First, when nonfinancial U.S. residents use brokers and dealers abroad to trade U.S. and foreign securities with foreigners, the transactions may not be recorded in the U.S. balance-of-payments statistics. Second, transactions in U.S. and foreign securities conducted in London and other foreign financial centers are reported as transactions for the countries in which the centers are located, not those in which the ultimate buyers and sellers reside. This has made it difficult to reconcile, for instance, U.S. and Japanese data on Japanese holdings of U.S. securities.[4] Third, data on stocks of foreign securities held by U.S. residents are difficult to interpret or use to estimate income flows because they are based on flow data classified geographically by the counterparty (buyer or seller), not by the issuing country.

There are fewer problems associated with the flow, stock, and income figures pertaining to transactions in U.S. securities than with the figures pertaining to transactions in foreign securities. Although there is uncertainty about the geographic location of foreign holdings of U.S. securities, there is no doubt about the issuing country of the stocks and bonds involved. As a result, there is good information about the interest rates, dividend payments, and yields when estimating income flows and adjusting

---

[4]Under the TIC system, Japanese sales and purchases of U.S. securities are based on transactions that have taken place within the United States, while Japan's records include its worldwide transactions in U.S. securities. However, this does not necessarily result in a mismeasurement of net global transactions in U.S. securities.

the values of holdings of U.S. securities by foreigners. When dealing with U.S. holdings of foreign securities, by contrast, there is no way to determine which countries' stocks and bonds are being traded. In addition, foreign holdings of U.S. securities are regularly surveyed, most recently in 1989, providing an up-to-date benchmark which can be used to make adjusted estimates for intermediate years. As noted above, until 1994 U.S. holdings of foreign securities had not been surveyed in a half century.

The Treasury Department has conducted benchmark surveys of foreign portfolio investment in the United States (inbound surveys) at least once every 5 years. These surveys collect information on foreign holdings of U.S. securities on a security-by-security basis. Approximately 4,000 U.S. firms that issue securities were included in the 1989 survey. The results of these benchmark surveys are intended to serve several purposes. First, they are used to update the cumulative transactions data with respect to both levels of foreign holdings and country of foreign investors. Second, they are used to improve estimates of the resulting income flows linked to the estimated stock of outstanding investment. Third, they are used to analyze foreigners' investment patterns in order to determine if these investments are of policy concern. Unfortunately, according to the Treasury Department, there are typically many errors in the initially submitted responses. In contrast to the regular TIC S forms, of which 80-90 percent are usable as submitted, only about 1 percent of submissions in the inbound survey can be used without extensive follow-up inquiries of the filers. The data eventually produced correspond well with position estimates based on the S form data, but the workload and reporting burden are substantially increased by the need for so much follow-up.

To improve data on transactions in foreign securities, the Treasury Department and FRBNY in recent years have undertaken several steps, the most important of which was a new outbound survey. The Treasury Department, in close consultation with BEA, the Federal Reserve Board, FRBNY, the Securities and Exchange Commission, and other government agencies, undertook a 1994 benchmark survey of the magnitude and composition of U.S. holdings of foreign securities. The survey collected detailed information on individual, foreign, long-term securities—both debt and equity—held by U.S. residents. When available, the results should improve estimates of the U.S. international investment position, as well as those of investment incomes associated with U.S. residents' investments in foreign long-term securities. They will also be a check on the accuracy of securities flow data. The outbound survey will focus on three types of institutions: (1) a small number of banks and brokerage firms operating as global custodians;[5] (2) a number of U.S. banks that may be operating as intermediary custodians for U.S. institutional and high-net-worth individual investors; and (3) large U.S. institutional investors active in international securities markets.

In addition, the FRBNY is undertaking a broad-based survey of U.S. holdings of short-term foreign securities to complement the outbound survey of long-term securities. The plan is to survey all current respondents to selected TIC forms on their foreign short-term assets.[6] Specifically, respondents will be asked about their foreign assets of both negotiable and nonnegotiable short-term instruments, their foreign currency denominated assets, and short-term assets they hold in custody. Short-term instruments will include commercial paper; short-term marketable notes; bankers and trade acceptances; certificates of deposits; short-term federal, state, and local government paper; and account receivables.

The Treasury Department also plans to include U.S. currency flows in the TIC reporting system. This information will improve U.S. international capital flow data, as well as estimates of U.S. monetary aggregates. This work is being carried out jointly by the Treasury Department's data management group, its financial enforcement offices (which are responsible for currency reports), and the Federal Reserve Board (see Chapter 5).

The Treasury Department, prompted by BEA's research, completed a small survey of international transactions by U.S. pension funds in 1991. This was followed by a broader survey for 1992-1993 by the Treasury Department and the FRBNY. Both surveys have helped the Treasury Department's efforts to expand the S form reporting panel. The pension fund survey suggested that many transactions had been carried out by offshore money managers and so had not been captured by the reporting system. The 1992-1993 effort also uncovered a large number of nonreporters and generated additional data. The inclusion of transactions undertaken by U.S. pension funds resulted in a 25 percent increase in the gross value of reported securities transactions for the 17 months ending May 1993, a total of about $170 billion.

---

[5]Global custodians are institutions that manage the custody of financial assets for clients; see Chapter 5.

[6]The survey will also include a sample of nonreporters who are thought to be actively engaging in these activities.

UNRESOLVED ISSUES

The present method of classification of securities transactions by country is appropriate for balance-of-payments estimates, but it leads to flaws in the data on transactions and holdings of securities and the corresponding estimates of income. When a U.S. resident buys a Japanese bond from a Canadian, the transaction appears, correctly, in the Canadian column of the U.S. balance-of-payments table, not the Japanese column. If it appeared in the latter, an error would be introduced into both countries' columns; there would be a payment to a Canadian with no capital flow to match it, and there would be a capital outflow to Japan with no payment to match it. However, the present method of classification does not provide estimates of holdings by the originating country of the security. In the absence of information on the nationality of the bond, it will be treated as a Canadian bond and thus added to U.S. holdings of Canadian securities. U.S. investment income from Canada will be overstated thereafter, and U.S. investment from Japan will be understated.

A similar problem exists regarding the treatment of foreign transactions in U.S. securities. A Japanese purchase of a U.S. bond in London does not and should not appear as a flow of Japanese capital into the United States. But Japanese holdings of U.S. bonds will be understated thereafter, along with Japanese earnings of investment income from the United States. Meanwhile, holdings and investment income earnings for the United Kingdom will be overstated.

There is no easy way to directly obtain correct, current information on the geographic classification of U.S. securities held by foreigners and the corresponding estimates of investment income, but use of the periodic benchmark survey results to make estimates for intermediate years could greatly reduce the problem. For foreign securities held by U.S. entities, there are two ways of getting more information: by supplementing the present monthly reports on purchases and sales of securities and by amplifying that system with periodic surveys on U.S. holdings of foreign securities, as is done for foreign holdings of U.S. securities. For example, institutions that currently report purchases and sales of foreign securities could be asked to file two sets of numbers— transactions classified by counterparty, like those now filed, and transactions classified by issuing country. The latter could be used to build more accurate estimates of stocks and thus to produce more accurate estimates of income.

In the process of designing the new outbound survey of foreign securities owned by U.S. residents, the Treasury Department concluded that most of the foreign stocks and bonds owned by U.S. residents are held with a small number of banks and brokerages that act as global custodians. It proposes to concentrate on them rather than the ultimate owners of the securities. If this method is successful, it may be possible to obtain quarterly data on actual holdings from the global custodians and use them to derive quarterly flow estimates for the balance-of-payments accounts, rather than basing the flow estimates on reported purchases and sales.

At least two problems would arise, however, if quarterly estimates of stocks were used to estimate net purchases and sales. First, it would be necessary to correct for price changes and exchange rate changes. That is necessary now, when estimates of holdings are built up year by year from estimates of previous holdings and transactions during the year. Under the present system, however, errors made in adjusting for price changes affect the stock and income estimates, but they do not affect the estimates of capital flows; the opposite would be true if quarterly estimates of stocks were used to estimate flows. Second, net changes in holdings, for example, of Canadian securities, would appear as transactions with Canada, even when the securities were not bought from a Canadian, and the errors in attribution would affect the estimates of the geography of capital flows rather than the stock and income estimates, as they now do. Consequently, it may be more appropriate to consider dual reporting of transactions in foreign securities, classified by country of the counterparty and by issuing country, although that may be burdensome to filers since it would entail doubling the number of reports they would have to file.

In June 1992 BEA introduced methodological changes intended to improve its estimates of income earned on U.S. holdings of foreign securities. The new method applies updated dividend yields by major countries to outstanding U.S. holdings of stocks in these countries.[7] However, its accuracy depends on accurate information about the nature of the foreign securities held. A different method seems possible: developing annual and benchmark estimates of income by gathering such data directly from the global

---

[7]The previous methodology was based on a cumulated flow of dividend receipts from the outdated 1943 benchmark survey and outdated dividend rates, both of which severely underestimated the flow of dividend receipts to the United States (Bureau of Economic Analysis, 1992a:73).

custodians. Since most interest and dividend payments must be made to them in the first instance, they should be able to supply more accurate income data than those presently or potentially obtainable by any indirect method.

RECOMMENDATIONS

• The Treasury Department and the Federal Reserve Bank of New York should mount a vigorous publicity campaign to bring the existence of the reporting requirements to the attention of all parties active in the international trading of securities, including pension funds, mutual funds, insurance companies, and individuals or businesses that serve as money managers and investment advisers. Special attention should be directed to institutional investors that deal directly in foreign markets. (3-6)

• To better assess the debtor/creditor position of the United States in the world economy, the outbound benchmark survey by the Treasury Department of U.S. holdings of foreign securities should be conducted not only in 1994 but also periodically thereafter—at least once every 5 years—to avoid cumulative errors. It can and should be carried out more frequently if a system is developed for collecting data from global custodians and the system is shown to be cost-effective. (3-7)

• The Treasury Department and the Federal Reserve Bank of New York should expand the TIC forms to improve the coverage of short-term securities, such as commercial paper. (3-8)

• To improve estimates of U.S. monetary aggregates, the Treasury Department, working with the Federal Reserve, should develop ways to monitor shipments of U.S. currency abroad. (3-9)

• For its inbound benchmark survey on foreign holdings of U.S. securities, the Treasury Department should improve the number of usable initial filings by continued educational efforts and other means to obtain the cooperation of filers. (3-10)

• To improve coverage of nonfinancial transactors, the Treasury Department and the Federal Reserve Bank of New York should change the language of the S form to make it clear that reporting is required not only of banks, brokers, and dealers, but also of U.S. residents who have reportable transactions with nonresidents in either U.S. or foreign securities, especially those through investment advisers and money managers. (3-11)

• The Bureau of Economic Analysis, the Treasury Department, and the Federal Reserve Bank of New York should explore the possibility of developing annual or benchmark estimates of income from U.S. holdings of foreign securities and foreign holdings of U.S. securities by gathering such income data directly from global custodians, instead of relying on indirect estimates based on security holdings. These agencies should also examine the feasibility of requiring filers to report an additional set of numbers, reflecting transactions by issuing country. Such data would be used to build more accurate estimates of stocks and to produce more accurate estimates of income. (3-12)

CLAIMS AND LIABILITIES

REPORTS OF U.S. BANKS

Except for the large potential for undercounting banks' custody transactions, as noted by BEA analysts, compilers and users of the TIC bank-reported data on U.S. bank transactions find no other glaring gaps or defects, and a recent study addressing the reliability of these data confirms this observation (Cayton, 1992). Since the current system emphasizes the transactions of banks, the compilers work closely with the reporting institutions, and they monitor and edit the data carefully.

It has been suggested, however, that the quarterly reports on foreign-currency claims and liabilities should be expanded to provide a currency-by-currency breakdown, at least for a few major currencies. As noted above in the discussion of transactions in securities, a breakdown by country is also needed. Without it, changes in claims and liabilities might be geographically misallocated, which will cause errors in the balance-of-payments accounts. Hence, a new breakdown by currency cannot replace the present one by country. For research and policy purposes, however, it may be important to know what currencies are held and owed as well as to know the geographic distribution of foreign-currency claims and liabilities.

Another vexing problem, which is not new but has become much more pervasive, concerns changes in official reserves, which have become a highly visible part of international capital movements. The most important component of official reserves is foreign exchange assets. Foreign exchange here refers to gross claims (securities, bank deposits, and the like) held by monetary authorities of one country and for which other countries have counterpart liabilities. Under the *Balance-of-Payments Manual* (International Monetary Fund, 1993a), external claims held by deposit money banks and readily available to authorities to meet a balance-of-payments need also may be counted as reserves. Many foreign central banks deposit their foreign-currency reserves in private institutions abroad or in domestic commercial banks. Those holdings, however, appear in U.S. statistics as liabilities to private institutions. This practice has sometimes led to serious interpretation problems of the reserves figures. Since the problem is one of interpretation and not a statistical one, it would be wrong to rearrange the data to deal with it. The United States has recently begun to publish data on its foreign-currency reserves, by currency (see Federal Reserve Board of Governors, 1994:587), but most other countries do not. It would be helpful if other countries published data on their reserves, showing currency composition.

REPORTS OF U.S. NONBANK INSTITUTIONS

There are serious and complex problems with regard to information on claims and liabilities of nonbank U.S. institutions, such as exporters and industrial and commercial firms. Other industrial countries have similar problems (see Appendix A). Nonbanks and individuals in the United States that have foreign claims and liabilities (above a certain reporting threshold level), other than holdings of long-term foreign securities, are supposed to report them on the TIC C forms. The amounts reported, however, appear to fall far short of the actual amounts—as measured by reference to the Bank for International Settlements (BIS) data—despite several attempts by the Treasury Department and FRBNY to increase the number of reporters. Data collected by the BIS, for example, suggest that foreign bank deposits held by U.S. residents are far larger than reported in the U.S. data, and Bank of England data indicate that U.K. banks hold large quantities of certificates of deposit in custody for U.S. residents. The difficulty of collecting comprehensive data on these claims and liabilities argues strongly for the use of partner country data, after careful analysis, for reconciliation and substitution purposes.

The IMF *Report on Measurement of International Capital Flows* (International Monetary Fund, 1992b) notes that there are particularly large differences for the United States between balance-of-payments data on nonbank capital outflows and inflows and those flows as calculated by reference to the banking statistics assembled by the BIS and by the IMF in its *International Banking Statistics* (IBS) series. For U.S. nonbanks, the differences between flows recorded in U.S. balance-of-payments compilations and flows derived from BIS and IBS figures averaged $20-25 billion per year during 1986-1989. These differences are attributable to the fact that, in the U.S. statistical system for balance of payments, reports on nonbank capital transactions are filed by only a few hundred large companies. "A large volume of transactions by individuals and by large and small businesses escape the [nonbank] reporting system entirely" (International Monetary Fund, 1992b:125). The IMF (p. 127) recommends that countries "systematically compare national data on nonbank capital flows with 'other party' measures of these items that can be derived from foreign-bank reports in the BIS/IBS system" in compiling balance-of-payments statistics, since almost all countries have good records of foreign transactions of their banks. Countries that have used international banking statistics (BIS/IBS figures) as a source for balance-of-payments data on assets of nonbanks include Canada, Germany, Ireland, Mexico, and the United Kingdom.

The Treasury Department and FRBNY have long been aware of shortcomings in U.S. statistics on nonbanks' international capital transactions reported on the C forms because of the difficulty of identifying reporters. A survey of 8,000 nonreporting firms in 1978 resulted in an addition of only about 1 percent to the reporting universe (in numbers) on the C forms. As discussed above, the Treasury Department recently surveyed pension funds to expand coverage of securities transactions. In this process, the pension funds were also asked about their short-term investments abroad that might be reportable on the C form. Even if it were possible to achieve relatively adequate coverage of sizable nonbank financial institutions, however, there is little likelihood that the system could be expanded to cover all significant capital transactions by nonfinancial companies and by individual investors. Thus, there is clearly a need to examine whether the records of financial institutions abroad could be used as a source of statistical data on international capital transactions by nonfinancial U.S. institutions.

Because of inadequacies of coverage in the nonbank data, BEA, in its compilation of U.S. nonbank claims on unaffiliated foreigners in the U.S. balance of payments, has begun to use BIS data. BEA also uses the data collected by the Federal Reserve Board on liabilities of foreign branches of U.S. banks in the Bahamas and the Cayman Islands to supplement the TIC data on U.S. nonbanks. BEA also has begun to use BIS data to estimate bank claims on U.S. nonbanks from Caribbean and Asian banking centers. The adjustments made by BEA resulted in an increase of $212 billion in the estimated outstanding claims of U.S. nonbanks on unaffiliated foreigners at the end of 1993. U.S. source data recorded these claims at $43 billion; with the substitution of BIS data this figure rises to $255 billion. U.S. nonbank liabilities to unaffiliated foreigners were adjusted upward for 1993 by $178 billion, from $55 billion to $233 billion (Bureau of Economic Analysis, 1994a:84).

An approach of using figures from international organizations and foreign central banks to improve current U.S. figures on international capital flows of nonbanks (actual or potential reporters on the C forms) does not eliminate the need for improving the coverage of the C form report, as well as of other reports. The C forms will be needed, in any event, to provide coverage of claims on and liabilities to countries that are not adequately covered in the international banking statistics. In addition, international banking statistics do not always conform to the balance-of-payments concept.

The Federal Reserve recently has begun to collect balance-sheet information for offshore branches of foreign-owned banks when these offshore offices are effectively managed by a U.S. agency or branch of a foreign bank.[8] The reports show claims on and liabilities to U.S. residents, by different types of claims and liabilities. Since Caribbean offices of foreign-owned banks have made most of the loans to U.S. nonbank customers from the Caribbean area (see Federal Reserve Bank of New York, 1992a:54), use of these new data should permit a major improvement in coverage of both the external assets and liabilities of U.S. nonbanks.

RECOMMENDATIONS

• Substitution by the Bureau of Economic Analysis of data from the Bank for International Settlements for data from U.S. sources has produced major improvements in coverage of the international claims and liabilities of U.S. nonbank firms and of investment income flows. BEA should continue its process of working with the BIS, the Federal Reserve, and the statistical authorities of other countries to seek further improvements in BEA's coverage

---

[8]Foreign banks' offices in the Cayman Islands report claims on U.S. nonbanks of $130 billion (see Federal Reserve Bank of New York, 1992a) and liabilities to U.S. nonbanks of about the same magnitude. These figures, which are collected annually by Cayman's authorities on report forms that have no reporting instructions, suggest that there is a substantial U.S. banking business being conducted through these branches that can be estimated only very roughly.

of international transactions through additional use of data collected by international organizations and foreign central banks. (3-13)

• The panel endorses the general recommendation of the IMF Working Group that foreign banks' liabilities to U.S. nonbanks be considered for substitution for reported U.S. nonbanks' claims on foreign banks. However, the panel stresses that U.S. programs to obtain data in this area from U.S. sources should be maintained and strengthened, even when partner country data are used instead of U.S. data, because U.S. compilers otherwise might become too reliant on the quality of other countries' data, over which they would have little control, and might be unable to detect new data needs and problems. (3-14)

• Following the current U.S. practice to publish data on the foreign exchange holdings of its monetary authorities, by currency, it would be helpful if other countries were to provide similar information. (3-15)

OFFICIAL GOVERNMENT TRANSACTIONS

CURRENT PRACTICES AND PROBLEMS

In general, problems in coverage of government international capital transactions appear less serious than those of private ones. Accounting systems in the federal sector have not greatly changed over the past 30 years, although significant changes have occurred in the composition of programs and how the programs are classified. A major difficulty with the government data is that a substantial number of agencies do not submit data in time for them to be included in current reports: most of them report after the close of the current quarter but before the next quarter. BEA believes that it can do a reasonably good job of estimating the transactions of the missing quarter accurately as long as it has the previous quarter's information, but not when data from two quarters are unavailable. To reinforce the need for timely reporting, BEA reminds delinquent agencies of their obligation to report in a more timely manner, and it has requested that the U.S. Office of Management and Budget (OMB) reinforce this effort by reissuing Directive 19. BEA has also asked OMB to "beat the drums" to emphasize the importance of these data.

The majority of the large agencies provide their data directly to the BEA on tape; small agencies with one or two programs provide their data on paper. All of the data are stored in a database whose managers must be flexible enough to adjust to a variety of events, such as the rescheduling of developing country debt by Congress. Moreover, since many government agencies report to Congress and OMB at the end of each quarter, there are other significant reporting requirements that coincide with BEA data needs. Reporting due to BEA invariably is not at the top of most agencies' lists of priorities; Congress and OMB come first. In addition, each agency may have a slightly different way of accounting for specific transactions, introducing another potential source of difficulty for BEA's compiling effort. For the most part, these differences are structural, in terms of the accounting systems and the accounts associated with the transactions. Nonetheless, some agencies clearly follow different accounting conventions, and they use varying definitions in defining transactions. Because agencies provide information in a consolidated format, they necessarily omit some data on individual programs. Some of these differences and omissions can be identified and corrected, however, when comparisons are made with the detailed accounting records the agencies produce for other purposes.

The number of transactions currently reported to BEA, even in a consolidated manner, is in the hundreds of thousands for every quarter. Thus, when performing edit checks, which require comparing current data with those of the previous quarter, BEA must make cross-comparisons among several hundred transactions. Types of transactions and their characteristics change over time. BEA follows two rules to ensure that transactions are properly listed in the accounts: comparison with other transactions and creating a new kind of transaction. Consider, for example, special assistance to a developing country for flood relief. If such a transaction appeared in a new quarter's report, BEA would search among the current transactions to find other instances of flood relief and to classify the new transaction consistently. If a new type of aid arose, such as assistance to Russia to set up a central bank, a new category of transaction would be set up. For the Persian Gulf war pledges to the United States, for example, one can find in the *Survey of Current Business* (Bureau of Economic Analysis, 1992a) a separate line for reporting of negative grants from countries supporting the United States in the Desert Storm operation.

RECOMMENDATIONS

• The panel recommends that the Office of Management and Budget reissue its Statistical Policy Directive 19 in the expectation that this action will help promote the objectives of more accurate and timely reporting. Increased emphasis on the importance of this reporting, coupled with electronic reporting, should enhance the accuracy and timeliness of the statistics on official government capital transactions. (3-16)

• The Bureau of Economic Analysis should examine the differences between the accounting reports submitted by federal agencies on their various military and foreign assistance programs to Congress and the Office of Management and Budget and the reports on official government international capital transactions they file with BEA. BEA should assess whether it can use the federal agencies' reports to Congress and OMB for balance-of-payments purposes. (3-17)

REPORTING BURDEN AND COMPLIANCE

A key to timely and accurate reporting of capital flow data is securing the cooperation of filers. Whether their reporting is complete and consistent depends on the manner in which their records are kept, their clear and uniform understanding of the types of transactions to be included, and their willingness to comply with the reporting requirements. The panel's canvass of data filers showed that they have a number of concerns about the reporting system (see Appendix B). With an understanding of filers' impressions of the reporting requirements, BEA, the Treasury Department, and FRBNY can better develop incentives to enhance compliance and to devise methods to improve the collection process.

TREASURY INTERNATIONAL CAPITAL SYSTEM

Table 3-1 shows the forms required under the TIC reporting system. In filing the B, S, and C forms, filers have to know the residence of the transactors in order to identify transactions between residents and nonresidents (foreigners). They also have to know whether the securities are domestic or foreign issues, whether the reportable transactions are debt or equity issues, and whether the financial instruments are short or long term. In addition, filers are required to provide a list of geographic allocations, based on the residence of the immediate transactors.

Given the dramatic changes in financial market practices and facilities in recent years, financial intermediaries now engage in a much more complicated business. A multitude of specialized departments and offices conduct transactions in many countries around

TABLE 3-1   Treasury International Capital (TIC) Forms

Form and Frequency	Who Must Report	Coverage	Currency
BC Monthly	All banks, other depository institutions (including commercial banks; banking Edge Act and Agreement Corporations; branches, agencies, and banking subsidiaries of foreign banks; building or savings and loan associations; mutual or stock savings banks; cooperative banks; credit unions; homestead associations; and consumer banks), International Banking Facilities (IBFs), bank holding companies, brokers and dealers located in the United States	Bank's own claims, and selected claims of brokers or dealers, on foreigners	U.S. dollars
BC (SA) Semi-annually	All banks, other depository institutions, IBFs, bank holding companies, brokers and dealers who are required to report on Form BC as of June 30 and December 31	Bank's own claims, and selected claims of broker or dealer, on foreigners in countries not listed separately on Form BC	U.S. dollars
BL-1 Monthly	All banks, other depository institutions, IBFs, bank holding companies, brokers and dealers who borrow federal funds from unaffiliated foreigners	Bank's own liabilities, and selected liabilities of broker or dealer, to foreigners	U.S. dollars
BL-2 Monthly	All banks, other depository institutions, IBFs, bank holding companies, brokers and dealers located in the United States	Custody liabilities of banks, brokers, and dealers to foreigners	U.S. dollars

TABLE 3-1 Continued

Form and Frequency	Who Must Report	Coverage	Currency
BL-3 Monthly	Any intermediary, i.e., any bank, other depository institution, IBF, bank holding company, broker or dealer located in the United States, that knows that it is being used as the U.S. address of foreigners in connection with the servicing of their loans to nonbank borrowers in the United States may be required to report on this form. For instance, a bank in the United States may be an intermediary for reportable foreign borrowings that are carried on the books of a "shell" branch or other related foreign office	Intermediary's notification of foreign borrowing	U.S. dollars
BQ-1 Quarterly	All banks, other depository institutions, IBFs, bank holding companies, brokers and dealers located in the United States that on their own account have claims on foreigners reportable on Form BC or on the account of their domestic customers have claims on foreigners	Reporting bank's own claims, and selected claims of broker or dealer, on foreigners; domestic customers' claims on foreigners held by reporting bank, broker, or dealer	U.S. dollars
BQ-2 Quarterly	All banks, other depository institutions, IBFs, bank holding companies, brokers and dealers located in the United States that, on their own account, have liabilities to or claims on foreigners denominated in foreign currencies, or on the account of their domestic customers have claims on foreigners	Liabilities to, and claims on, foreigners of reporting bank, broker or dealer; domestic customers' claims on foreigners held by reporting bank, broker, or dealer	U.S. dollar equivalents

continued on next page

TABLE 3-1 Continued

Form and Frequency	Who Must Report	Coverage	Currency
BL-1 (SA) Semi-annually	All banks, other depository institutions, IBFs, bank holding companies, brokers and dealers who are required to report on Form BL-1 as of June 30 and December 31	Bank's own liabilities, and selected liabilities of broker or dealer, to foreigners in countries not listed separately on Form BL-1	U.S. dollars
BL-2 (SA) Semi-annually	All banks, other depository institutions, IBFs, bank holding companies, brokers and dealers who are required to report on Form BL-2 as of June 30 or December 31	Custody liabilities of reporting banks, brokers, and dealers to foreigners in countries not listed separately on Form BL-2	U.S. dollars
CM Monthly	All U.S. persons other than banks and other depository institutions; IBFs; bank holding companies and their domestic, majority-owned subsidiaries; security brokers and dealers; savings and loans and other thrift institutions; and the U.S. government and its agencies, corporations and other instrumentalities who on their own account or on the account of other U.S. persons, have liabilities to, or claims on, unaffiliated foreigners, unless the amounts fall below exemption levels specified for each form. Among the types of persons to whom this reporting requirement applies are exporters, importer, industrial concerns, nonbank holding companies, nonbank	Dollar deposit and certificate of deposit claims on banks abroad	U.S. dollars
CQ-1 Quarterly		Financial liabilities to unaffiliated foreigners; financial claims on unaffiliated foreigners	U.S. dollars

TABLE 3-1 Continued

Form and Frequency	Who Must Report	Coverage	Currency
CQ-2 Quarterly	financial institutions (e.g., insurance companies and money market funds), leasing concerns, nonprofit institutions, trading companies, charitable organizations or foundations, foreign sales corporations incorporated in the United States or its possessions, whether sole proprietorships, partnerships, associations or corporations, and the agencies, branches, subsidiaries and other affiliates of foreign business enterprises located in the United States. (The exemption level for C forms is aggregate levels of reportable claims or liabilities of $10 million or more.)	Commercial liabilities to unaffiliated foreigners; commercial claims on unaffiliated foreigners	U.S. dollars
S Monthly	All banks, other depository institutions IBFs, bank holding companies, brokers, dealers, nonbanking enterprises or other persons in the United States who on their own behalf, or on behalf of customers, engage in transactions in long-term securities directly with foreigners (i.e., do not use a bank, broker, dealer, or other intermediary located in the U.S.); institutions that execute transactions by order of their domestic clients, who, in turn, are acting on behalf of foreigners; brokers who clear for other brokers and dealers who engage in long-term securities transactions with foreigners.	Purchases and sales of long-term securities by foreigners	U.S. dollars

the clock. Under these circumstances, filers may not have available the information required for TIC forms, or they may have to expend considerable effort in order to report timely and accurate data. Specifically, most of the TIC reporting is prepared by comptrollers of financial intermediaries. To prepare the TIC reports, they have to accumulate, review, and process information obtained from offices in many different locations. They also have to identify the types of securities, a task that has become increasingly difficult in modern markets. The reporting of zero-coupon bonds or repurchase agreements, for example, is particularly difficult. The securitization of items traditionally on banks' balance sheets has created further possibilities for ambiguity and misunderstanding. There are also difficulties in recognizing international transactions in the newer, short-term financial instruments and derivatives. These problems can lead to incorrect reporting by filers, as can other difficulties discussed in the rest of this section.

Filers' Understanding of TIC Reporting

According to filers, they are unfamiliar with the purpose and the use of the required data, and they complain about the long time lag for the Treasury Department and FRBNY to respond to their requests for guidance on treatment of new financial instruments. To assist them in completing the forms, filers would like an understanding of the objectives and specific uses of the requested data. In addition, filers would find it useful if additional examples of transactions were included in the instructions.

Number of Reports and Data Consolidations

Depending on the organizational structure of a filer's operations and the level of automation, reporting entities frequently experience difficulty in compiling data at the required consolidation level—for example, bank, nonbank, and international banking facilities. In some instances, financial institutions find it easier to submit one consolidated report for a bank holding company than multiple reports. Other institutions find it easier to submit data by legal vehicle, business segment, or division or department. Filers stated that currently, for example, there are ten separate TIC forms applicable to banking institutions. Since separate reports are required for several consolidation levels, there may be an annual requirement of numerous forms, many of which are prepared manually. Filers would like to reduce this burden by eliminating some forms.

Inconsistencies Between TIC and Accounting Systems

Filers said that the TIC reporting requirements are often impractical, in that they exceed the capabilities of financial institutions to capture and report data. A bank's automated system is generally geared to one set of reporting criteria or classifications. Filers pointed out that inconsistencies between TIC reports and their own accounting systems make it difficult to construct criteria that can be uniformly applied. For example, many operating systems do not contain information that distinguishes a customer by location. A system may have been devised only to name the holdings of the bank's customer (for example, Bank of Tokyo) and not to distinguish between that bank's New York agency and its parent bank in Japan. Thus, to respond to the TIC reporting requirements that make the residence distinction is often a burdensome manual process. Even when a system has an address field, the instrument may only give the name of the organization and cite a U.S. or foreign paying agent. Thus, it is not known whether the issuer is the U.S. branch or agency of the foreign organization or the foreign parent.

Filing Deadlines

Filers also indicated that the 15-calendar-day period for filing reports is inadequate because operating systems and financial staffs in the reporting institutions are fully occupied with their own accounting tasks from the end of one month through the first ten business days of the next one. In addition, information from branches and subsidiaries located outside the United States is generally mailed to the reporting institution and may not be available by the reporting deadline. Moreover, the process of compiling data in the required format generally is a manual one. Filers would like to have at least 15-20 business days or 20 calendar days.

FRBNY Questions on TIC Reports

According to filers, FRBNY frequently queries them about the reported TIC data after it has compared entries on the TIC reports with those on other Federal Reserve reports. The time required of filers to respond to such queries often takes longer than to prepare the original report. This FRBNY follow-up is a necessary part of the effort to obtain accurate and complete data, but to the filers, this represents an additional reporting burden. According to filers, the queries raised often are due to definitional and timing differences between the TIC and other Federal Reserve reporting requirements.

In addition, although FRBNY frequently advises filers on the application of particular reporting requirements to specific capital transactions and provides interpretations to the instructions, these interpretations are not always formalized, standardized, and distributed regularly to all filers. To ensure consistent application of reporting requirements in comparable situations, filers would like FRBNY to document and periodically distribute such supplementary reporting guidance.

BEA Direct Investment Reporting System and Other Reporting Requirements

Table 3-2 shows the forms required by BEA on direct investment. In response to the panel's survey, several large U.S.-based multinational enterprises with numerous foreign affiliates indicated that reporting requirements for the 5-year benchmark surveys are particularly burdensome. Several employee-years may be required to complete these forms (see Appendix B). These U.S. firms have to submit individual reports to BEA for their subsidiaries overseas, which often involves reviewing different sets of company accounts and in different languages. At the same time, few respondents to the panel's survey were familiar with BEA publications on direct investments. Nonetheless, they expressed interest in knowing how the data they report are tabulated by BEA and what the final products look like.

Respondents reported that the instructions for the BEA forms are fairly clear and that sufficient help can be obtained by calling the assistance number. Their views, however, were divided regarding whether the data required of them are generally available from their accounting and management records. Most did agree that providing information by geographic allocations is difficult due to differences between their accounting systems and the statistical reporting requirements. It should be noted that some companies establish and maintain supplementary data systems for statistical reporting purposes. Most respondents would like

TABLE 3-2   Direct Investment Data Forms, Bureau of Economic Analysis

Report and Frequency	Who Must Report	Coverage
BE-11 (all forms) Annually	Nonbank U.S. persons having a nonexempt nonbank foreign affiliate. An affiliate is exempt if none of its exemption level items exceeds $15 million, if it is less than 20-percent-owned, directly and/or indirectly, by all U.S. reporters of the affiliate combined, if its U.S. parent is a bank, or if it is a bank	U.S. direct investment abroad, including current economic data on the operations of U.S. parent companies and their foreign affiliates
BE-11A Annually	U.S. reporters meeting requirements for filing form BE-ll (see above) report data for consolidated domestic enterprise	Financial and operating data of U.S. reporters, including information on balance sheet items, distribution of sales or gross operating revenues, and U.S. merchandise trade
BE-11B Annually	U.S. reporters meeting requirements for filing Report BE-11 (see above) report data on majority-owned affiliates	Financial and operating data of majority-owned foreign affiliates, including information on balance sheet items, income statement, composition of external finances, distribution of sales or gross operating revenues, and U.S. merchandise trade
BE-11C Annually	U.S. reporters meeting requirements for filing Report BE-11 (see above) report data on minority-owned affiliates	Financial and operating data of minority-owned foreign affiliates, including information on total assets, annual sales or gross operating revenues, net income (loss), U.S. merchandise trade, and employment and employee compensation

continued on next page

TABLE 3-2 Continued

Report and Frequency	Who Must Report	Coverage
BE-13 Upon acquisition	A U.S. business enterprise when a foreign person establishes or acquires directly or indirectly through an existing U.S. affiliate a 10 percent or more voting interest in that enterprise, including an enterprise that results from the direct or indirect acquisition by a foreign person of a business segment or operating unit of an existing U.S. business enterprise that is then organized as a separate legal entity or an existing U.S. affiliate of a foreign person when it acquires a U.S. business enterprise, or a business segment or operating unit of a U.S. business enterprise, that the existing U.S. affiliate merges into its own operations rather than continuing or organizing as a separate legal entity	Information related to initial foreign direct investment transaction, including identification and ownership structure of new U.S. affiliate or newly merged portion of a U.S. affiliate, financial and operating data, investment and services provided by state of local governments, and identification of foreign parent and ultimate beneficial owner, and cost of investment
BE-14 Upon direct investment	A U.S. person—including, but not limited to, an intermediary, a real estate broker, business broker, and a brokerage house—who assists or intervenes in the sale to, or purchase by, a foreign person or a U.S. affiliate of a foreign person, of a 10 percent or more voting interest in a U.S. business enterprise, including real estate or a U.S. person who enters into a joint venture with a foreign person to create a U.S. business enterprise	Information related to purchase or sale transactions or related to joint ventures

TABLE 3-2 Continued

Report and Frequency	Who Must Report	Coverage
BE-15 (long and short forms) Annually	Each nonbank U.S. business enterprise that was a U.S. affiliate of a foreign person at the end of its fiscal year, if on a fully consolidated, or, in the case of real estate investments, an aggregated basis, one or more of the following three items for the U.S. affiliate (not the foreign parent's share) exceeded cutoff levels at the end of its fiscal year: total assets, sales or gross operating revenues, excluding sales taxes, or net income after provision for U.S. income taxes. Cutoff levels are as follows: less than $10 million, exempt; between $10 and $20 million, file short form; greater than $20 million, file long form	Covers financial and operating data of U.S. affiliate, including information on balance sheet items and schedule of employment, land and other property, plant, and equipment, changes in retained earnings or incorporated U.S. affiliate or in total owner's equity of unincorporated U.S. affiliate, distribution of sales or gross operating revenues, employee compensation, taxes and research and development, and merchandise trade of U.S. affiliate
BE-133B and BE-133C Semi-annually	Each nonbank majority-owned foreign affiliate of a nonbank U.S. parent, if any of the following three items for the affiliate is expected to be outside the range of negative $10 million to positive $10 million in any of the years to be reported: total assets, annual net sales or gross operating revenues, excluding sales taxes, or annual net income (loss) after foreign income taxes	Schedule and follow-up schedule of expenditures for property, plant, and equipment of U.S. direct investment abroad
BE-507 Upon acquisition or change of industry classifi-cation	Each foreign affiliate newly established or acquired by a U.S. person and required to be reported on form BE-577, BE-133B, or BE-133C; each U.S. person who becomes a new U.S. reporter by virtue of establishing or acquiring a	Industry classifications of U.S. reporter and foreign affiliates

continued on next page

TABLE 3-2 Continued

Report and Frequency	Who Must Report	Coverage
	foreign affiliate; or existing foreign affiliate or U.S. reporter whose industry classification has changed from that on a previous form	
BE-577 Quarterly	U.S. persons who hold 10 percent or more of voting stock or equivalent interest in a nonexempt foreign business enterprise. If none of the three items listed below for a foreign business enterprise are outside the range of negative $15 million to positive $15 million, that enterprise is exempt from reporting	U.S. reporter's equity in foreign affiliate's, receipts and payments between U.S. reporter and foreign affiliate during quarter, debt and other intercompany balances between foreign affiliate and U.S. reporter, change during the quarter in U.S. reporter's equity in capital stock and/or additional paid-in capital of incorporated foreign affiliate or equity investment in unincorporated foreign affiliate, and U.S. reporter's share in annual income and equity position
BE-605 Quarterly	Every U.S. business enterprise, except an unincorporated bank, in which a foreign person had a direct and/or indirect ownership interest of 10 percent or more of the voting stock if an incorporated business enterprise or an equivalent interest in an unincorporated business enterprise at any time during the reporting period	Foreign parent's direct equity in U.S. affiliate's, direct payments to and receipts from foreign parent by U.S. affiliate, as consolidated, during quarter, intercompany debt balances between U.S. affiliate and foreign parent, change during the quarter in foreign parent's equity in U.S. affiliate, annual income and equity position, direct transactions or accounts between U.S. affiliate and foreign affiliates of the foreign parent

TABLE 3-2 Continued

Report and Frequency	Who Must Report	Coverage
BE-606B Quarterly	Every unincorporated U.S. banking branch or agency in which a foreign person had a direct and/or indirect ownership interest of 10 percent or more at any time during the reporting period. The report is to cover direct transactions and positions between the unincorporated U.S. banking branch or agency (U.S. affiliate) and the foreign parent	Changes during quarter in foreign parent's permanent invested capital, certain realized and unrealized gains (losses), net of tax effect, and foreign parent's charges to U.S. affiliate, net of U.S. affiliate's charges to the foreign parent during the quarter
BE-10A, BE-10A-Bank, BE-10B, BE-10B-Bank Benchmark	U.S. persons who hold 10 percent or more of voting stock or equivalent interest in a foreign business enterprise and foreign affiliates of U.S. direct investors	Complete financial and operating data for U.S. persons who are direct investors abroad for each foreign affiliate; data on investment position and transactions between foreign affiliates and U.S. direct investors
BE-12 Benchmark	U.S. business enterprises (affiliates) in which one foreign person holds 10 percent or more of voting stock or equivalent interest	Complete financial and operating data for each U.S. affiliate of foreign direct investors; data on investment position and transactions between U.S. affiliates and foreign direct investors

more time to file the forms. They also would like BEA to consolidate forms with other federal ones that collect the same data.

As can be seen in Tables 3-1 and 3-2, BEA and the Treasury Department use many forms to collect data on direct and portfolio investment transactions between U.S. residents and foreigners. In addition, other federal agencies that have oversight, supervisory, and regulatory responsibilities for the nation's financial systems require financial institutions to report certain data on their business activities. (There are also state agencies that monitor financial institutions.) Federal banking regulatory agencies include the Federal Reserve Board, the Federal Deposit Insurance Corporation (FDIC), and the Office of the Comptroller of the Currency. These three regulatory authorities also act through the Federal Financial Institutions Examination Council (FFIEC). Other regulatory agencies include the Securities and Exchange Commission, which oversees the nation's securities markets, and the Commodities Futures Trading Commission, which regulates activities in futures exchanges. Table 3-3 shows the reports required by the Federal Reserve Board and the FFIEC; Table 3-4 shows those required by other federal and some state agencies.

ASSESSMENT

According to respondents to the panel's survey of filers of BEA and Treasury Department reports, it is not uncommon for an internationally active financial institution to file almost all of these forms, and sometimes multiple copies of each, for their various affiliates and subsidiaries. One such institution reported that it files 1,300 statistical and reporting forms annually. Filers, in general, find the statistical and regulatory data reporting burdensome. They also complain about inconsistencies in reporting requirements, duplicative efforts, and the high costs of compliance. Respondents also note that they find little direct benefit to the management of their complex businesses from the required reporting.

The panel's survey of BEA, Treasury Department, and FRBNY staff to ascertain their perspectives on the efficiency of the existing data collection system on U.S. international capital transactions yielded similar observations. All recognized there is need to improve the existing system to close data gaps. In particular, BEA staff noted that the U.S. system suffers from gaps in coverage, duplication of effort, increasing respondent burdens, outdated data processing and collection methods, and inadequate or outdated estimation methodologies. BEA staff also noted that improvements in the efficiency of the existing data systems would be possible through access to banking and credit card clearance information; increased use of publicly available financial data; and increased use of regulatory information from agencies such as the Federal Reserve, the Securities and Exchange Commission, and the Commodities Futures Trading Commission (see Appendix B).

The panel agrees with the above assessment. It believes that an effective response to the growing reporting burden and diminishing usefulness of some of the reported data requires three steps: (1) to reexamine vigorously the various statistical and regulatory reports; (2) to identify and eliminate duplications and inconsistencies; and (3) to the extent possible, combine similar reports and simplify others. The goal is to redirect the systems to collect data that are of maximum use at minimum cost to both filers and compilers. Toward this end, federal regulatory and statistical agencies will have to work together to streamline existing reporting systems and to eliminate low-priority programs. This is in line with the mandates of the FDIC Improvement Act, which encourages the FFIEC to consider eliminating the numerous differences between regulatory accounting principles (RAP) and the generally accepted accounting principles (GAAP) used in the preparation of corporate financial statements. Streamlining of reporting requirements will not only ease the reporting burden, but will also reduce the need to reconcile different databases. The resulting savings can be used to improve data quality, enforce reporting compliance, and strengthen data analysis efforts.

Data filers also report that disparate statistical and regulatory reports have hampered their electronic reporting; it is difficult to develop in-house automated data recording, management, and reporting systems to meet different reporting requirements. Coordinated efforts by federal regulatory and statistical agencies to develop consistent approaches to their data collection methods could greatly help the nation to move toward an electronic data collection system (see Chapter 5).

Since the 1987 stock market crash, federal regulatory agencies have worked together more closely on their supervisory responsibilities. Further coordination of these agencies with their statistical counterparts on data reporting will strengthen the effectiveness of both the regulatory and the data reporting systems, essential for monitoring the financial conditions of U.S. economy.

Because the structure of financial markets and the nature of financial instruments have changed dramatically over the past decade and will continue to evolve, a vigorous review of the disparate regulatory and statistical reporting forms is needed to ensure that only relevant data useful for public policy making are collected and that irrelevant data are not. Such a review is critical to enhance the cost-effectiveness of the existing data collection systems to cover adequately the burgeoning volume of financial transactions in various forms and levels of complexity. Coordinated efforts by regulatory and statistical agencies to streamline reporting requirements in consultation with filers is likely to engender filers' cooperation and compliance, yielding more accurate and timely data.

TABLE 3-3   Forms on Activities of Financial Institutions, Federal Reserve Board, and Federal Financial Institutions Examination Council

Report	Frequency	Coverage
FC-1	Weekly	Foreign currency report of banks in the United States
FC-2	Weekly	Consolidated foreign currency report on foreign branches and subsidiaries of U.S. banks
FC-3	Monthly	Assets, liabilities, and positions in specified foreign currencies of firms in the United States
FC-4	Quarterly	Consolidated report of assets, liabilities, and positions in specified currencies of foreign branches and subsidiaries of firms in the United States
FFIEC 004	Annually	Indebtedness
FFIEC 009	Quarterly	Country exposure report of banks in the United States
FFIEC 019	Quarterly	Country exposure report of foreign branches and subsidiaries of U.S. banks
FFIEC 030	Annually	Foreign branch report of condition
FFIEC 031	Quarterly	Consolidated Reports of Condition and Income (Call Report)
FFIEC 032	Quarterly	Consolidated Reports of Condition and Income (Call Report)
FFIEC 033	Quarterly	Consolidated Reports of Condition and Income (Call Report)
FFIEC 034	Quarterly	Consolidated Reports of Condition and Income (Call Report)
FFIEC 035	Monthly	Foreign currency report (domestic and foreign)
FR 2006	Monthly	Bankers' acceptances created by the bank
FR 2042	Monthly	Various time deposit instruments outstanding
FR 2050	Weekly	Selected deposits in foreign branches held by U.S. addresses
FR 2069	Weekly	Assets and liabilities for large U.S. branches and agencies of foreign banks
FR 2077	Weekly	Liabilities to/and custody holdings for U.S. addresses (foreign branches)
FR 2415	Weekly	Daily outstanding balances of selected borrowings
FR 2416	Weekly	Statement of condition for management's domestic offices and subsidiaries detailing assets, liabilities, and certain supplementary data
FR 2502	Monthly	Foreign branches assets and liabilities
FR 2502S	Quarterly	Foreign branches assets and liabilities
FR 2573	Monthly	Total dollar of debits to demand and savings deposits

TABLE 3-3   Continued

Report	Frequency	Coverage
FR 2900	Weekly	Daily outstanding balances of demand, time and savings accounts, daily outstanding balances of cash items and balances on deposit with other banks. Used for computing management's reserve requirements
FR 2950	Weekly	Certain Eurocurrency transactions done with foreign entities
FR Y6	Annually	Bank holding companies
FR Y6A	Quarterly	Selected data for nonbank subsidiaries of bank holding companies
FR Y7	Annually	Annual report of foreign banking organizations
FR Y8	Semiannually	Report of bank holding company's intracompany transfers and balances
FR Y9C	Quarterly	Consolidated financial statements for bank holding companies
FR Y9LP	Quarterly	Parent company only financial statements
FR Y11AS	Annually	Combined financial statements of nonbank subsidiaries of bank holding companies, by type of nonbank subsidiary
FR Y11Q	Quarterly	Combined financial statements of nonbank subsidiaries of bank holding companies
FR Y20	Quarterly	Financial statements for a bank holding company subsidiary engaged in ineligible securities underwriting and dealing
FR Y111	Annually	Selected financial data for nonbank subsidiaries of bank holding companies

RECOMMENDATIONS

• In response to the growing complexity of transactions and organizational structures of financial institutions, the Treasury Department and the Federal Reserve Bank of New York (FRBNY) should work together with data filers to streamline TIC reporting requirements (including level of details, frequency of reports, and exemption levels), clarify reporting instructions and guidelines, and determine how particular transactions should be reported. A major objective should be to eliminate unnecessary details, explore the feasibility of obtaining certain data on a quarterly instead of monthly basis (for example, data on country details), and simplify reporting forms. Periodic meetings between staff of the Treasury Department and FRBNY and filers should be held for these purposes. (3-18)

TABLE 3-4   Other Reports Required of Financial Institutions

Agency and Report	Frequency
Federal Deposit Insurance Corporation	
FDIC Assessment	Semiannually
FDIC Survey—Summary of deposits by domestic branch	Annually
FDIC Examination	Every 5 years
Federal Financial Institutions Examination Council	
Federal Reserve Board and New York State Bank Examination	Annually
Directors' examination	Annually
Trust examination	Annually
Abandoned property examination	Every 5 years
Securities and Exchange Commission	
Form 10-Q financial report	Quarterly
Form 10-K financial report	Annually
State and other agencies	
Section 121 Report	Monthly
Legal Lending Limit	Quarterly
New York State Report of Abandoned Property	Annually
Housing and Urban Development Survey	Quarterly
National Securities Clearing Corporation (NSCC) Survey	Quarterly
English Companies Act	Annually

• The Treasury Department and the Federal Reserve Bank of New York should conduct an active educational campaign for data filers covering the purposes and uses of the required data. This would be especially helpful to foreign-owned financial intermediaries operating in the United States. (3-19)

• The Treasury Department and the Federal Reserve Bank of New York should formalize their consultation processes with filers. A manual of instructions and administrative guidance should be distributed to filers. The manual could be in the form of diskettes or a loose-leaf binder, in which updated instructions would replace old ones. (3-20)

• The panel recommends consideration of streamlining of reporting in four areas:

1. The FFIEC 035 monthly foreign-currency report (see Table 3-3) contains substantial information on foreign-currency exposures. The additional requirement for financial institutions to file the weekly foreign-currency reports (FC-1, FC-2, FC-3, and FC-4) (see Table 3-3) for domestic offices and foreign offices seems unneces-

sary. The Federal Reserve Board and the Treasury Department should examine the two sets of forms to determine if the more detailed monthly FFIEC reports are sufficient to meet their needs for information on foreign-currency exposure.

2. Through the quarterly Call Report (FFIEC 031, 032, 033, and 034) (see Table 3-3), the Federal Reserve Board, the FDIC, and the Office of the Comptroller of the Currency collect detailed information on the financial conditions of all banking institutions in the United States. In view of the volume of data gathered in the Call Report, the Treasury Department, in collaboration with the Bureau of Economic Analysis, should thoroughly review the usefulness of the TIC B forms, which collect monthly, quarterly, and semiannual information on banks' assets and liabilities with foreigners (see Table 3-1). If duplications exist or certain reported TIC data are no longer useful and meaningful, the TIC forms should be simplified.

3. In view of the incomplete coverage under the TIC C form on nonbank commercial claims and liabilities with unaffiliated foreign firms, such as trade credit and accounts receivable and payable (see CQ-2 in Table 3-1), the Treasury Department and BEA should consider integrating Treasury's CQ-2 form with BEA's direct investment forms (see Table 3-2). In addition to direct investors, BEA should require firms that generate significant commercial credit and liabilities through trade to file the integrated form. Major U.S. and foreign exporters and importers located in the United States should be targeted. In addition, harmonizing the definitions of accounts payable and receivable used in balance-of-payments reporting and those used by firms in financial accounting under generally accepted accounting principles would help improve coverage. Under such principles, cash items are not included in accounts receivable or payable; they are, however, included in balance-of-payments reporting.

4. The panel attaches great importance to BEA's 5-year censuses of outward and inward direct investments because they yield basic information on the economic effects of these enterprises. However, the panel notes that the list of questions and the degree of detail have multiplied over the years and is concerned that the reporting burden may outweigh the benefits. Accordingly, the panel recommends that BEA, in consultation with data users, review the need for each of the major sections of the censuses and the breakdowns, taking into account the extent to which the data developed are of good quality and used. (3-21)

4
Financial Derivatives: Data Gaps and Needs

$\mathbf{A}$mong the most important changes in world financial markets over the past two decades has been the emergence of a myriad of new and rediscovered financial instruments in the form of derivative products. Financial derivatives include swaps, options, forwards, and futures for interest rates, currencies, stocks, bonds, indexes, and commodities. Many derivative transactions are international, involving residents of different countries, and they are often conducted in multiple currencies. Their rapid growth can be attributed to the need of investors and borrowers to manage risks in an environment of fluctuating exchange rates, interest rates, and commodity prices. Adverse changes in exchange rates, for example, can eliminate a firm's overseas profits; commodity price fluctuations can increase input prices of production; and changes in interest rates can put pressure on a firm's financial costs.

The wave of financial deregulation, technological innovation, and competition among market participants has further facilitated the development of derivatives. In addition, the cost-saving features of these products and the flexibility they afford investors and borrowers have fueled their expansion. They have been used not only for hedging, but also for trading activities.

Particularly since the early 1980s, derivatives have come to account for a significant share of international financial transactions. Since derivative products appear in numerous forms and

114

are used for various purposes in financing and portfolio management strategies, they have complicated many aspects of the accounting, regulating, and statistical reporting of financial transactions.

This chapter explores the revolutionary changes that financial derivatives have brought to world financial markets and their implications for the collection of accurate, timely, and relevant data for public and private decision making. It is important to understand the basic features and uses of these instruments and how they have affected the coverage of the existing balance-of-payments data and their interpretation.

USES AND GROWTH OF FINANCIAL DERIVATIVES

Financial derivatives are secondary instruments, the values of which are dependent on changes in the value of the underlying financial instrument or commodity. They are generally linked to a primary financial instrument or an indicator (such as foreign currencies, government bonds, corporate equities, certificates of deposit, stock price indices, and interest rates) or to a commodity (such as gold, petroleum, copper, wheat, coffee, and cattle). They usually do not result in a transfer of the underlying primary instrument or commodity at the inception of a contract. Instead, they usually entail an exchange between the counterparties to the contract at some future date. Derivatives can generally be classified as either "option-like" or "forward-like." Options give the holder the right—but not the obligation—to purchase (or sell) an underlying financial instrument or commodity at a specified price at a future date. Forwards are a commitment to purchase (or sell) an underlying financial instrument or commodity at a specified price at a future date.

Derivative products can take the form of one or a combination of several basic financial contracts:

• A *financial option contract* gives the purchaser of the option the right to buy, sell, or exchange specific financial instruments at a fixed or determinable price (called the exercise or strike price) at the exercise of the option. Examples include currency, interest rate, stock, index, and commodity options.

A *warrant* can be considered as a type of option: it is a contract that entitles the holder to subscribe to a specified number of shares or bonds at a fixed price during a set period. Like options, warrants can be purchased and sold independently of the underlying shares or bonds.

• A *financial forward contract* is one in which two parties agree to exchange specific financial instruments at a future date on predetermined terms. Examples are foreign exchange forwards and interest rate forwards.

• A *swap contract* is the binding of two parties to exchange two different payment streams over time, the payments being tied, at least in part, to subsequent and uncertain market developments. Examples include swap contracts on interest rates and foreign currencies, equities, and commodities (notably gold and petroleum products). A swap can be considered as a series of financial forwards, except that the underlying credit risks of the two types of instruments can be different.

• A *futures contract* requires the delivery of a specified amount of an underlying asset at some future date at a price agreed on the day the contract is made. Examples are currency futures, interest rate futures, index futures, and commodity futures. Futures contracts can also be considered as a form of forward contract traded on public exchanges, except that the underlying credit risks of the two types of contracts can be different.

BASIC FEATURES AND USES

A primary purpose of these secondary instruments is to hedge against exposure to risk. Most, therefore, are designed to transfer one or more of the financial risks inherent in an underlying primary financial instrument or commodity to a third party willing to accept the risks. The counterparty (buyer or seller) to the transaction assumes the risk either for speculative purposes or to hedge an offsetting exposure of its own. Some derivative instruments are not new but have been rediscovered and promoted since the early 1980s. Others are new products designed to enable borrowers and investors to deal with volatility in exchange rates, interest rates, and stock and commodity prices.

In principle, portfolio managers can realign financing risks through cash markets without using financial derivatives. For example, borrowers and investors can diversify their foreign exchange risks by holding assets and liabilities in different currencies. A company that wants to lock in an attractive interest rate to meet future financing needs can issue the debt in the cash market before the funding is needed. In practice, however, the transaction costs of cash market strategies can be daunting, and their liquidity and credit risk implications can be unacceptable. Also, there may be regulatory barriers and tax disincentives. When used prudently, derivatives can offer cheaper alternatives than cash market products to achieve the same hedging or trading objectives.

Derivatives are also designed to provide borrowers and investors with flexibility to unbundle and hedge different risks separately. In the case of foreign exchange futures contracts, a U.S. exporter can transfer its foreign exchange risk to a firm with the opposite exposure or to a firm in the business of managing foreign exchange risks, leaving the exporter free to focus on its core business. This strategy will avoid the risk of loss if exchange rates move against the firm before payments for the goods are received. Furthermore, financial derivatives can be combined with a debt issuance to unbundle the financial price risk from other risks inherent in the process of raising capital. By coupling its bond issues with swaps, for example, a firm can separate interest rate risk from traditional credit risk (Rawls and Smithson, 1989).

Yet another use of derivatives relates to home mortgages. Innovative financial derivatives have been one means to support residential refinancings in the United States. During 1993, as U.S. interest rates declined to their lowest levels in a number of years, refinancings of residential mortgages reached record high numbers. Prepayments reduced the income stream of mortgage holders. To hedge against bursts of prepayment exposure, some mortgage bankers and other financial institutions were able to transfer prepayment risk by turning to reversed indexed principal notes (see Feigenberg et al., 1993). Such instruments are designed to extend cash flows to financial institutions as interest rates decline and to shorten cash flows as interest rates rise. The more prevalent approach to handling prepayment risk, however, has been through the securitization of mortgage assets through collateralized mortgage obligations.

Derivatives such as futures and options tend to involve lower transaction costs, and at times they offer higher liquidity than cash markets (for example, through index trading). This higher liquidity is useful for investors who can also use derivatives to change their risk exposures—by hedging against downside risk, swapping bond coupons for equity dividends, diversifying into foreign markets—without having to buy or sell the underlying securities. An investor holding a long-term bond can protect asset value through a period of expected interest rate turbulence by a swap with floating rate income during that period, rather than selling the holding outright.

Active participation in derivatives markets requires capital strength, in-depth market information, and technical expertise. Consequently, derivative instruments, and the rights and obligations underlying them, are for the most part created by financial enterprises—either acting as agents or brokers in setting up contracts between two other parties or as principals in contracting with a customer. That is, activities in financial derivatives are largely conducted at the "wholesale" rather than at the "retail" level. An indication of the institutional nature of swap transactions comes from the International Swap Dealers Association (ISDA), an international group of commercial, investment, and merchant banks and other swap dealers: the average size of the swap transactions in the portfolios of the respondents surveyed in 1992 was about $27 million. Major users of financial derivatives include large business enterprises, banks, savings associations, insurance companies, institutional investors, government agencies, and international organizations.

Derivatives can be traded on organized exchanges or they can be over-the-counter (OTC) contracts.[1] Exchange-traded instruments are in standardized forms, amounts, terms, maturities, and delivery dates. OTC instruments are generally customized to clients' needs; they often specify commodities or instruments and terms not offered on exchanges. OTC market transactions are generally negotiated over the telephone before being confirmed in writing. As in the case of cash instruments, it is not uncommon for financial derivatives to be cross-listed in international capital markets. Through arbitrage, these secondary instruments link different derivative markets, as well as the cash markets.

There are major risks in the use of derivatives—risks both for individual firms that are users or dealers in derivatives and potential risks for the financial system as a whole. At the level of the individual firm or other user, there have been several recent cases of major financial losses through the use of derivatives in often complex and highly leveraged transactions. Among the more widely publicized cases are those of Codelco, Metalgesellschaft, Procter and Gamble, Gibson Greeting Cards, and Orange County, Califor-

---

[1]In the United States, exchanges in which derivatives contracts are traded include the American Stock Exchange, the Philadelphia Stock Exchange, the Chicago Mercantile Exchange, the Chicago Board Options Exchange, and the Chicago Board of Trade. Unlike exchange markets, in which orders are brought to a central facility (a "floor") to be executed, OTC orders are handled by dealers working over the telephone or through a computerized order execution system.

nia. The need for a more disciplined approach by users of derivatives and for greater senior management attention and responsibility has been recognized, and a set of "best practices" for the handling of these instruments proposed by industry sources through a report of the Group of Thirty (1993).

The issue of systemic risk, that is, the potential impact of derivatives on the financial system as a whole, is also a subject of debate. Questions have been raised about possible scenarios in which derivatives might be a source of a widespread disturbance in the financial system. One area of concern has focused on the high degree of concentration of derivatives' trading in a small number of institutions: the question is whether the failure of a major derivatives dealer could impose credit losses on a large number of counterparties, threaten their financial health or solvency, and endanger the financial system more broadly. A second area of concern has centered on the issue of whether certain risk management techniques, such as dynamic hedging of options positions— techniques that lead market participants to buy assets when prices are rising and sell when prices are falling—can disturb markets by exacerbating volatility.

Recent Growth

From a limited beginning in financial forward and futures contracts in the late 1970s have come a plethora of currency, interest rate, and commodity options, futures, and swaps instruments and many combinations of them. Among derivatives, swaps have grown the fastest in recent years. Most swap activity to date has been concentrated on interest rates. According to market participants, swaps are attractive as a way to either hedge against existing risks or transform exposures from one source of risk to another. In addition, financial swaps are simple in principle and unusually versatile in practice. They are therefore revolutionary, especially for portfolio management. A swap coupled with an existing asset or liability can radically modify effective risk and return.

Swaps have been a powerful force in integrating global capital markets. Increasingly, they link currency and money markets and erode price discrepancies that result from differences of liquidity and credit standing across markets. Globally, the key uses of swaps lie in the arbitrage of yield and credit differentials across borders, the management of interest and exchange rate risk, and the global diversification of funding and investing. Swaps can be tailored to meet a variety of needs, often as major components of elaborate structured financings.

Comprehensive statistics are not available on the levels of activity in derivative instruments, but several sources do collect data on these instruments:[2]

- The Bank for International Settlements (BIS) publishes estimates of market size for selected derivative financial instruments. Estimates are in notional (principal) amounts. BIS estimates are based on its own calculations and data from various other sources, including the International Swap Dealers Association, futures and options exchanges worldwide, industry associations, and U.S. organizations, such as the Commodity Futures Trading Commission (CFTC) and the Options Clearing Corporation.[3]
- The CFTC, which oversees the U.S. commodity futures market, collects data from reports on large trades submitted by exchanges' clearinghouses. There is a very high cutoff point for these reports.
- The Chicago Board Options Exchange collects proprietary data on foreign holdings of U.S. options. These unpublished data include the number of covered long and short call and put contracts and the number of uncovered calls and puts traded on the Chicago Board Options Exchange.
- The National Futures Association collects data for the CFTC on foreign options and futures traded by U.S. residents. These unpublished data cover the total number of contracts by brokerage firms and by general geographic distribution, but they are not distinguished by type.
- The Intermarket Surveillance Group collects daily data on U.S. options traded by foreign residents on all U.S. exchanges and provides data to member exchanges and other board members.
- The Federal Reserve, the FDIC, and the Office of the Comptroller of the Currency, using the Call Report, collect data on interest rate contracts, foreign exchange rate contracts, and contracts on other commodities and equities, as well as on other off-balance-sheet items. The data are limited to derivatives transac-

---

[2]Ann M. Lawson of the Bureau of Economic Analysis assisted with the compilation of these sources.

[3]The ISDA conducts surveys every six months on turnover and every year on outstanding positions. Their coverage of derivative products and markets is limited, however.

tions of banks, and they do not show the direction of trade or residency of trader. The data are available to the public.

The explosive growth of financial derivatives has been charted by the BIS, with data covering outstanding (open) instruments throughout the world; see Table 4-1. The notional amount of exchange-traded interest rate and currency futures and options outstanding was estimated to be $7.4 trillion at the end of 1993, a more than tenfold increase from $684 billion in 1987. Interest rate futures and options accounted for about 98 percent of the total. The notional value of OTC swaps and swap-related derivatives was about $8.5 trillion at the end of 1993. About 75 percent of these derivatives were interest rate swaps.

In addition to the currently available data, 26 central banks planned to conduct a global survey of derivative markets in April 1995. The survey was to be performed in conjunction with the triennial central bank survey of foreign exchange markets. In addition to data on the cash foreign-currency markets, the 1995 survey was to collect data on derivative markets in foreign exchange, interest rates, equities, and commodities. The survey will provide data on the size and structure of derivative markets. Market size will be measured in terms of both notional amounts and market values, and the data will be broken down by counterparty type as well as whether it is a domestic or international transaction. The national data will be published by each of the 26 central banks, and global statistics will be compiled and published by the BIS.

REPORTING DERIVATIVES TRANSACTIONS

Unlike traditional financial instruments, such as loans and deposits, which can easily be defined as assets and liabilities and recognized in accounting systems when they are acquired, derivatives can create either future or contingent financial assets and liabilities. Actual financial assets and liabilities are balance-sheet transactions; contingent ones are off-balance-sheet items.

BASIC CONCEPTS AND PRACTICES

Derivative transactions can be measured in terms of either notional amount or market (cash) value. Notional values represent the face value of the principal of the underlying contract on which the derivative instruments are based. They are the underlying

TABLE 4-1 Derivative Contracts Traded Over the Counter, Notional Principal Amounts (in billions of U.S. dollars)

Instrument	1987	1988	1989	1990	1991	1992	1993
New contracts							
Interest rate swaps	387.8	568.1	1,347.2	1,769.3	2,332.9	3,717.0	5,516.9
Currency swaps[a]	86.5	124.3	833.6	1,264.3	1,621.8	2,822.6	4,104.7
			178.2	212.8	328.4	301.9	295.2
Other swap-related derivatives[b]	—	—	335.5	292.3	382.7	592.4	1,117.0
Amounts outstanding at end-of-year							
Interest rate swaps	682.9	1,010.2	1,502.6	3,450.3	4,449.4	5,345.7	8,474.6
Currency swaps[a]	183.7	319.6	449.1	2,311.5	3,065.1	3,850.8	6,177.3
				577.5	807.2	860.4	899.6
Other swap-related derivatives[b]	—	—	—	561.3	577.2	634.5	1,397.6
Memorandum items: exchange-traded financial instruments	683.9	1,234.2	1,654.2	2,126.0	3,308.7	4,392.2	7,433.8
Interest rate futures and options	610.3	1,174.6	1,588.5	2,053.6	3,229.7	4,287.6	7,322.8
Currency futures and options	73.6	59.6	65.7	72.4	79.0	104.6	110.9

NOTE: Data collected by the International Swaps and Derivatives Association (ISDA) only; the two sides of contracts between ISDA members are reported once only; excluding instruments such as forward rate agreements, currency options, forward foreign exchange contracts and equity and commodity-related derivatives.

[a]Adjusted for reporting of both currencies, including cross-currency interest rate swaps.
[b]Caps, collars, floors, and swaptions.

SOURCE: Bank for International Settlement (1994a).

amounts used to calculate contract cash flows. With the important exception of currency swaps, principal is usually not exchanged in a swap transaction. For example, the notional amount of an interest rate swap is the reference or benchmark amount used to calculate the periodic interest payments of either leg of the swap. A fixed and a floating interest rate are multiplied by the respective notional values to determine the amounts to be exchanged by the parties to the swap. In this example, the market or cash value of the derivative contract is determined by calculating the present value of all expected future cash flows (interest payments) under the contract. Since the expected cash flows normally are just a fraction of the notional amount, the cash value (or replacement cost) is only a fraction of the notional value (Federal Reserve Board of Governors et al., 1993). Therefore, notional value is a misleading indicator of the economic significance of derivative transactions; it is, however, a useful measure for comparing relative importance of differing types of derivatives and their growth.

The *cash*, or market, value of a derivative is the appropriate measure for estimating, at a particular moment in time, the economic value of the derivative transaction. The notional value of the derivative is an inappropriate measure because it is a reference amount on which payments are determined and is not itself exchanged. For example, the cash payment initiating a stock option contract would consist of the fee or premium paid for the purchase of the option and the cash margin required by the exchange during the life of the contract. The notional value, in this example, is the value of the stock on which the option has been written. Only if the option is exercised (i.e., the stock is actually purchased by the holder of the option) does a transaction equal to the value of the stock occur.

In balance-of-payments accounting, which relies heavily on national accounting practices for compilation of data from balance-sheet assets or liabilities, any change in ownership of an asset or liability gives rise to a balance-of-payments transaction if a counterparty is a nonresident. Derivatives that give rise to off-balance-sheet (future or contingent) assets and liabilities become reportable in the balance of payments only when the contractual obligation is actually carried out and a payment is made in the form of a capital or income flow or service charge.

In theory, the cash value of cross-border derivatives transactions, including the capital gains and losses, should be covered in the U.S. balance-of-payments data. In practice, however, only limited information on the cash value of derivatives transactions is captured by the current data collected on U.S. international capital transactions. The lack of standard accounting practices and designated reporting, the complexity of the instruments, the multiple purposes they serve, and the growing volume of derivative transactions, especially in OTC markets, have posed difficulties for their coverage in the balance of payments. These difficulties include, among others, identifying derivatives transactions, determining their cash (and "marked-to-market" or fair position) values, and allocating them to the current or the capital account under the balance-of-payments framework. Specifically, under the Treasury International Capital (TIC) system, reporters are instructed to include warrants and options pertaining to long-term securities in their reporting of international sales and purchases of long-term securities only when the underlying security is a stock or long-term bond. Data on purchases and sales of warrants and options are not separately reported but are commingled with purchases and sales of long-term securities.[4] All other options and warrants are omitted from the current TIC system.

For futures and options contracts, BEA measures trading by foreigners in U.S. futures exchanges in this country in an effort to improve the data in the U.S. balance of payments. BEA's estimates include two major components: commissions received by U.S. brokerage firms from foreign traders, which are estimated by applying average commissions (derived from the schedules of major brokerage firms) to the number of contracts closed with foreign residents; and profits and losses and the margin requirements and subsequent changes of foreign traders between two consecutive quarters, which are estimated from the "large trade" data of the CFTC. According to BEA, it does not estimate U.S. receipts and payments related to U.S. residents' transactions in foreign futures because of the lack of data. No other derivatives transactions are covered. The limited information on derivatives transactions presently available is inadequate for BEA's purposes of estimating corresponding balance-of-payments transactions.

The panel's canvassing of TIC data filers also confirms that filers believe that they are not required to report on their deriva-

---

[4]Transactions in claims on specific coupons or principal payments stripped from an underlying security (for example, TIGR, Treasury Investment Growth Receipts, or CATS, Certificates of Accrual on Treasury Securities), are commingled with reported purchases and sales of U.S. Treasury bonds and notes. Collaterized mortgage obligations are commingled with reported transactions in long-term debt securities.

tives transactions, whether tradable or not, and that the TIC forms (except the S forms, as discussed above) do not specifically request such information. The guidelines currently being developed by the U.S. accounting profession and international organizations (see below) will help the TIC data collection system to capture such transactions.

Derivatives in Balance-of-Payments Analysis

As discussed above, most derivative transactions are not included in the balance of payments. The absence of these data can mislead analysts in evaluating the economic or market significance of recorded capital flows. Some examples can illustrate how derivatives can substitute in practice for types of assets or liabilities that are a part of the U.S. balance of payments. A German export company that is selling goods for dollars but wishes to be protected against a decline in the deutsche mark (DM) value of the dollar during the interval before it receives the dollars, could do so in several ways. Only one of them, however, would probably appear fully in U.S. balance-of-payments data. The German company could borrow dollars from a U.S. bank, expecting to repay the loan with proceeds from the export; this transaction would increase claims on foreigners reported by U.S. banks for inclusion in U.S. balance-of-payments statistics. There would be an offset to the claims in increasing liabilities to foreigners, as the German company would hold the dollar proceeds of the loan until receiving payment for the goods. Derivatives transactions that accomplish the same purpose would largely be excluded from balance-of-payments data. The German exporter might buy a DM forward from a U.S. bank, anticipating paying for this purchase with dollars received from the export. The exporter might buy DM futures from a U.S. exchange, expecting to pay for the purchase with dollars received from the export. Only a small portion of either transaction, representing margin requirements and perhaps a commission paid by the exporter for the purchase, would be reflected in U.S. balance-of-payments data. The exporter might also purchase a call option from a U.S. bank to buy DM for dollars or purchase a put option to sell dollars for DM. These option transactions could also protect the exporter if the dollar weakened against the DM, and they, too, would not appear in U.S. balance-of-payments data.

Similar examples can be constructed for other capital account transactions. For example, a Japanese investor in U.S. securities could hedge a purchase either by borrowing dollars from a U.S. bank or by the use of derivatives—such as a sale of forward dollars, a sale of dollar futures, or transactions in call or put options. The dollars borrowed from a U.S. bank would enter the U.S. balance of payments, but the value of the derivatives would not.

An analyst examining balance-of-payments data and noting the rise in U.S. bank claims on foreigners in one case and not the other might be misled about the nature of exchange market pressures during the period. If the analyst assumed that the absence of bank borrowing meant the transaction was unhedged, she or he might conclude that the securities purchase was a source of more upward pressure on exchange markets than it actually was. Borrowing from a bank by a foreigner to help finance and hedge a long-term security purchase reduces the upward pressure on the dollar from the purchase, since the buyer is to that extent initiating less net new demand on the cash foreign exchange market. Had the securities purchase been hedged by a derivative transaction, the analyst, lacking information on the derivative transaction, might overestimate the net new demand in the exchange market. If the related derivatives data were available, the analyst would be in a better position to assess the likely net effect on exchange markets, as well as the structure of interest rates and of capital flows.

Somewhat similar examples can be constructed for currency swaps. A U.S. borrower who has a choice of borrowing abroad in yen or dollars might choose to borrow in yen and to enter into an interest rate swap so that the payments would be in dollars. Since U.S. balance-of-payments data do not distinguish between borrowing in yen or dollars, knowledge about currency swaps might not be especially helpful. If currency distinctions were made in the U.S. balance of payments, however, capital account data would be more revealing, and supplementary information about currency swaps could be informative. Knowledge of derivatives is also important both for U.S. agencies like the Treasury Department and the Federal Reserve and for private participants in the exchange markets or firms that have exposure to foreign-currency developments.

The flows in the capital account of the balance of payments need to be supplemented by knowledge of activities in the derivatives market in interpreting the international sources of exchange market and interest rate pressures. That is not an argument for changing the capital account or for eliminating it, nor is it an argument for giving up a balance of payments based on national borders; rather, it is an argument for recognizing that there are now international financial transactions that are not registered in the capital account in their full dimension and that they can affect interpretation of international financial flows.

Yet another point relates to the U.S. net investment position. To assess potential exchange market pressures in today's globalized economy, it is useful to know whether U.S. obligations to foreigners are denominated in dollars or foreign currencies. If a foreigner borrows in the United States and invests the funds in the United States, there is no net additional dollar exposure (the U.S. international investment position would not show a net increase in debt). However, if a foreigner invests in the United States and is fully hedged in the derivatives market (through a currency swap, for example), the U.S. international investment position shows a net increase in debt but does not show whether the foreign claimant has taken a dollar risk. (There is clearly a credit risk taken by a U.S. obligor.) From the foreigner's perspective, the debt is fully hedged, so that from that transaction alone there is no future dollar exposure when interest and principal come due. (There may be an exposure, depending on how or whether the banks in the middle have covered their risks.) These kinds of transactions raise issues about the implications of derivatives on foreign—and even domestic—attitudes toward the dollar.

Overall, data on derivatives are useful in gauging potential exchange market and interest rate pressures. Evidence of a strong build-up in short positions against the dollar might be useful in judging the timing and extent of exchange market intervention. Data on derivatives may also help in judging whether foreigners— or even residents—are willing investors in the United States. If they are willing investors, monetary policy might not need to be so tight as otherwise to ensure enough of a capital inflow to avoid currency instability and undue weakness in bond and stock markets in the face of a persistent current account deficit.

Experts responsible for the revisions of the International Monetary Fund (IMF) *Balance-of-Payments Manual* and the System of National Accounts (SNA) have developed guidelines for the compilation of data on derivatives. In addition, the U.S. Financial Accounting Standards Board is formulating standards for the treatment of derivatives, and federal regulatory agencies are collecting some data on these financial transactions. However, the proposed treatments of derivatives, as developed by the various expert groups, are not identical (see below).

Improved data on these transactions will facilitate assessments of the risks associated with these products, enhance the coverage of the capital and current account data, and assist in the interpretation of the balance-of-payments data. Derivatives transactions have considerable bearing on international financial services in the form of fees and commissions, which also are components of the current account of the balance of payments.

PROPOSED IMF BALANCE-OF-PAYMENTS AND SNA TREATMENT OF DERIVATIVES

The importance of financial innovations has been explicitly recognized in the recent revisions of the IMF's *Balance-of-Payments Manual* (International Monetary Fund, 1993a) and the international System of National Accounts (see United Nations et al., 1993). The revisions to these systems present closely coordinated criteria for determining whether derivative instruments are classified as financial assets that should be recorded in the SNA financial account, the balance-of-payments capital account, and the national and sectoral balance sheets. The fifth edition of the IMF *Manual* emphasizes the linkages of the balance of payments, international investment positions, and the external sector accounts of the SNA as a set of integrated national accounts. The treatment of derivatives in the IMF *Manual* parallels that proposed in the SNA.

In the IMF *Manual*, "financial derivatives" are classified within the portfolio investment category. In addition, the coverage of portfolio investment has been widened to include, in addition to equities and long-term debt securities (bonds and notes), short-term (money market) debt instruments and financial derivatives. Financial derivatives—options, traded financial futures, and others—are to be classified as financial assets and thus included in the portfolio investment category.

Essentially, the *Manual* distinguishes between assets, which represent actual claims, and the authorization, commitment, or extension of an unutilized line of credit or the incurring of a contingent obligation, which does not establish such a claim. According to the *Manual*, options, futures, and warrants give rise to transactions in current periods that create current assets and liabilities. Other derivative instruments yield contingent liabilities and assets. The *Manual* notes, however, that it cannot provide standards to cover all circumstances because of the complexity and diversity of the instruments. Its proposed treatments are to be applied to the most common instruments in their basic uses.

The SNA revision, jointly produced by statistical agencies of the United Nations, the IMF, the Organization of Economic Co-operation and Development (OECD), the European Community, and the World Bank, proposes that contingent or future liabilities and assets not be included in the balance sheets for the current period, since financial transactions would arise in a future period only if the contingency arose, or when the future asset or liability became a current one. Secondary instruments that are market-able, however, would be included. These marketable instruments have characteristics that give rise to actual financial assets or liabilities in the current period, such as a required margin pay-ment or a current resale value.

ACCOUNTING AND REGULATORY ISSUES

Currently, the treatment of secondary financial instruments in the accounts of corporate enterprises varies according to the pur-pose for which the instrument is being held—that is, whether it is used for hedging, investment, or trading. This treatment affects the valuation and time of recording of transactions in the ac-counts and makes data collection on a consistent basis more diffi-cult than otherwise would be the case.

Contingent liabilities and assets are usually mentioned in the notes to corporate accounts rather than in the balance sheets. The premium paid for an option is entered in the balance sheet as an asset—usually as an investment within current assets. In con-trast, the premium received by the writer of an option is not entered as a liability, as the premium is not repayable to the purchaser. Premiums received are credited to profit-and-loss ac-counts, but they are usually offset by a provision of the same amount in order to defer recognition of the receipt of income until the outcome of the option is known. The treatment of traded options by the writer (seller) of an option, however, is dif-ferent: these are entered in the accounts of corporate enterprises as a liability (or negative asset), reflecting the fact that sales of these contracts produce short positions in these instruments, in contrast to the long positions reflected in the accounts of a pur-chaser.

Concerns about the accounting and reporting of financial de-rivatives have by no means been confined to matters of collecting balance-of-payments data. In the United States, both the accounting standards authorities and federal regulatory agencies have taken great interest in these instruments. On the issue of market par-ticipants' public disclosures relating to derivatives, some observers have come to the conclusion that traditional accounting approaches have limited ability to encompass financial derivatives. New approaches to reporting and disclosure that focus on exposures to underlying risk factors (for example, exchange rate risk, interest rate risk) may be more informative than the traditional accounting focus on balance sheet categories and instrument definitions. In this alternative approach, derivatives would not be viewed in isolation, but instead would be considered in the context of a portfolio of cash market and derivatives positions exposed to the same underlying risk factors.[5]

Financial Accounting Standards Board

The Financial Accounting Standards Board (FASB) added to its agenda in May 1986 a project on financial instruments and off-balance-sheet financing. This project was to develop broad standards for resolving the accounting issues raised by off-balance-sheet instruments and transactions, as well as those raised by the inconsistent accounting guidance and practice that have developed for financial instruments over the years. Furthermore, the project was to provide a consistent conceptual basis for resolving financial instrument accounting issues—those issues that have already been identified as well as the many issues that have arisen as financial innovation continues. In October 1994 the FASB issued Standard 119 pertaining to disclosure and fair valuation of derivatives (Federal Accounting Standards Board, 1994).

Early in its project, FASB proposed interim steps to improve disclosure about financial instruments while it considered more difficult and time-consuming issues of recognition and measurement. Work on such disclosure resulted in two FASB statements (Financial Accounting Standards Board, 1990a, 1991a). Statement No. 105 (1990a) extends present disclosure practices of some entities for some financial instruments by requiring all entities to disclose certain information about financial instruments with off-balance-sheet risk of financial loss. Statement No. 107 (1991a) requires disclosure of fair value of financial instruments for which it is practical to estimate fair value, including those not recognized in the statement of financial position.

---

[5]Several recent reports by U.S. and international groups address issues of proper accounting and public disclosure: Bank for International Settlements (1994b, 1994c, 1995), Federal Reserve Bank of New York (1994), Group of Thirty (1993), and Institute of International Finance (1994).

Following these interim steps, FASB proceeded to the recognition and measurement part of its project. It issued a discussion memorandum on that subject (Financial Accounting Standards Board, 1991b) that delved into such basic issues as what financial assets or liabilities should be recognized in financial statements, how they should be reported, and how they should be measured. Questions directly relating to derivative and off-balance-sheet financial instruments were raised: "What should be the accounting for financial instruments that are intended to transfer market or credit risks—for example, futures contracts, interest rate swaps, options, forward commitments, nonrecourse arrangements, and financial guarantees—and for the underlying assets or liabilities to which the risk-transferring instruments are related?"

The new Standard 119 applies to futures, forwards, swaps, options, and other financial instruments with option- or forward-like characteristics. It requires disclosure of the contract amount or notional equivalent of derivatives. In addition, it requires a discussion of the credit and market risks, cash requirements and accounting policies associated with these instruments. It also amends Statements 105 and 107 to require greater disaggregation of information, including information about fair value and risk.

Federal Bank Regulators

Federal bank regulatory authorities have been interested in derivatives and off-balance-sheet financial instruments for prudential reasons, reflecting their concern about the safety and soundness of U.S. banking institutions. In accordance with the Basle Capital Accord, the three federal bank regulatory agencies—the Office of the Comptroller of Currency, the Federal Deposit Insurance Corporation, and the Federal Reserve System—in 1989 adopted risk-based capital requirements for the banks under their supervision. To monitor banks' risk-based positions, the three regulatory agencies, acting through the Federal Financial Institutions Examination Council (FFIEC), now require banks to submit certain information about derivatives. Currently, the quarterly Call Report covers financial contracts on interest rates, foreign exchange, and stock indexes as well as those on commodities and individual stocks (see Table 3-3 in Chapter 3).[6] Bank holding companies

---

[6]Financial guarantees (such as guarantees of loans, performance bonds, and letters of credit) are also covered by the Call Reports.

provide similar data in their quarterly (Y-9C) reports, filed with the Federal Reserve (see Table 3-3). Both reports cover the notional values of interest rate swaps, futures and forward contracts, option contracts, and similar contracts involving commodities and equities. They exclude market value data for certain exchange-traded contracts, as well as foreign exchange contracts with original maturities of less than 14 days. Annual report disclosures of the "amount of accounting loss," as required by FASB's Statement No. 105, generally include these contracts. Such disclosures in annual reports of corporations may also differ from the market value data included in Call Reports and Y-9C reports, depending, for example, on how the organization discloses contracts that are used for hedging purposes. Other than these differences, market value disclosures in both reports are generally similar to disclosures of the amount of accounting loss in corporate annual reports.

The information reported on the Call Reports and the Y-9C differs from that required for balance-of-payments purposes in various ways. Specifically, the Call Report information is submitted on a consolidated basis, by institution, with each U.S. bank including in its report the aggregate of its worldwide activities, including those activities of its overseas branches. Contracts are not disaggregated in terms of residents and nonresidents, and a single amount would be reported for the total value of a reporting bank's holdings of, for example, interest rate swaps, with no separate reporting of the amount of those swaps contracted between resident and nonresident parties.

More recently, federal bank regulators, again operating through the FFIEC, introduced a limited but focused reporting form (FFIEC 035), the Monthly Consolidated Foreign Currency Report of Banks in the United States. It is required only of banking institutions that engage in significant amounts of foreign exchange activities: generally, U.S.-chartered banks and U.S. branches and agencies of foreign banks that have more than $1 billion in commitments to purchase foreign currencies and U.S. dollar exchange. Again, the data are reported on a consolidated basis, with each U.S. chartered bank that files reporting its worldwide activity. However, the FFIEC 035 focuses *not* on all the off-balance-sheet activity of a bank, but rather on the institution's foreign-currency exposure. Thus, it calls for reporting items that affect the institution's foreign-currency position: both off-balance-sheet activities (contracts to buy or sell foreign currencies, spot or forward, through OTC or organized exchanges; foreign-currency options, written or purchased;

interest rate swaps *if* there is a cross-currency exchange included) and on-balance-sheet activity (in the form of "noncapital" assets and liabilities denominated in foreign currencies).[7] The FFIEC 035 asks filers to submit the data disaggregated by individual foreign currency: each filing institution reports for both major types of off-balance-sheet contracts (options, futures, etc.) and on-balance-sheet items the assets and liabilities in each of the major foreign currencies (German deutsche marks, Swiss francs, British pounds, etc.). This monthly report thus provides data on the filing institutions' consolidated long positions and short positions in specific foreign currencies.

Data collected in the five FFIEC reports (031, 032, 033, 034, and 035) are primarily intended for bank supervisory and regulatory purposes. Aggregated data are published in the *Federal Reserve Bulletin* and in the Federal Reserve's *Annual Statistical Digest.* The Call Report data are also included in the Uniform Bank Performance Report and the annual report of the FFIEC.[8]

RECOMMENDATIONS

• An interagency group led by the Federal Reserve and including the Federal Reserve Bank of New York, the Treasury Department, the Bureau of Economic Analysis, the Securities and Exchange Commission, the Commodity Futures Trading Commission, and other financial regulatory bodies, should be established to undertake several tasks. Specifically, the interagency group should identify the major participants in financial derivatives markets, the intermediaries involved, and the various forms of transactions. It should also examine the coverage, quality, and consistency of the limited data on financial derivatives currently collected by the Federal Financial Institutions Examination Council, the Commodity Futures Trading Commission, the Securities and Exchange Commission, and private institutions and determine ways to expand coverage, eliminate duplication, standardize definitions, and, whenever appropriate, integrate the data. The group should

---

[7]In addition, Section 305 of the FDIC Improvement Act requires increased disclosure of derivative exposures, and Section 308 requires banks to establish standards to evaluate their exposure to weak institutions, including those arising from derivative products (see Federal Reserve Board et al., 1993).

[8]Call Report data are available to the Reserve Bank staff through the Federal Reserve Board's computer facility, and to the public on magnetic tape through the National Technical Information Service subscription files.

work closely with market participants, industry groups, and the accounting profession to ensure harmonization of accounting, regulatory, and statistical reporting practices, especially for classifying derivatives transactions and recognizing their market values, income flows, and gains and losses. It is important that the group secure the cooperation of filers and that filers have an appreciation of the purpose and significance of the transactions they are required to report. Because many of the fastest growing derivatives transactions are international in nature, consideration should be given to collecting data on such activities from large financial institutions and multinational corporations, and to classifying the data by major financial instruments and in key currencies. Over the long term, harmonization of international reporting standards for derivatives is desirable. (4-1)

• Data on financial derivatives are needed for interpretation of market developments for macroeconomic policy purposes, as well as for regulatory purposes. These data also are needed for the more specific purpose of improving the measurement of the capital account of the balance of payments. Better coverage of U.S. international currency exposure also is needed as an addendum to the data on the U.S. international investment position. The Federal Reserve, other financial regulators, the Treasury Department, and the Bureau of Economic Analysis should work together, in consultation with data providers, to define the most important data needs and to develop procedures for data collection. (4-2)

• As a near-term step, using the guidelines contained in the IMF *Manual*, the Treasury's TIC data collection program should be expanded to cover derivatives transactions that represent on-balance-sheet activities. The panel believes that the concepts and procedures proposed in the *Manual* and in the revised international System of National Accounts are useful to facilitate the development of data reporting frameworks on financial derivatives for balance-of-payments purposes. Nonetheless, given the complexity of these instruments and differences in national accounting systems, it is important that the U.S. data compilers work with the U.S. accounting profession and market participants to refine the guidelines for firms reporting in the United States. (4-3)

5

Alternative Data Sources and Collection Methods

$\mathbf{A}$s noted throughout this report, the data collection system for U.S. international capital transactions has relied heavily on manual reporting by large financial intermediaries located in the United States, with an emphasis on banking activities. However, liberalization of world capital markets, securitization of transactions, emergence of new financial products, the rise in nonbank participants in markets, and increased use of offshore financial centers have given rise to numerous transactions beyond the reach of the traditional system. Data gaps are most severe for international transactions of U.S. nonbanks, U.S. residents' direct sales and purchases of foreign securities overseas, and cross-border derivatives transactions. At the same time, data filers have noted the burden of having to complete numerous forms whose purposes they do not fully understand. Data compilers, for their part, have had to contend with outdated collection methods and demands to collect information on increasing volumes of transactions with limited resources.

Clearly, the existing system is under stress, and there is a need to develop alternative data collection methods to improve its efficiency and effectiveness. In view of the global nature of transactions and their rapid expansion, improvements over the medium term in the coverage and accuracy of data, without substantial increases in resources, lie in drawing on information from existing custodians of financial assets and from large-payment, clearance, and settlement systems. Over the long term, as rising numbers of multinational corporations and financial institutions commit large sums to develop in-house international information and communications systems to meet their operational needs, the possibility of collecting balance-of-payments data electronically increases, as has recently been analyzed by a task force of the Statistical Office of the European Community (EUROSTAT). This chapter explores the feasibility of gathering securities data from global custodians, payment and settlement organizations, and clearinghouses in the medium term and from automated data exchange systems over the long term.

DATA SOURCES

GLOBAL CUSTODIANS

Global custodians are institutions that manage the custody of financial assets in multiple markets for clients, most of which are institutional investors. Many global custodians are leading commercial and investment banks and large brokerage houses. Over the past decade, these financial institutions have invested heavily in automation. They use their automated data systems not only to meet their own operational needs, but also to offer various fee-earning services to other financial institutions and money managers. Global custody is one of these services. Actual physical custody of assets is usually maintained by foreign local subcustodians, who keep the assets in the country of origin. The main role of a global custodian is that of master record-keeper and reporter. Every client is provided a monthly or quarterly report detailing information on assets held, including value and transaction date. Information on the national residence of the client is also available. Global custodians therefore appear to have much of what is needed to compile data on the U.S. positions (holdings) of foreign securities and changes in those positions.

Economies of scale provided by information technology have given rise to a relatively small number of very large global custodians around the world. Some of these include Bankers Trust, Chase Manhattan, Citibank, Morgan Stanley, Salomon Brothers, and State Street Bank in the United States, as well as Barclays Bank in the United Kingdom. These global custodians could serve as prime sources of information on international portfolio investment positions and their changes; in addition, with such data the quality of transaction data would also be improved.[1]

Global custodians have highly automated record-keeping and reporting systems. It would appear, therefore, that they could retrieve the necessary information at relatively low costs. Although automated systems of global custodians vary, there is uniformity in information maintained because of the record-keeping requirements of the 1974 Employee Retirement Income Security Act (ERISA) pension fund laws and the requirements of the Securities and Exchange Commission (SEC).[2]

An advantage of developing this data collection method is that many custodians are now building large telecommunications and information networks. This bodes well for the future development of an automated data collection system (see the discussion on electronic data exchange, below). A drawback is that not all major U.S. investors use global custodians in the United States to manage the records of their financial assets; some rely on custodians in other countries. Thus, U.S. global custodians would not have coverage of all U.S. holdings of foreign securities. However, since major U.S. investors do have to report their holdings directly to the Treasury Department (with the assistance of their foreign global custodians), some of the data would be available.

FINANCIAL CLEARINGHOUSES AND
PAYMENT AND SETTLEMENT SYSTEMS

Payment, clearance, and settlement organizations are institutions that process financial transactions. These organizations settle trades (transactions) by delivering the asset and payment, or, in the case of financial derivatives, by satisfying the terms of the contract. Most of these organizations have highly automated record-keeping systems. Economies of scale made possible by advanced

---

[1]Global custodians were a main source of data in the Treasury Department's 1994 outbound portfolio investment survey of U.S. holdings of foreign securities because of this improved coverage potential. Authority to obtain data from global custodians, as well as from U.S. investors, was provided by the International Investment and Trade in Services Survey Act.

[2]The purpose of ERISA is to ensure that employees and retirees of private firms receive the pensions they have been promised as a condition of their employment. To protect employees against loss from financial hazards, ERISA requires pension plan sponsors to disclose to participants all of the provisions and financial conditions of their pension plans. Similarly, SEC Rule 17F-5 governs the management of custody of the portfolio investments of mutual funds.

telecommunications technology have led to a moderate number of large clearance and settlement organizations around the world that handle most of the transactions. Most countries have only one major clearance and settlement organization; in the United States, a small number of organizations provide clearance and settlement services for the various types of transactions.

Some of the U.S. organizations provide services to members at the "retail" level, matching the orders of buyers and sellers, keeping track of accounts of clients, and settling the trades generally through major banking institutions. Others, the large-value payments systems, provide the "wholesale" settlement networks. There are 3 clearinghouses and 3 depositories that serve the nation's stock exchanges and over-the-counter dealers; 9 that serve the 14 futures exchanges (such as the Commodity Clearing Corporation); and 1 that serves equity options markets (the Options Clearing Corporation) (U.S. Office of Technology Assessment, 1990:81). These organizations typically serve their clients at the retail level and interact with (settle with and obtain credit from) depository institutions or banks, which, in turn, have access to this country's two large-value payment and clearance networks: Fedwire and the Clearing House Interbank Payments Systems (CHIPS).[3] Both Fedwire and CHIPS are on-line, real-time electronic payment systems. Fedwire is the wire transfer network of the Federal Reserve, which electronically transmits funds and Treasury securities (on a book-entry basis) among banking institutions. CHIPS is a private electronic payment system owned and operated by the New York Clearing House Association, whose members are 11 New York money-center banks.[4] These systems have grown dramatically with the explosion of domestic and international financial activities. The feasibility of collecting data from Fedwire and CHIPS is discussed below.

Fedwire

According to the Federal Reserve, a depository institution can use Fedwire for access to its account at its local Federal Reserve

---

[3]In Europe, large multinational clearing and settlement organizations include CEDEL and Euroclear.

[4]Member banks include the Bank of New York, Chase Manhattan Bank, Citibank, Morgan Guaranty Trust Company of New York, Chemical Bank, Bankers Trust Company, Marine Midland Bank, United States Trust Company of New York, National Westminster Bank USA, European American Bank, and Republic National Bank of New York.

bank to transfer securities or funds to any other domestic depository institution that has an account with a Federal Reserve bank. Depository institutions include all domestic commercial banks, foreign banks with branches or agencies in the United States, trust companies, savings banks, savings and loans associations, and credit unions that are covered by the Federal Deposit Insurance Corporation (FDIC). These institutions can transfer cash and securities both for themselves and for their customers, which include correspondent banks, governments, corporations, institutional investors, and individuals.

The method by which depository institutions secure access to the Fedwire system generally depends on their volume of use. Institutions with large volumes of securities or fund transfers usually have a computer-to-computer link with their local Federal Reserve bank. Institutions with relatively low volumes are connected by telephone lines to their Federal Reserve banks through personal computer links that use the Federal Reserve software, known as Fedline. Institutions that use Fedwire infrequently can get access to Fedwire off-line, by telephone calls to personnel at the Federal Reserve banks (Federal Reserve Board of Governors, 1992:730-731).

A Fedwire fund transfer message identifies the sending and receiving institutions, the dollar amount of the transfer, and the beneficiary of the transfer (if the institutions itself is not the beneficiary). A securities transfer message identifies the sending and receiving institutions, describes the securities issue and amount of funds to be transferred, and records the actual payment (if the securities are delivered against payments). The computer verifies that the sending and the receiving institutions have the securities or funds in the designated accounts. When the processing is complete, both institutions receive acknowledgments.

CHIPS

CHIPS is the central clearing system in the United States for international transactions, handling more than 95 percent of all dollar payments moving between the United States and the rest of the world. In addition to the 11 members of the New York Clearing House Association, CHIPS users include many other commercial banks with headquarters in New York, more than 95 New York branches or agencies of foreign banks, and a number of other banking offices. Currently, about 140 financial institutions use

CHIPS. About two-thirds of all CHIPS participants are foreign banking institutions in the United States.

CHIPS payments executed during a day are irrevocable and made final through settlement at the end of the day. CHIPS settles its net balances each evening with the Federal Reserve Bank of New York (FRBNY). A CHIPS settlement account at FRBNY is funded by the settling participants in a net debit position and drawn down by the New York Clearing House Association to pay those participants in a net credit position. After completion of daily processing, records of transactions are sent to participants by CHIPS.

CHIPS transfers and settles in U.S. dollars for international and domestic business transactions. These transactions are conducted by banks for their customers and for their own accounts, supporting the various financial service and intermediary functions required by businesses and governments. CHIPS serves as the conduit for moving dollars between participant banks for a wide variety of transactions, including:

- foreign and domestic trade services (letters of credit, collections, and reimbursements);
- international loans (placements and interest disbursements);
- syndicated loans (assembly, placement of funds, and interest);
- foreign exchange sales and purchases (spot market, currency futures, interest and currency swaps);
- Eurodollar placements;
- sale of short-term funds;
- funds movement and concentration; and
- Eurosecurities settlement.

The operation of CHIPS is based on a structured record format that embodies fixed and variable data fields. It is highly conducive to computer automation at both originating and receiving banks. By taking advantage of this structure, many participants send payment messages between dissimilar systems without any manual intervention. CHIPS can accept, for example, identification numbers from SWIFT (Society for Worldwide Interbank Financial Telecommunications) and automatically cross-reference them to the CHIPS Universal Identification Numbers (UIN). SWIFT is a European-headquartered electronic payments system for international transactions; it is a cooperative company created under Belgian law.

According to a recent FRBNY study (Federal Reserve Bank of

New York, 1987-1988), CHIPS handles payments for almost all foreign exchange transactions. In contrast, Fedwire accounts for virtually all payments related to transactions for securities, purchases, redemptions, financing, and federal funds purchases and sales. Significant overlap between the two systems exists, however, in the categories of payments related to bank loans, commercial and miscellaneous transactions, settlements, and Eurodollar placements.

Three categories of information that can be gleaned from both systems:

• transactors: brokers/dealers, investor customers, security issuers, own accounts, own trading accounts, own investment accounts;
• kind of investments: commercial paper, bankers' acceptances, domestic certificates of deposit (CDs), book-entry securities (Fedwire), Euro CDs, mortgage-back securities, municipal securities, and other or unspecified; and
• nature of transactions: secondary markets, new issues, payments at maturity, and unspecified.

In addition, four other categories of information are sometimes available:

• purpose of transaction: investment, trading, repurchase agreement, safekeeping, other or unspecified;
• numbers of transactions and dollar amounts of each item: investment, trading, repurchase agreement, safekeeping, other or unspecified;
• originating place of transactions: outside or inside the United States; and
• transactions for foreign customers and for banks' own foreign offices.

Clearly, not all the data that would be needed to record international capital transactions for balance-of-payments purposes are currently available from Fedwire and CHIPS. The information in the payment and clearance networks is purposefully kept to a minimum to lower clearing and settlement costs. In some cases, not all of the information currently being requested is available to the sending and receiving institutions or supplied by them, and not all of the information requested is needed to execute the transfers.

Nonetheless, it is technologically feasible for the systems to add information, as illustrated by the SWIFT payment system, which allows 100 additional characters to be included for each transaction, either in numerical or alphabetical form. There are also optional fields available in both the Fedwire and CHIPS networks.[5] Of course, to require a private electronic clearance system to obtain and provide new information would probably require new legislation and, possibly, compensation. According to the Federal Reserve staff, the development of such new data formats would require a lead time of 2-3 years at a minimum.

Large-value payment systems are integral parts of the monetary institutions in a country. They are also key mechanisms in the operations of the global financial system. As such, their safety and soundness are crucial to national and international financial stability. Currently, industrial countries are working toward a set of common practices and standards to improve clearing and settlement of global trading of securities and multilateral banking transactions.[6] Uniform codes of operation and system design to be developed for these financial information networks, under these private and public initiatives, will facilitate the introduction of electronic data interchange as a method of data collection in the future (see below).

RECOMMENDATIONS

• The potential for using global custodians as a new source of data appears promising. In addition to information on securities holdings, the Treasury Department and the Federal Reserve Bank of New York should actively explore the feasibility of gathering flow data on securities transactions from global custodians and assess its cost-effectiveness. (5-1)

---

[5]However, there is a lot of demand for the optional space in SWIFT, CHIPS, and Fedwire: for example, law enforcement agencies in various countries would like to use the optional space to identify parties to the payments to assist in money-laundering investigations.

[6]The Group of Thirty, a private organization of international bankers, economists, and business executives, issued a study recommending such steps to maximize the efficiency of clearance and settlement for the world's securities markets (see Group of Thirty, 1989). The Basle Committee on Payment and Settlement Systems, an international committee of central bankers, has been studying this issue as it relates to the safety and soundness of large payment systems (see Basle Committee on Payment and Settlement Systems, 1992).

- On the basis of the information currently available on Fedwire and CHIPS, it appears that it would be possible to secure statistical data on U.S. international capital transactions from the two systems. The Treasury Department and the Bureau of Economic Analysis should conduct a rigorous study to explore such feasibility by undertaking an in-depth analysis of a sample of transactions that pass through Fedwire and CHIPS. They should also determine whether cost savings would result from using data from Fedwire and CHIPS. If data for analysis cannot be released by CHIPS or Fedwire to outsiders due to privacy concerns, the Treasury Department and BEA could request the staffs of Fedwire and CHIPS to devise ways of providing the data without violating individuals' privacy. (5-2)

COLLECTION METHODS

ELECTRONIC DATA INTERCHANGE

An important recent development in information technology with powerful implications for the automated collection of economic data has been the emergence of electronic data interchange (EDI). EDI refers to the electronic transfer of computer-processable business data among the computer systems of different organizations using an agreed standard to structure the data. EDI is especially useful for frequent substantive exchanges of routinized information. Under certain circumstances, through the use of standard formats, it can allow businesses to reduce the use of paper purchase orders, invoices, shipping forms, and technical specifications. EDI can improve data accuracy while reducing data entry, mailing, and paper handling costs. Indirect benefits also arise from modified business practices, including reduced inventory, better cash management, reduced order time, greater sales through improved customer satisfaction, and more accurate and timely information for decision support.

The data standard that is taking the lead in the EDI field is EDIFACT—which stands for EDI for administration, commerce, and trade. Developed by the United Nations, it has been adopted on an international level. More than 130 EDIFACT messages have been established for the purpose of preparing invoices, customs declarations, and the transfers of funds, among others. EDIFACT messages are increasingly used in Europe in various economic sectors (such as construction, the social and health fields, and national accounts). In addition to exporters and importers in merchandise trade, the banking community is showing interest with pilot projects, both nationally and internationally. SWIFT uses the EDIFACT standard, and European business administrations increasingly communicate in EDIFACT terms.

In the United States, the Accredited Standards Committee X12 chartered by the American National Standards Institute (ANSI) has developed the X12 standard. Although EDIFACT and X12 are separately established, they are considered similar families of standards, and the ANSI-X12 committee has played a key role in the definition of the EDIFACT. The committee is also committed to the convergence of X12 with the EDIFACT standard.

Under the aegis of EUROSTAT, a task force since July 1991 has been exploring the feasibility of using EDIFACT messages for collecting data on balance of payments and international investment positions. The task force is led by experts from De Nederlandsche Bank (the Netherlands Central Bank). The anticipation that paper recording of individual transactions may cease, causing the existing transaction (ticket) data collection system used in continental Europe to break down (see Appendix A), has been a major driving force behind the European balance-of-payments compilers' interest in EDIFACT. The movement toward the creation of a single capital market in Europe has also provided an impetus toward harmonizing balance-of-payments data across member states of the European Community.

The rationale for this approach is that business organizations are the source of balance-of-payments data. If they increasingly use EDIFACT messages, it would seem efficient that these messages be used for reporting balance-of-payments data. It capitalizes on the development of EDIFACT messages for commercial purposes by requiring the commercial originators of such messages to send copies or extracts to the balance-of-payments compilers. In this way, the collection of data for the balance of payments should become, in principle, cheap, simple, and quick. For items of data needed for official but not commercial purposes, separate data would be collected: in principle, this can be achieved by including an extra field (or fields) on the commercial electronic messages for official purposes. The EUROSTAT task force is working on a system for implementing this approach and for exchanging aggregated data among official bodies using the same EDI techniques and the same EDIFACT standard. It would be possible, in theory, to collect data on all cross-border transactions as they occur.

Under this approach, data on balance-of-payments and international investment positions would be filed with balance-of-payments data compilers using electronic messages. Messages could relate to transaction data or survey data as appropriate. For transaction data, messages would cover transactions reported by customers through a commercial bank or directly to the balance-of-payments compiler, as well as banks' own transactions and customer transactions reported by banks to the balance-of-payments compiler. Reporting by the balance-of-payments compiler to international statistical bodies can also be done in electronic format.

In researching the possibilities of using EDIFACT messages for reporting balance-of-payments data, the EUROSTAT task force developed a data flow analysis that traces the information exchanged between the various parties. A summary of the data flows identified by the task force is shown in Figure 5-1.

The balance-of-payments messages to be used fall in two categories: those that use existing, but slightly adjusted EDIFACT messages, and those for which new messages would be developed. The messages would cover all data collection systems and provide all information needed. The approach followed in developing messages would be flexible in that the use of all segments of the messages would be optional; however, national guidelines or regulations could make the use of all or part of these messages mandatory.

The compilation of balance-of-payments data requires the reporting of incoming and outgoing payments, that is, transactions between residents and nonresidents. The key, in most cases, is to allocate the transactions to the correct period, appropriate category, and geographic area. The principal data for balance-of-payments compilation in an electronic data system include:

- identity of the resident engaged in the transaction (name and address, additional identification number, such as SIREN [in France], a VAT [value-added-tax] number, or other national registration number);
- (industrial) activity of the resident engaged in the transaction;
- country of the nonresident partner to the transaction;
- date of the transaction;
- total amount of the payment (possibly broken down, for instance, in the case of a composite payment on a loan, to interest and redemption payment);
- currency of the transaction;
- nature of the transaction, in code and in verbal description (about 200 kinds of balance-of-payments items are differentiated

according to regulations from EUROSTAT, the Organization for Economic Cooperation and Development (OECD), and the International Monetary Fund (IMF); in some cases as, for example, that of outward direct investment, this might involve additional geographic data if the country of the payee differs from the country in which the direct investment took place, which is relevant for balance-of-payments data);

- identity of the nonresident engaged in the transactions;
- date of the message;
- identification of the resident banking intermediary and of the banking intermediary of the nonresident; and
- bank reference number.

The compilation of the data on international investment positions requires the reporting by residents of their stocks of foreign assets and liabilities, by value and function. The data needed include:

- identity of the reporting resident;
- debtor or creditor country;
- value;
- currency;
- kind of stocks and flows;
- date of the reported position;
- type and sector of the reporting resident; and
- identity of the nonresident.

A paperless process of reporting information to statistical authorities has potential benefits for both data compilers and data filers. The European compilers believe that automated reporting will be more timely and is likely to result in higher quality data. In addition, they expect that the switch from reporting by paper forms to reporting by electronic messages will bring about large cost savings because manual data transcription work, with possible typing errors, is significantly reduced. Increases in the accuracy and timeliness of data would also reduce follow-up costs. Banks, which act as intermediaries in collecting balance-of-payments data under an electronic reporting approach, can save costs by using EDIFACT messages. In the long run, the use of internationally exchanged EDIFACT balance-of-payments messages will save banks in a number of countries the costs of collecting forms to be used for reporting external transactions.

According to the EUROSTAT task force, savings also will ac-

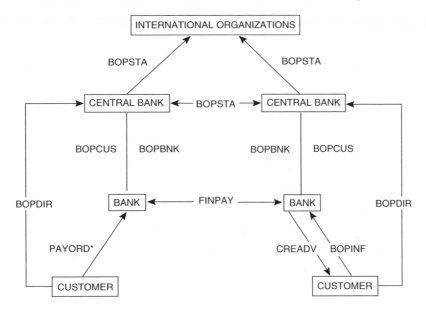

* Read as PAYORD/PAYEXT/PAYMUL

Message	Transferred Information
PAYORD/ PAYMUL/ PAYEXT	Payments messages sent by a customer to the customer's commercial bank to make payment by debiting the customer's account. The same applies to extended payment orders (PAYEXT) and multiple payment orders (PAYMUL).
BOPCUS	Messages covering individual customer transactions (payments/receipts) sent by banks to the balance-of-payments compiler.
BOPBNK	Messages sent by banks to balance-of-payments compiler reporting banks' own transactions, aggregated individual customer transactions, portfolio transactions, and banks' asset and liability positions.
FINPAY	Messages for making payments involving banks in two different countries.

Message	Transferred Information
BOPINF or CREADV (for crediting information)	Receipt messages sent by a customer to the customer's commercial bank giving information on the nature of the transaction when the customer's account is credited. This information is forwarded to the balance-of-payments compiler.
BOPDIR	Messages sent by nonbank enterprises directly to balance-of-payments compiler, reporting information on amounts received from nonresidents via resident banks, settlements via external bank accounts, current accounts held abroad with nonbanks, nonbanks' foreign assets and liabilities, participation in an international clearing system, or responses to statistical questionnaires.
BOPSTA	Messages sent by balance-of-payments compilers reporting aggregated balance-of-payments data to international statistical bodies and/or other balance-of-payments compilers.

FIGURE 5-1 Data flows in EDIFACT for balance-of-payments data.

crue to customers because they will in most cases no longer have to report the transactions to national compilers. This saving assumes that customers' resident banks will have all the necessary balance-of-payments information, which will be supplied by foreign payors in EDIFACT messages received through SWIFT or other international networks. Of course, this would require harmonized balance-of-payments data collection systems among countries and international networks, such as SWIFT, to transmit the messages.

An important aspect of this electronic approach is the development of standardized information codes and statistical systems for information extraction. It is important that national data compilers become involved in the development of the coding systems. It is crucial that the necessary information be coded so as to minimize retrieval costs. With regard to extraction systems, a crucial issue is the determination of how and when to aggregate information. This decision will affect costs because of the huge volume of information available. It will also bear on whether the anonymity of individual buyers and sellers can be maintained: in the absence of such anonymity, many buyers and sellers may be unwilling to reveal even their national origin. Confidentiality rules among nations will need to be set up for electronic data collection.

In the United States, the Bureau of the Census and the National Center for Education Statistics have laid the groundwork for using EDI to collect statistical data by developing transaction sets for economic and education information. Both approaches build on the standards established by ANSI. Under the proposed framework, these federal statistical agencies would be able to accept information based on different record-keeping systems (such as payroll, revenue, and cost data based on different definitions). Agencies could accommodate a variety of record-keeping formats used by individual businesses by translating the respondents' reports to agency standards. This approach is believed to have the potential to reduce reporting burden on both small and large businesses, increase response rates, and improve the quality of data collection (U.S. Office of Management and Budget, 1993).

To coordinate the U.S. work on EDI with international developments in this area, the U.S. Office of Management and Budget (OMB) has established liaison with the EUROSTAT task force. In addition, a working group of U.S. statistical agencies interested in EDI has been established to explore EDI capabilities in the private sector, develop plans for use of EDI to improve data collection methods, and promote convergence of the national and international standards. Nonetheless, progress in this area is likely to take some time because of the complexity of harmonizing international standards, which entails commitment, resources, and consensus of market participants, regulators, and national governments.

INTERNATIONAL DATA EXCHANGE AND COORDINATION

Internationalization of financial markets has meant that data compilers can no longer rely solely on domestic data sources. Coordination and cooperation among countries to exchange data is needed to improve coverage of individual countries data. The IMF and the Bank for International Settlements (BIS) maintain extensive databases on international banking transactions that can be used to cross-check and improve national balance-of-payments data. The IMF/BIS databases are especially useful in improving information on transactions of domestic nonbank entities with banks abroad. As discussed in Chapter 3, BEA has recently increased utilization of data obtained by BIS from central banks, and it also exchanges data directly with authorities in other countries to improve the balance-of-payments data on portfolio transactions of nonbanks. BEA is reviewing the feasibility of further expanding the use of such data.

There are differences in definition and coverage among reporting systems of countries that submit banking data to the IMF and the BIS. Major differences exist in data reported by banks on their custody accounts, definitions of instruments (such as deposits and repurchase agreements), and geographic allocations. Placing these data on a basis consistent with U.S. concepts has required and will continue to require cooperative efforts of the IMF, BIS, central banks, and national statistical authorities.

RECOMMENDATIONS

- In the United States, the Federal Reserve, the Treasury Department, and the Bureau of Economic Analysis should allocate resources to study the systems architecture of information technology adopted by financial institutions and multinational corporations and to investigate ways to facilitate the development of these automated data collection systems to prepare for the emerging electronic global trading environment. (5-3)
- Data exchanges and the use of the databases of international

organizations require that the data of different countries be comparable in coverage, definitions, and concepts. Despite recent efforts of various countries to bring about greater convergence, significant conceptual differences and data inconsistencies among countries remain. This circumstance points to the need for careful and systematic comparisons of bilateral data, as well as for comparisons between national data and information contained in international databases, before substituting or making adjustments to national databases. This process is inevitably labor-intensive and time-consuming. One approach would be to focus on the countries of greatest quantitative importance and data that offer the most possibilities for improvement. Another promising approach is for U.S. statistical officials to consult closely with statistical experts in countries with which the United States is engaged in data exchanges. The aim would be to enhance understanding of how the bilateral statistical systems, definitions, and concepts can be modified to make the systems more consistent. (5-4)

• An essential step toward harmonizing data on international transactions of various countries is to encourage national compilers to adhere to standards currently being developed by international organizations, such as the International Monetary Fund, the Bank for International Settlements, the United Nations, the Organization for Economic Cooperation and Development, and other international securities and financial groups. In addition, different international organizations need to establish guidelines showing how their different databases can be reconciled. (5-5)

As national data compilers strive to adjust to the internationalization of capital transactions, the challenge is how to improve data collection systems to reflect several factors: the needs of data users; the growing number and diversity of institutional and private players engaging in international capital transactions; the changing role of intermediaries and financial instruments; the complexity of financial transactions; and the costs versus the benefits of collection. Only when this challenge is met will U.S. analysts, business people, and policy makers be in a position to adequately understand the impact of international financial activity on the U.S. economy and the role of U.S. financial institutions in the world economy.

APPENDICES

A

Monitoring Capital Transactions in the United Kingdom, Germany, and Japan

The same underlying forces that have affected international capital transactions in the United States—and made information on such activities increasingly important in recent years—have come into play in the economies of the country's major trade partners. In this appendix we consider the reporting systems that three of those partners—the United Kingdom, Germany, and Japan—use to compile their statistics on international capital transactions and how they have sought to adapt them to take account of the new demands on those systems. Whenever possible, we note commonalities and differences with the U.S. system. Together with the United States, these countries account for approximately 80 percent of the world's capital flows.

THE U.K. SYSTEM[1]

There are two aspects of the U.K. system for monitoring international capital data that are particularly noteworthy. The first is that the U.K. balance-of-payments account is conceptually identical with its overseas-sector account within the national economic and financial accounts framework. The second is that, like the United States, the United Kingdom uses a survey system, generally under the purview of the Central Statistical Office (CSO),

---

[1] We thank Robert Heath of the Bank of England for providing information on the U.K. data system.

with the Bank of England providing data mainly on banking and capital flow activity. The fact that surveys are conducted to obtain data for broader purposes than just the balance of payments limits costs and adds to the consistency of data across a range of economic statistics, such as the national accounts and the money supply. Because many statistics are collected for purposes other than balance-of-payments ones, however, the system can be slow to adapt to new developments or to adjust reporting requirements to capture the growth of derivative instruments. In addition, problems can arise when the ultimate uses of the data are not clear to filers.

Recently, the view has emerged that the quality of statistical reporting will be improved by the centralization of data compilation in one organization to provide a clear line of responsibility, namely, the CSO. This was the conclusion, for example, of the Pickford Report (Pickford, 1989), which examined the adequacy of government statistics. Its findings led to the transfer of many statistical functions from other government departments to the CSO. In 1990 Chancellor of the Exchequer John Major launched another initiative to improve economic statistics. Among areas that needed improvement were balance-of-payments data. A senior government statistician, Richard Eason, was asked to conduct a thorough investigation of the balance-of-payments compilation system. One theme of his report (Eason, 1991) was the need for centralization of data collection and compilation.

In the United Kingdom, the Bank of England had had a long tradition of producing data for the capital account—more than 60 years. In the 1930s the bank monitored U.K. banking and other short-term liabilities. In 1954 it became responsible for compiling the whole of the balance of payments, which was logical in view of the reliance on exchange control data. In 1960 responsibility for data compilation was transferred to the CSO because of the need to ensure integration of the balance of payments with the national accounts. However, the bank has continued to have a significant role in the production of data.

The Bank of England compiles data on new net issues of securities. This is an area in which the bank's expertise in international markets is of particular help to the CSO. The bank has long had an interest in the efficient functioning of the international financial system: for example, it has in recent years monitored and analyzed developments in Euromarkets, the international debt crisis, and the recycling of the surpluses of oil-exporting countries. The bank's International Division has created an extensive database of announcements of both securities and credits in the international markets. The database on international bonds alone extends back to 1971 and has more than 26,000 individual records. It is one of the most comprehensive databases of its kind in the world, and data from it are supplied to both the Bank for International Settlements and the Federal Reserve Bank of New York. The bank obtains its data from market sources, and it partly cross-checks them with other sources, such as data from the International Securities Market Association. The database stores information on the residency of the issuer, the names of the lead managers, the interest rate or rates, and the amounts raised, as well as many other attributes. However, these data, which are from market sources, are not used for official statistical purposes, primarily because they concentrate on announcements of facilities and not on amounts drawn. Instead, the data on net new issues by U.K. corporate entities used in the balance of payments are compiled by CSO's Financial Statistics Division, drawing on the bank's expertise and knowledge.

Since the release of the Eason report (Eason, 1991) some of the Bank of England's compilation responsibilities, primarily for nonbank financial institutions, have been shifted to the CSO. The bank's role in the production of data is to be concentrated primarily on those markets and institutions in which the bank has a close policy, operational, or supervisory interest. This mandate covers principally banks, government accounts, and capital markets. In this manner, the bank's expertise in financial markets is still available to the CSO.

THE GERMAN SYSTEM[2]

Centralization is also a hallmark of the German reporting system, in which the Bundesbank and its branches are preeminent. At the same time, the German system in some respects resembles that of the United States. The German reporting system for international capital transactions, like the U.S. one, is based on two types of reports: the first is concerned with position statistics and treats the external position of banks and nonbanks, that is, claims on and liabilities to foreigners as well as direct investment relations; the second concerns flow statistics and deals with transactions or payments.

The German reports on the external claims and liabilities re-

[2]We thank Rudolph Seiler of Deutsche Bundesbank for providing information on the German data system.

semble those used in the United States, at least with regard to concepts and coverage of assets and liabilities. German nonbanks have to report their external financial and commercial claims and liabilities regularly. The number of reporters is much higher in Germany (about 13,000) than in the United States (about 400), however, and reports must be filed monthly in Germany, not quarterly as in the United States. German banks also have to submit comprehensive and detailed reports on their external assets and liabilities, also on a monthly basis. At the time of this writing, there were about 480 such filers in Germany, compared with close to 1,000 in the United States. Both German banks and nonbanks have to report their direct investment positions annually. The reports consist of major items from the affiliates' balance sheets.

The most important transactions or payments reports filed in Germany concern the purchase or sale of securities. German banks and nonbanks also have to report on all other long-term capital transactions.

All of the reports are filed with one agency, the Bundesbank, and its branches. Because of the legal requirement for such reporting, the use of simple forms, and the existing long-established reporting relationship, the rate of compliance and the quality of the data submitted are high. With such reports, the Bundesbank is able to provide a relatively detailed breakdown of capital transactions of nonresidents 3 to 4 weeks after the end of a given month. Data on direct investment are obtained from the reports of German parent companies or from reports of German subsidiaries of foreign companies on payments of capital. Data are collected on flows of equity capital and long-term intercompany debt. Reinvested earnings, which are shown under direct investment, are calculated from the balance sheets of resident and nonresident associated companies.

It is assumed that almost all direct investment flows are recorded in the German balance of payments, although perhaps after some delay. The Bundesbank has good reporting contacts with large enterprises. As in the United States, however, there may be considerable reporting gaps in the case of real property transactions, which fall under direct investment. Such nonreporting is a particularly acute problem in the case of the real estate investments of private individuals.

In contrast to U.S. practice, the portfolio transactions shown in the balance of payments are based almost exclusively on banks' payment reports. The banks report German residents' securities transactions with nonresidents by submitting special forms, by providing copies of their securities settlement statements, or by communicating the required data on magnetic tapes. This method of data collection, based on transaction records, is commonly known as the ticket or transaction system.

The "other capital" transactions are broken down between banks and nonbanks. For banks' long-term capital transactions, payment reports and stock figures from external position are available. With these two sources of data, banks' long-term capital transactions can be accurately monitored. For short-term capital flows, transactions shown in the balance of payments represent changes in claims on and liabilities to foreigners derived from the banks' external position reports. Because of good reporting ethics, a relatively low reporting threshold, and means of double-checking, German authorities are reasonably confident that they have good data on the international capital transactions of Germany's banking sector.

The long-term capital transactions of nonbanks are recorded by means of payment reports. In addition, stock reports on the long-term assets and liabilities (excluding securities) of nonbanks are available. As for the banks' reports, a comparison of the payment and stock reports is possible. This sector appears to be relatively well covered by the reports because the long-term capital transactions mainly involve large enterprises, which generally fulfill reporting obligations.

The short-term capital transactions of nonbanks are identified with the help of stock reports. Nonbanks have to report the level of their external assets and liabilities every month. These data lend themselves to detailed breakdowns of short-term capital transactions. Nonetheless, it is not always possible to differentiate the effects of exchange rate fluctuations and changes in asset prices.

THE JAPANESE SYSTEM[3]

Institutionally, the Japanese compilation system is also highly centralized. The role of the Ministry of Finance in Japan in many respects parallels that of Germany's Bundesbank and the U.K.'s Central Statistical Office. Moreover, the Japanese system, much like the German one, tends to compile information on all transactions, as opposed to the survey approach used by the United Kingdom and the United States.

---

[3]We thank Shinichi Yoshikuni of the Bank of Japan for providing information on the Japanese data system.

The Japanese reporting system seeks to take account of all transactions between residents and nonresidents. It relies on estimation procedures only in a few limited cases for which complete reporting is not feasible. By most accounts, the Japanese system has been quite successful in ensuring accuracy, as evidenced by the very small numbers of errors and omissions in the data. This was particularly the case before 1988; since then, reported errors and omissions have increased (see below).

Underpinning the Japanese system of reporting all cross-border transactions are two principles. One is that all such transactions, or those involving the exchange of foreign currency, must be made through the accounts of banks designated by the Ministry of Finance. The other principle relates to the system of designated securities companies: the purchase and sale of foreign securities must be conducted through securities companies designated by the Ministry of Finance; for other transactions, individuals must submit a report on each transaction. Such arrangements ensure that, under most circumstances, authorities compiling data have information on all international transactions.

Every cross-border transaction that exceeds a certain amount (about $40,000) must be reported to the Bank of Japan, which has been designated by the Ministry of Finance as the sole compiler of balance-of-payments statistics. In practice, authorized foreign exchange banks serve as the agents of the Bank of Japan and submit appropriate remittance forms on behalf of their customers. The reports specify the amount and purpose: loan, direct investment, or other capital transactions. In addition, they cover invisible transactions, such as the receipt and payment of interest and dividends, grants, and contributions. Accordingly, all balance-of-payments items, with few exceptions, are theoretically covered by these remittance and customs reports. Authorized foreign exchange banks, for their part, are required to submit reports on the monthly movement of their external assets and liabilities.

For some balance-of-payments items, reports other than remittance ones are used; most notably for the compilation of portfolio investment data. Portfolio investment, as part of the long-term capital account, covers most transactions in foreign and domestic securities that have no contractual maturity or have a maturity of more than 1 year.

For outward portfolio investments, the most important sources of data are the reports of designated securities companies, which are required to file monthly statements on the purchase and sale of foreign securities both for their own accounts and those of their customers. There were more than 100 such securities companies when this report was being written. Like the designated securities companies, some financial institutions are required to file similar monthly portfolio investment reports. In addition, anyone who buys foreign securities (over a specified minimum) directly from overseas intermediaries must submit notification describing the details of each such transaction. Issuers of foreign bonds in Japan are required to submit certain reports to the minister of finance through the Bank of Japan.

Inward portfolio investments, which involve investments by nonresidents in Japanese securities, are classified into stocks, bonds, and overseas bond issues by residents. Data regarding stocks and bonds are collected on a settlement basis from designated securities companies, authorized foreign exchange banks, and individual transactors. Data for bond issues by residents are obtained through special reports called Notification Concerning Issue or Flotation of Securities and Report on Invisible Trade Payment.

The valuation method used is relatively simple. Securities transactions denominated in currencies other than U.S. dollars are converted to dollars using basic exchange rates set by the Ministry of Finance. Outward investments in stocks and bonds are geographically allocated into ten major markets: the United States, the United Kingdom, Germany, France, Luxembourg, the Netherlands, Canada, Switzerland, Australia, and "others." Allocation is made according to the location of the market in which the transaction occurred. Inward investments are allocated by the domicile of the transactor. Accordingly, they can be allocated to individual countries, but they are aggregated into the same geographical breakdown as outward investments. Stock data are compiled from flow data. As a result, most items are recorded at transaction value rather than at market value. An exception is made for Japanese equities held by nonresidents: these values are adjusted periodically to reflect market levels. In addition, adjustments are made in the case of yen-denominated bonds to reflect changes in exchange rates.

RECENT CHANGES

Despite the strengths of the U.K., German, and Japanese reporting systems, certain inadequacies in them were becoming increasingly apparent by the late 1980s, as they were in the United States.

In the United Kingdom, for example, it became clear that greater resources had to be devoted to adjust to the rapidly changing domestic and international financial environment. In 1979 U.K. exchange controls were completely removed; this change, together with deregulation of domestic financial markets, led to a surge in financial transactions. Capital inflows and outflows to the United Kingdom were some 14 times larger in the decade after the lifting of exchange controls than before. Errors and omissions also rose: for the 3 years before 1978, errors and omissions in the balance-of-payments accounts were about $4 billion a year; in 1988, they were approximately $18 billion.

A second problem discovered was incomplete reporting by the corporate sector. As in the United States, it was determined that more comprehensive coverage was needed of transactions involving nonbank financial institutions and industrial and commercial companies: considerable data clearly were not being collected on overseas transactions of the corporate sector.

A third shortcoming of the U.K. system that became evident was that there was inadequate data on the financial transactions of the household sector. Although some data on outward portfolio investment could be derived from reports by intermediaries, it was generally seen as unsatisfactory. At the same time, inward portfolio investment was identified as a particularly weak part of the accounts. During the past decade, the United Kingdom has generally had positive errors and omissions, implying either unrecorded credits in the current account, such as investment income, or unrecorded net capital inflows. The Bank of England concluded that it seemed likely the bulk of the errors and omissions were portfolio flows (Bank of England, 1990).

Similarly, in the German case, reporting gaps became evident in the late 1980s when German private individuals increasingly started to avail themselves of foreign banking services, which led to various kinds of errors. For example, if a German investor bought a German government bond through a Luxembourg bank, the transaction then appeared in the German balance-of-payments statistics as a purchase of German securities by a nonresident. As in the United Kingdom, Germany's errors and omissions in the balance of payments had significantly increased by the end of the 1980s. In theory, the German reporting system should have been able to close such gaps. In the example above, the private German investor should have reported the purchase of German or foreign securities through the Luxembourg bank. In practice, however, either deliberately or through ignorance, the reporting requirement often is not met. The result of purchases of deutsche mark securities by German investors through nonresidents, therefore, is an overestimation of Germany's external liabilities or, in the case of purchases of foreign securities, an underestimation of the stocks of foreign securities held in Germany.

Japanese financial observers have encountered similar difficulties in recent years. The Japanese system was quite successful in ensuring the accuracy of statistics until recent years, as evidenced by the very small errors and omissions in their data up to 1988. Since then, however, problems have arisen with the capital account data. Errors and omissions increased dramatically in 1989 and 1990, reflecting the growing proportion of international transactions conducted outside the reporting system. Clearly, the increased scope and sophistication of the activities of Japan's financial institutions have placed a substantial burden on the reporting system. At the same time, these developments have made it necessary for compilers to obtain more information directly from nonfinancial private institutions. In addition, Japan is one of the industrial countries that does not include reinvested earnings from direct investment in investment income.

Like their counterparts in the United States, compilers in the United Kingdom, Germany, and Japan have also had to deal with the difficult problems of valuation and geographic allocation. When exchange rates fluctuate, the exchange rate used to convert foreign currencies to national ones for statistical purposes can differ substantially from the rate that prevailed at the time of the transaction, causing discrepancies in statistics. Similarly, allocating transactions geographically has become problematic.

The United Kingdom, Germany, and Japan all have begun to adjust their reporting systems in an attempt to reverse the perceived decline in the quality of data and ensure that the systems keep pace with the rapidly evolving international financial markets.

In the United Kingdom, such efforts have centered on major reviews of the adequacy of the U.K. balance-of-payments data and, when possible, corrective actions. Impetus for such reviews had come from a combination of rising errors and omissions, on one hand, and a growing current account deficit, on the other. U.K. efforts to improve the capital account data have, pursuant to the recommendations of the Eason report (Eason, 1991) led to a greater centralization of data collection. In addition, steps have been taken to deal with incomplete reporting by the corporate sector. The result has been a more comprehensive coverage of nonbank financial institutions and commercial companies. This has been accomplished by collecting more data on overseas transactions directly from the corporate sector and by reducing reliance on data from intermediaries. For example, a new survey of securities was conducted in 1989. It was followed by an expansion of coverage of the financial assets and liabilities of nonfinancial institutions at the end of 1990 and an exploratory survey of fund managers in 1991. Consideration also has been given by U.K. authorities to improving data on transactions in the household sector. The proposal is to survey individuals to learn more about their overseas transactions in securities. Another proposal under consideration is to assess these transactions through surveys of fund managers' private client business. Since the measures have been undertaken, the net errors and omissions have decreased.

For data on inward portfolio investment—that is, data on foreign investment in U.K. equities—improvements were made as a result of the introduction of a share register survey at the end of 1989. This survey, carried out on behalf of the CSO by a private company, showed that the overseas sector held about $33 billion more equity than had previously been estimated from data on transactions provided by financial intermediaries. In early 1990, the method of compiling data on foreign investment in U.K. company bonds was changed from a reliance on survey data from intermediaries to calculating net overseas investment as a residual from total net new issues by U.K. companies obtained by the Bank of England, primarily from market sources and net acquisitions reported by domestic sectors.

German compilers likewise took steps to adjust to the changes in international capital markets that occurred during the 1980s. They sought to deal with the increasing volume of securities transactions, especially those involving nonresidents, by relying more heavily on electronic data processing. Difficulties related to the recording of data on new financial instruments and related innovations was dealt with by seeking closer cooperation with banks. The German compilers believe that major reporting gaps did not arise from the internationalization of institutional investors' business because the number of such institutions in Germany is generally limited, and they are generally sympathetic to statistical reporting requirements. The German compilers also believe that data gaps attributed to the growing international diversification of private individuals' portfolios can be improved as long as these transactions are handled and reported by the German banking system.

In Japan, efforts are also under way to adjust to the new reporting environment. Now under consideration are proposals to make more frequent use of sample estimations of certain balance-of-payments items, such as international investment position and reinvested earnings.

B
Views of Data Compilers, Filers, and Users

Many members of the Panel on International Capital Transactions are long-time users of data on U.S. international capital transactions. They considered it essential to consult with the data compilers and a broad range of data filers and data users to assess the adequacy of the existing data collection system. In order to understand compilers' perspectives, the panel invited staff of the Bureau of Economic Analysis (BEA) of the U.S. Department of Commerce, the U.S. Department of Treasury, and the Federal Reserve Bank of New York (FRBNY) to assess the efficiency, accuracy, coverage, timeliness, and relevance of the existing data system. The panel also asked filers to comment on the existing reporting requirements (in terms of content, detail, and frequency), the reporting methods, and areas for improvements. And the panel canvassed users on the kinds of data on capital transactions with which they are familiar, what they do with the data, their perceptions of the quality of the data, their current unmet data needs, and their suggestions for improving existing data. This appendix summarizes the results of the these panel activities. The last section presents the results of the panel's literature search of studies using data on international capital transactions.

DATA COMPILERS

The panel queried BEA, Treasury Department, and FRBNY staff on three key aspects of the U.S. system for collection of data on international capital transactions: (1) the efficiency, coverage, accuracy, timeliness, and relevance of the data collected; (2) the reporting burden; and (3) suggestions for improvements in the data collection methods and procedures.

EFFICIENCY, COVERAGE, ACCURACY, TIMELINESS, AND RELEVANCE

As one might expect, BEA staff are reasonably satisfied with the collection of data on direct investment, especially given the agency's current resource constraints. They recognize, however, that improvements are needed in data on foreigners' purchases of U.S. real estate. Likewise, Treasury Department and FRBNY staff, who have primary responsibility for portfolio investment data on banking, nonbanking, and securities transactions, expressed confidence in the Treasury International Capital (TIC) data, in particular, the banking data. They attribute the strength of the banking data to the close association of many TIC components with reporting by banks to federal regulatory agencies (through, for example, the Call Reports).

Treasury and FRBNY staff view nonbank coverage as more problematic. They also concede that such products as derivatives are not adequately covered. The staff of BEA, a major user of the TIC data, share this perspective. They attribute gaps in coverage of portfolio transactions to a dependence on reporting by financial intermediaries rather than by principals. They note that these problems in coverage are exacerbated by the fact that an increasing number of transactions bypass traditional financial channels and the existing data collection system.

On timeliness, BEA staff judge that the quarterly U.S. balance-of-payments data are released in a timely manner. They note, however, that some countries provide these data on a monthly basis. They believe that the timeliness of U.S. balance-of-payments data could be improved through greater use of electronic filing, access to bank or credit card clearance information, improved compliance on surveys, and better processing procedures. Treasury Department and FRBNY staff stated that most respondents submit their data by prescribed deadlines and that estimation techniques are used in cases in which the data submitted are incomplete.

On questions of relevance, BEA and Treasury Department staff regard the U.S. international capital data as highly relevant and important to construct the U.S. balance-of-payments accounts and the U.S. international investment position. However, FRBNY staff noted that users are best positioned to judge the relevance of the data. They also questioned the value of reporting counterparties by country, particularly on the S form, pointing out that the majority of the countries reported are major financial hubs and not the ultimate owners. The FRBNY staff suggested that data on country breakdown be collected on a less frequent basis than monthly, since monthly collection is time consuming for respondents and compilers alike. Alternatively, the data could be made more relevant if they were redefined in a way that permitted identification of the issuer of a foreign security or the ultimate recipient or payee of a flow of funds. In this way, the country breakdowns would be more relevant.

REPORTING BURDEN

BEA staff believe they have made efforts to minimize the reporting burden on respondents. Further reductions in the reporting burden are likely to be realized not so much from reducing data items collected as from the application of more modern technology to the collection, processing, and estimation of data. Electronic data collection and development of more sophisticated estimation techniques, for example, could reduce the number of companies required to report data.

Treasury Department staff noted that the burden associated with TIC reporting is reasonable, but FRBNY staff said that the current system may ask too much of smaller institutions. The latter suggested consideration be given to raising exemption levels when it would reduce the reporting burden without substantially degrading coverage.

AREAS FOR IMPROVEMENT

BEA staff provided the panel with a long list of suggestions on improving data on both direct and portfolio investment. In the area of direct investment, principal suggestions included increasing data exchanges with other federal agencies, such as the Treasury Department, to identify gaps and overlaps between data sets; improving the coverage of foreign direct investment in U.S. real estate; increasing data exchanges with other countries to improve the comparability of data across countries; and further improving on-line computerized processing procedures.

For portfolio investment, BEA staff suggestions included coordinating data collection efforts among BEA, the Treasury Department, and the FRBNY and exchanging data among them to reduce gaps and overlaps in coverage, duplication of effort, and reporting burdens on filers; integrating TIC C form reporting with BEA direct investment reporting; improving coverage of direct transactions by pension and mutual funds and short-term securities; and investigating new sources of information such as bank and credit card clearance and regulatory information.

Treasury Department and FRBNY staff indicated that a benchmark survey on U.S. holdings of foreign securities is a priority. FRBNY staff also urged benchmarking to improve the banking data and a study of off-balance-sheet items, such as derivatives, to determine their effects on balance-of-payments flows. Treasury Department staff believe improvements are needed in the coverage of derivatives transactions, commercial paper, and zero-coupon issues.

Both BEA and FRBNY staff maintained that corporations and financial institutions need to be held responsible for reporting through legal fines and greater efforts to ensure that they are aware of their reporting obligations.

DATA FILERS: TIC REPORTING SYSTEM

The panel received detailed responses to its canvass from six internationally active banks and securities firms that file reports in the TIC system. The panel subsequently met with more than 20 representatives from large commercial and investment banks and securities firms. Respondents indicated that they file B forms (for reporting claims and liabilities by banks, brokers, and dealers) and S forms (for reporting purchases and sales of long-term securities). None files C forms for nonbank reporting.

There is wide agreement among respondents that the current forms and instructions are difficult to follow and that a general discussion, in lay terms, of the objectives and specific uses of the reported data would help filers to understand the importance of the data and the need for their compliance with the reporting requirements. In addition, respondents would like the FRBNY and the Treasury Department to ensure that reporting guidance given to individual reporting institutions is consistent and that examples of how new transactions should be reported are included in the filing instructions.

Respondents pointed out that the TIC forms are not a standard size, making them cumbersome not only to handle, but also to file and photocopy, and they recommended standardizing the size of the different TIC reports. Also, they noted that since some banks are allowed to submit modified reports, such options should be made known to all filers.

Respondents asserted that the existing TIC reporting system is not cost-effective. Filers are often queried by FRBNY on the data filed; they, in turn, need to work with various units of their organizations to respond to the FRBNY's inquiries, creating a hidden reporting burden not addressed by the U.S. Office of Management and Budget when it authorized the reporting requirement. Respondents claimed that discrepancies are often due to different interpretations by FRBNY and filers of what data should be included. Both FRBNY and filers spend an inordinate amount of time and resources in reconciling their differences. Respondents believe that discrepancies could be drastically reduced if there were clearer instructions and an understanding of the purpose of the data. Respondents want to understand what the Treasury and Federal Reserve need to know and why. Furthermore, respondents pointed out that the consolidation of data from numerous internal reports and the internal reconciliation process used by the filers can lead to significant rounding of figures. They asserted that many questions raised by the FRBNY relate solely to such rounding differences.

The filing of forms generally involves two basic processes. First, data are extracted from various internally generated computer reports, either from different accounting systems or from different submitting departments. Then the data are manipulated so that they are in the form that FRBNY requires. Because of the complexity of the forms, this identification and manipulation of data is at least partly manual. Methods used to complete the forms include consolidating information from different departments and areas, such as the general ledger and demand deposit system, into a final spreadsheet report; having each submitting department utilize its own system to accumulate necessary data; and using automation involving computer mainframe and personal computer applications.

Sources of Errors and Omissions

According to respondents, all areas of the reporting system are vulnerable to errors or omissions when the forms are being completed. This is especially true, however, because the data are, at least in part, manually identified and manipulated. Although respondents indicated that most errors are detected by routine internal controls before filing, problems occur if items are coded incorrectly in internal systems, if units in a financial institution are unaware of the need to report certain items, or if there is difficulty in interpreting the instructions for handling specific situations.

Determining the occurrence of U.S. transactions abroad can be especially vulnerable to omissions when they are of only minimal amounts and infrequently reported by a financial institution. It is particularly difficult to maintain accurate and complete reporting when the units compiling data for the reports are only occasionally called on to identify necessary information. Because of the complex manipulation process, there may be omissions in the information provided to the TIC reporting unit.

The identification of the country of residence for U.S. transactions abroad also poses difficult questions that can generate reporting errors. Most respondents cite problems with three issues related to country of residence. First, transactions with multilateral lending institutions, such as the International Bank for Reconstruction and Development (the World Bank) and the International Monetary Fund (IMF), can be miscoded as domestic transactions and therefore be inadvertently omitted from the reports, since both of these organizations have U.S. addresses. Similar errors can occur if international or regional organizations that carry the code of the country in which they are domiciled are not manually adjusted to match the requirements of TIC forms.

Second, transactions with U.S. branches and agencies of foreign banks and institutions in the United States provide a dilemma for data filers on several fronts, the first of which is definitional. In one instruction (general instruction D,3,d), U.S. offices of foreign governments are to be considered foreign. In a later instruction (general instruction D,4,a), U.S. offices of foreign official banking institutions are to be considered domestic. Errors and omissions can easily result from these conflicting instructions when dealing with U.S. offices of nationalized or central banks of foreign countries. On another front, the operating systems of financial institutions may use country codes for purposes that conflict with the form S definition of foreign customer, making it necessary to identify and temporarily reclassify U.S. branches of foreign banks each time an S form is filed. For example, the New York branch office of the Reserve Bank of Australia is coded as a U.S. resident for the purpose of addressing transaction confirmations and other documents, but it must be classified as foreign for S form reporting. Another problem with U.S. branches of foreign banks arises because operating systems of reporting financial institutions may have limited information, which requires manual identification and verification. A system may have been devised to name the holdings of the bank's customer (e.g., Bank of Tokyo) and not distinguish between the New York agency and the parent bank in Japan. Even if an address field is incorporated in the operating system, it does not determine whether U.S. branches and agencies of foreign banks are acting on behalf of their foreign parent; it only provides the name of the organization and cites a U.S. or foreign paying agent. Thus, it is not known whether the issuer is the U.S. branch or agency of the foreign bank or the foreign parent.

Third, the TIC instructions require that an individual must reside in a foreign country for 1 year to be considered a resident of that country. This information is difficult for reporting units to determine.

Entering the correct U.S. dollar amounts is not considered a significant source of error because these amounts can be checked by internal systems. Nonetheless, financial institutions that have multiple feeder systems—that is, numerous departments contributing data to be consolidated by the TIC reporting group—are vulnerable to duplication errors. Moreover, monthly TIC forms are now reported in millions of dollars, while the semiannual forms are required to be reported in thousands: this difference often results in reported amounts on semiannual forms being erroneously inflated by 1,000.

Errors and omissions can also arise when instructions are not clear about reporting new types of instruments. In general, reporters are not aware of or are confused about filing requirements. Examples of financial instruments whose inclusion is often questioned are certificates of deposits, repurchase agreements ("repos"), and "other deposit balances." There are also certain transactions whose treatment is not discussed in the instructions but for which the Federal Reserve banks have verbally indicated the approved treatment. For instance, buy- and sell-back trades are to be treated as repos and resales, according to the verbal instructions of the

FRBNY, but these transactions are not mentioned in the written instructions.

Most respondents engage in financial derivative transactions with foreign entities. Such off-balance-sheet transactions are not reported on TIC forms, however, because instructions do not specifically include derivatives as reportable items. Instructions for the BL-1 and BC forms specifically exclude swaps, futures, foreign exchange forwards, options, and warrants. One respondent noted that, to the extent that the transactions create assets and liabilities for the bank, it reports such assets or liabilities on Forms BC or BL, as appropriate, although another respondent stated that it reports foreign positions not on TIC forms but on Treasury forms FC-3 and FC-4.

The respondents did not indicate awareness of private international capital transactions not covered in the TIC system and, understandably, they did not call for additional data to be reported within the system. Some suggested, however, expanding the CM, CQ, and CQ-2 forms to capture transactions that bypass financial intermediaries.

FORM-SPECIFIC PROBLEMS

Many specific sections of the instructions were reported as unclear or inconsistent by respondents. Their comments are listed in this section by forms.

General

• Instructions are unclear on whether domestic operating subsidiaries (nondepository) of a bank are to be included in the bank or nonbank reports.

• The treatment of bankers' acceptances executed by a U.S. head office on behalf of its foreign branches is unclear. Because the foreign office has the claim on the foreign customer, some banks treat the head office claim as a claim on its own foreign office. Because the head office creates the bankers' acceptance, other banks treat the claim as a third-party one on a foreign customer. The instructions are unclear regarding the appropriate classification.

• It is not clear what entities are reportable in the "own foreign office" category. It appears that only transactions with foreign branches or majority-owned subsidiaries of the filer are to be included. It is not clear whether transactions with other related parties are reportable (e.g., a U.S. bank's liability to a foreign subsidiary of its parent bank holding company or a foreign branch of another U.S. bank that is part of the same holding company).

• Claims are not sufficiently defined. Definitions should be consistent with other regulatory reports: for example, the Country Exposure Report includes accrued interest receivable and long-term securities.

• The term *transaction* is defined neither in the TIC form general instructions nor in the specific reports. It is not clear whether the term is limited to purchases or sales or also applies to conversions, exchanges, etc.

• It is not clear how to report commercial paper issued by a U.S. subsidiary of a foreign company but guaranteed by the foreign parent. The converse is also not clear. Informing filers of the purposes and objectives of the TIC reports could help answer these kinds of questions.

• The TIC data requirements are often impractical to implement, since they exceed the capabilities of financial institutions to capture and report the data. Generally, a bank's automated system(s) is tailored to one set of reporting criteria or classifications. The inconsistencies in the TIC reports make it difficult to construct criteria that can be applied uniformly.

B Forms

• Instructions are confusing regarding mutual funds (BL-2) as they relate to trust business.

• The terms *foreign public borrowers* (form BC, column 1) and *foreign official institutions* (form BL-1, columns 1 through 3) in two different reports cover similar institutions (including central banks). However, column titles are different for each report, which causes confusion. Filers suggest that references to foreign public borrowers be eliminated and that the entities covered under foreign official institutions be expanded to include additional entities currently included in foreign public borrowers.

• Claims on form BC exclude long-term securities. Because of the increased securitization of assets by banks, the distinction between long-term loans and long-term securities has become blurred. Consideration should be given to including both classes of assets on form BC.

• The instructions for form BL-2 are confusing. The title of the form refers to custody liabilities to foreigners; however, the instructions require the reporting of claims on U.S. persons.

• Form BL-2 instructions (page 2) contain the phrase "financial claims" but do not define it.

• Form BC requires U.S. banks to report monthly their claims on foreigners payable in dollars. Form BQ-1 requires U.S. banks to report quarterly those same claims and domestic customer claims on foreigners payable in dollars. The purpose of having two overlapping reports is not clear.

S Form

• The reporting requirements of the S form are difficult to follow. The title of the S form indicates that the report covers purchases and sales of long-term securities by foreigners. However, the instructions require the reporting of redemptions as purchases or sales. This seems inconsistent.

• If a stock is purchased from a foreigner, it is to be reported as a "sale," and sales are to be reported in the "purchaser" column. This is because the form is structured from the standpoint of foreigners. From the viewpoint of the staff of a domestic reporting financial institution, this is confusing. It is also confusing when viewed in terms of other TIC reports in the series.

• In completing the S form, the location of a foreign broker with whom a trade for a U.S. customer is made is said to determine the "foreign country" line on which the transaction is to be reported. This seems to contradict the purpose of the report, which seems to suggest reporting the issuer. For example, the purchase of German securities from a U.K. broker would be reported as a purchase from (sale by) the United Kingdom.

REPORTING BURDEN

Generally, respondents indicated that the 15-calendar-day period for filing reports is inadequate. They note that consideration should be given to allowing 15 or 20 business days, or 20 calendar days, for several reasons.

• Operating systems and financial staffs are occupied with other priorities during the period from the end of one month through the first 10 business days of the next month.

• Information on the activities of branches located in U.S. possessions or on subsidiaries located outside the city where the head office is located is generally mailed to the head office and may not be available by the reporting deadline.

• The FRBNY frequently raises questions that relate to the TIC reports after comparing the TIC data with other reports. (The time required of the filers to respond to questions often is longer than that required for the actual preparation of the reports.) There are several issues related to the FRBNY's telephone inquiries. For several reasons, respondents think that much of this questioning could be eliminated. Because of time differences, in the cases of certain transactions, the reports of international branch offices will not match. For example, the head office of a bank may deposit funds with its London branch on the afternoon of September 30. Because of time differences (London is already closed), the London branch will not record this transaction until October 1. In this case, the head office will show a "due" from London on its BC report for September 30. However, the London branch will not report the off-setting "due" to its parent corporation on FR 2502 for September 30, since the transaction did not appear on the books in London until the following day. For a branch like that in London, the fluctuations or differences can be extremely large. At present, the FRBNY receives copies of all tickets generated from foreign official purchases and sales of U.S. long-term securities, that is, all the information on these transactions required on the S form. Reporting by financial institutions on these transactions should be eliminated, since it poses an unnecessary reporting burden on filers to report duplicative information. Differences between data on copies of the tickets the FRBNY receives on foreign official purchases and sales of long-term securities and information on such transactions submitted by filers on the S form at times can be attributed to the inclusion of financing charges in the total amounts of transactions by filers.

Respondents believe that consolidation and elimination of reports could reduce reporting burden.

• Depending on the organizational structure of a bank's operations and level of automation, reporting entities frequently experience difficulty in compiling data at the required consolidation level (i.e., bank, nonbank, and IBF). In some instances, it is easier for financial institutions to submit one consolidated report for the entire bank holding company than multiple reports. For other institutions, filers believe that it is easier to submit data by legal vehicle, business segment, division, or department.
• Currently, there are ten separate TIC forms applicable to banking institutions. Since separate reports are required for at least three

consolidation levels, this translates into numerous forms, many of which are prepared manually. Respondents proposed that long-term securities be included on the BC form, eliminating the need for the S form.

• Suggested modifications to the present system that would reduce the reporting burden without sacrificing what the respondents considered important information included cutting or eliminating detail (or asking for detailed breakouts in the original forms, rather than asking for them after the reports have been filed), reporting less frequently, and modifying the report formats. Specific suggestions included making semiannual reports data reportable in millions, if not eliminating them altogether; changing monthly reports to quarterly ones, consistent with quarterly publication of the U.S. *Treasury Bulletin*; and modifying the reporting format to include all countries in alphabetical order, rather than by hemisphere.

There was no consensus among respondents with regard to electronic data filing: some said it is feasible; others said it is not because there are many different accounting systems in banks and securities firms and it would be difficult to develop a standardized format that all could use. For those respondents who assume they would not have to change accounting formats, on-time transmission and CD-ROM are the preferred filing methods.

There are respondents from whom the FRBNY receives duplicate copies of all foreign official purchases and sales of long-term securities. Respondents suggest that a system could be established whereby financial institutions under such circumstances would provide the FRBNY with a computer run or tape of all such transactions into which they have entered. The FRBNY would compare its information captured from the duplicate tickets to the computer run and question the financial institutions about differences between the two information sources. Respondents believe such a system would reduce the burden of unnecessary reporting while improving data accuracy.

DATA FILERS: BEA'S SURVEYS OF U.S. DIRECT INVESTMENT ABROAD

Seven large U.S.-based multinational corporations provided substantive responses to the panel's invitation for comments on BEA's surveys of U.S. direct investment abroad.

The response was split regarding reporting burden. Some respondents stated that the information requested is generally available from accounting and management records; others indicated that there are major problems in obtaining it. The latter respondents noted, for example, that units preparing reports need to work with subsidiaries overseas to obtain data not available locally. Furthermore, they indicated that the BE-10 and BE-11 forms often require nonaccounting data or data tabulated in ways that are different from the way they are normally collected by companies (especially for their reporting to the Securities and Exchange Commission or the Internal Revenue Service). All respondents who have significant financial claims or liabilities with nonaffiliated foreign entities indicated that they report them on TIC nonbanking C forms.

The level of detail requested is at times beyond that in available records. Respondents' comments show that the number of employee hours required to complete each of the forms varies widely from company to company.

The experience of one major U.S. multinational corporation—which is shared by others that have extensive direct investment abroad—is worth noting. The corporation estimated that the periodic (i.e., 5-7 years) BE-10 form requires approximately 3 employee-years to complete the individual forms for its several hundred foreign affiliates and to consolidate data from the numerous domestic affiliates that qualify. It noted that it has not been cost-effective to develop a completely computerized collection system for the benchmark BE-10 because of its periodic nature; consequently, some manual transmission, completion, and assembly are required. The annual BE-11 form requires approximately 1 employee-year to complete individual forms for the several hundred affiliates and to consolidate the records of the numerous domestic affiliates that qualify. The BE-11 is submitted on the company's own computer-generated forms. The quarterly BE-577 requires approximately 2 employee-months, to complete each quarter's individual forms for the more than 100 foreign affiliates subject to reporting requirements. The BE-577 is also submitted on the company's own computer-generated forms. The corporation also noted that the information needed to complete these BEA forms is not always available in its U.S. headquarters location. Generally, responses to the more detailed questions on forms BE-10 and BE-11 must be requested from the field: such items include geographic allocations of revenues and balance sheet items, as well as imports and exports into and out of the United States. This information requires the company to establish and maintain a supplementary data collection system.

The corporation further pointed out that there are difficulties in reconciling the reporting requirements with the company's accounting system. Internal collection of financial data is by individual affiliate. In a number of cases, several affiliates operate in the same country. Ownership of these companies by the U.S. filer can be either direct or indirect. The reporting of consolidated data to the BEA on several foreign affiliates directly owned by the U.S. filer would require considerable effort. In addition, the corporation indicated that the reporting of branch earnings is subject to different interpretations. The annual profit or loss reported by a foreign branch results in an increase or decrease in the payable (receivable) with the U.S. home office. The actual transfer of funds offsets this accounting entry. It is not clear which of these transactions should be reported in the BE reports.

Furthermore, the corporation noted that matching exports from the U.S. parent company to its foreign affiliates with records of imports from the U.S. parent company kept by these foreign affiliates becomes difficult because trading companies are used as intermediaries in these transactions. The U.S. exporter does not always know the final destination of its goods. Likewise, the importing foreign affiliate may not record the country of origin in its purchase records, making a detailed review of its transactions time-consuming.

Respondents' suggestions on how to reduce the reporting burden without sacrificing data were both general and specific. General suggestions included requesting information in a manner consistent with accounting systems, being able to answer questions by referring to annual reports, and extending the time allowed for filing. An example of a specific suggestion was that filers should not be required to obtain information from foreign entities in which they have only a minority ownership interest. Respondents indicated that any reduction in the reporting burden, whether by following general or specific suggestions, would improve the quality of data they submit to BEA.

Respondents also noted that improving the clarity of the instructions could ease the filing burden. Cross-referencing, both between sections of one form and between different forms, would be helpful. They added that it would be helpful to explain in the general instructions the purpose of the data filing, how the data are tabulated, and what the final publications look like. The respondents were not familiar with BEA publications that report the data supplied by filers. None indicated that they use the data (in large part because they work in accounting offices, not economic offices); one requested that copies of the published report be sent to it.

Some respondents would like to have additional time to file reports. Others would like definitions to conform as closely as possible to accounting practices used in their businesses or required in submissions to the Securities and Exchange Commission or the Internal Revenue Service. Some respondents would like to file reports in electronic form; others want to continue to process and file data manually. A number of respondents proposed higher exemption levels for reporting; they asserted that this would reduce the reporting burden and cut errors.

DATA FILERS: BEA'S SURVEYS OF FOREIGN DIRECT INVESTMENT IN THE UNITED STATES

Substantive responses about BEA's surveys of foreign direct investment in the United States were received from four large U.S. affiliates of foreign firms. All indicated that they have the information available for completion of BEA forms, but none of them uses (or is familiar with) the resulting statistical output published by BEA. Respondents suggested providing more time for filers to complete reports, restricting inquiries of filers to areas that involve direct investment, and consolidating these reports with other federal ones that collect the same data. Some suggested that the reports be consolidated with other government statistical reports collecting the "same" data.

Quarterly and annual reports (BE-605, BE-606B, and BE-15) were commonly recognized as reports filed. Although most respondents stated that the information requested is generally available from accounting and management records, they indicated that there are some items that are so irrelevant that they would not be tracked were it not for the reporting forms. In addition, data on specific locations required on the forms necessitates investigation because records are not kept on that basis. The amount of time required to complete the reports varied.

Most respondents indicated that the instructions are fairly clear or that sufficient help can be obtained by calling the assistance number. They also believe that the coverage is complete.

Respondents indicated that they do not use BEA publications that report direct investment data. Respondents who have significant financial claims or liabilities with nonaffiliated foreign entities indicated that they report them on CQ-1 and CQ-2 forms. Other comments concerned the term *parent company*. A 10 percent investment by a single foreign entity in a U.S. business is considered a parent company according to BEA filing instructions, but respondents from companies that have more than 10 percent foreign ownership stated that they are not affiliates of foreign parent companies. Others resented the implication that they are subsidiaries of foreign companies that own 25 percent of their common stocks.

DATA USERS

In addition to two large industry groups that expressed the collective views of their members, nearly 40 other respondents provided comments on the capital account data in the U.S. balance of payments. Respondents in the canvass include experienced researchers and policy analysts who fall into four principal groups: staff of federal agencies or international institutions, academic users, staff of private financial institutions or research organizations, and people associated with industry or commerce. Since the perspectives of these user groups differ, we report their comments separately, after presenting a few general views that were shared by most of the respondents.

Overall, users are generally satisfied with the data, although a considerable number of frequent users would welcome more timely data (mainly banking and securities data). These requests were primarily from private-sector users, who reported that a 3-month delay in publication makes the data difficult or impossible to use for market analysis. Users from U.S. government agencies also indicated they would like timeliness improved; academic users were not troubled by current publication schedules.

Users generally believe that improving data comparability among different sectors of the economy and standardizing data standards among countries are essential to enhance the usefulness of existing data. Users also urged that up-to-date data be provided on the market value of U.S. holdings of foreign securities. Some also recommended categorizing securities data along the format used by large financial institutions, which group data by country; region; security type (bonds versus stocks); maturity, and indices of volume and price; and purposes of investments, differentiating corporate acquisitions (such as in mergers and acquisitions) and institutional investment for portfolio reasons.

Federal and International Agency Staffs

In considering the various types of capital flow data, respondents from federal and international agencies were most familiar with data on foreign direct investments in the United States, followed by U.S. direct investments abroad, and U.S. banks' claims on foreigners. There was little familiarity with data on nonbanks' international assets (other than securities or direct investments). Consistent with users' familiarity with direct investment data, the most frequently cited data source was the *Survey of Current Business* and related Commerce Department publications, followed by the *Treasury Bulletin*. Other than BEA and Treasury Department sources, respondents make use of publications from the IMF and the Organization for Economic Cooperation and Development (OECD), the balance-of-payments accounts of other countries, and country exposure reports.

Most of the respondents in this group use the data to prepare internal reports for the management of their agencies and for other reports. In evaluating the published data, most respondents judged coverage as "good," a few said "excellent"; accuracy was judged mainly "good," a few "excellent," some "unknown"; timeliness was judged mainly "good" or "excellent," but some said "poor"; and judgments about relevance were divided equally between "good" and "excellent." Respondents noted, however, that the errors and omissions in the U.S. balance-of-payments accounts are large, that there is inadequate detail on portfolio data, and that the data are not available electronically.

There were several suggestions for improvement: (1) to publish securities data by categories similar to those used in analyses of domestic financial markets, that is, to show flows before and after valuation changes, give more country detail, and use more position country data; (2) to provide time-series data; (3) to publish on a more timely basis; and (4) to make data available electronically, in the form of diskettes, CD-ROM forms, and other methods.

Academic and Public Policy Researchers

Academic and public policy researchers expressed greatest interest in direct investment data, almost equal interest in each of the other principal categories of capital flows, and least interest in the more amorphous nonbank portfolio data. Most described the quality of the U.S. data as "good"; a few characterized it as "excellent." Some, however, consider the country identification of security holdings to be useless.

The most frequently cited source of data is the *Survey of Current Business*, followed by the *Treasury Bulletin*. Also used are the IMF's *International Financial Statistics* and OECD publications. Many respondents indicated that they use the data for general research purposes. A few mentioned specific projects involving exchange rates, trade, the service sector, valuation of assets and liabilities, and teaching.

Suggestions to augment the data included: (1) providing currency details; (2) establishing closer concordance between direct investment and trade data; (3) publishing data on a more timely basis; and (4) providing up-to-date market valuations for data on securities holdings.

Users in Financial Institutions

Replies from individuals in financial organizations—banks, securities dealers, and financial research institutions—indicated that they are especially interested in the data on international transactions in U.S. and foreign securities and, to a lesser extent, in the data on direct investments. Most find the quality of the data "good" in general and "excellent" in some respects; only timeliness was rated "poor."

Most of these respondents use the data as published in the *Survey of Current Business* or *Treasury Bulletin*, but there is also considerable dependence on industry sources (for example, Data Resources Inc.), and the Federal Reserve Board's flow-of-funds data. A wide variety of additional data sources was also mentioned, including publications by the IMF, the OECD, industry and trade associations, and government of Japan data (in part because they are not revised). The principal use of the data is market research of various kinds. Other uses mentioned included interest and exchange rate forecasts, internal planning, and training courses.

This group of respondents also noted that revisions in Treasury data are difficult to follow over time, and data are not sufficiently timely. Among data not now published that would be useful are more detail on foreign dealings in U.S. government securities, data on U.S. activities in specific foreign financial markets, separation of short-term and long-term transactions, data on joint ventures and mergers, and detailed data on securities held in the U.S. and foreign portfolios. Other suggestions for improvement were to revise data presentation using selected industry presentations as models and to provide detailed information on the basis for revisions in the data. Most often, respondents recommended publication on a more timely basis.

Users in Commerce and Industry

Two major industry groups responded to the panel's canvass. In both cases the emphasis was on data on inward and outward direct investments. One industry group rated the data as "excellent" in most respects and "poor" in none; the other rated the information generally between "good" and "poor." Both industry groups rely primarily on BEA publications. In both cases, the data are used regularly in the preparation of reports, testimony before Congress, and general policy analysis. Other data sources used by these groups include the IMF, the OECD, and European Community publications.

Several suggestions were made by these two industry groups: (1) to standardize industry codes across sectors in the economy; (2) to standardize country codes among databases; (3) to identify data on flows pertaining to offshore banking centers; (4) to provide longer time series for direct investment data; and (5) to furnish industry breakdowns of direct investments in wholesale and retail trade.

USE OF DATA IN PUBLISHED STUDIES

Our literature search revealed that there are more published studies using BEA's information on direct investment than the Treasury Department's TIC data on portfolio investment. Although most of these studies appear in the References and Bibliography, the selected list below (Figures B-1 and B-2) shows them by topic.

FIGURE B-1 Selected Published Studies Using BEA Data on Foreign Direct Investment in the United States and U.S. Direct Investment Abroad

GENERAL

Caves, R.E.
  1982 *Multinational Enterprise and Economic Analysis.* New York: Cambridge University Press.
Hufbauer, G.C.
  1975 The multinational corporation and direct investment. Pp. 253-319 in P.B. Kenen, ed., *International Trade and Finance: Frontiers for Research.* New York: Cambridge University Press.
Stekler, L., and G.V.G. Stevens
  1991 The adequacy of direct investment data. In P. Hooper and J.D. Richardson, eds., *International Economic Transactions.* Chicago: University of Chicago Press.
Stevens, G.V.G.
  1974 The determinants of investment. Chapter 3 in J.H. Dunning, ed., *Economic Analysis and the Multinational Enterprise.* London: George Allen & Unwin.

SHARE OF DIRECT INVESTMENT ENTERPRISES IN A
MARKET OR THE ECONOMY

Eisner, R., and P.J. Peiper
  1988 The World's Greatest Debtor Nation? Paper presented to Joint Session of North American Economics and Finance Association. New York.
Stekler, L., and G.V.G. Stevens
  1991 The adequacy of direct investment data. In P. Hooper and J.D. Richardson, eds., *International Economic Transactions.* Chicago: University of Chicago Press.
Ulan, M., and W.G. Dewald
  1989 *The U.S. Net International Investment Position: The Numbers Are Misstated and Misunderstood.* Washington, D.C.: U.S. Department of State.

DIRECT INVESTMENT, TRADE, AND COMPETITIVENESS

Bergsten, C.F., T. Horst, and T.H. Moran
  1978 *American Multinationals and American Interests.* Washington, D.C.: The Brookings Institution.
Bloomstron, M., R.E. Lipsey, and K. Kulchycky
  1988 U.S. and Swedish direct investment exports. In R.E. Baldwin, ed., *Trade Policy Issues and Empirical Analysis.* Chicago: University of Chicago Press.
Kester, Anne Y., ed.
  1992 *Behind the Numbers: U.S. Trade in the World Economy.* Panel on Foreign Trade Statistics, Committee on National Statistics. Washington, D.C.: National Academy Press.

FIGURE B-1 Continued

Lipsey, R.E., and I.B. Kravis
   1987   The competitiveness and comparative advantage of U.S. multinationals, 1957-1984. *Banca Nazionale del Lavoro Quarterly Review* 40(161):147-165.
Lipsey, R.E., and M.Y. Weiss
   1981   Foreign production and exports in manufacturing industries. *The Review of Economics and Statistics* 63(4):488-494.

FORECASTING DIRECT INVESTMENT FLOWS IN MACROECONOMIC MODELS

Helkie, W., and L. Stekler
   1987   *Modeling Investment Income and Other Services in the U.S. International Transactions Accounts.* International Finance Discussion Paper No. 319. Washington, D.C.: Board of Governors of the Federal Reserve System.

DETERMINANTS OF MULTINATIONAL BEHAVIOR

Corbo, V., and O. Havrylyshyn
   1982   Production Technology Differences Between Canadian-Owned and Foreign-Owned Firms Using Translog-Production Functions. NBER Working Paper No. 981. Cambridge, Mass.: National Bureau of Economic Research.
Courtney, W.H., and D.M. Leipziger
   1975   Multinational corporations in LDC's: the choice of technology. *Oxford Bulletin of Economic Statistics* 37(4):297-304.
Froot, K.A., and J.C. Stein
   1989   *Exchange Rates and Foreign Direct Investment: An Imperfect Capital Markets Approach.* NBER Working Paper No. 2914. Cambridge, Mass.: National Bureau of Economic Research.
Lim, D.
   1977   Do foreign companies pay higher wages than their local counterparts in Malaysian manufacturing? *Journal of Development Economics* 4(1):55-66.
Lipsey, R.E., I.B. Kravis, and R.A. Roldan
   1982   Do multinational firms adapt factor proportions to relative factor prices? In A.O. Krueger, ed., *Trade and Employment in Developing Countries: Factor Supplies and Substitution.* Chicago: University of Chicago Press.
Morley, S.A., and G.W. Smith
   1977   The choice of technology: multinational firms in Brazil. *Economic Development and Cultural Change* 25(2):239-264.
Ray, E.J.
   1989   The determinants of foreign direct investment in the United States: 1979-1985. In R. Feenstra, ed., *Trade Policies for International Competitiveness.* Chicago: University of Chicago Press.

continued on next page

FIGURE B-1 Continued

Reuber, G.L.
  1973 *Private Foreign Investment in Development.* Oxford: Clarendon Press.
Stevens, G.V.G.
  1969 Fixed investment expenditures of foreign manufacturing affiliates of U.S. firms: theoretical models and empirical evidence. *Yale Economic Essays* 9(1):137-198.
  1972 Capital mobility and the international firm. In F. Machlup, W. Salant, and L. Tarshis, eds., *The International Mobility and Movement of Capital.* New York: National Bureau of Economic Research.
Stevens, G.V.G., and R.E. Lipsey
  1992 Interactions between domestic and foreign investment. *Journal of International Money and Finance* 11(1):40-62.
Wells, L.T.
  1973 Economic man and engineering man: choice in a low-wage country. *Public Policy* 21(Summer):219-242.

DIRECT INVESTMENT AND ECONOMIC WELFARE

Encarnation, D.J., and L.T. Wells
  1986 Evaluating foreign investment. In T.H. Moran, ed., *Investing in Development: New Roles for Private Capital?* New Brunswick, NJ: Transactions Books.
Graham, E.M., and P.R. Krugman
  1989 *Foreign Direct Investment in the United States.* Washington, D.C.: Institute for International Economics.
Little, I.M.D., and J.A. Mirrlees
  1974 *Project Appraisal and Planning for Development.* New York: Basic Books.
Musgrave, P.B.
  1975 *Direct Investment Abroad and the Multinationals: Effects on the United States Economy.* U.S. Congress, Senate Subcommittee on Multinational Corporations of the Committee on Foreign Relations, 98th Congress, 1st Session. Washington, D.C.
Roemer, M., and J.J. Stern
  1975 *The Appraisal of Development Projects.* New York: Praeger.
Stekler, L., and G.V.G. Stevens
  1991 The adequacy of direct investment data. In P. Hooper and J.D. Richardson, eds., *International Economic Transactions.* Chicago: University of Chicago Press.
U.S. General Accounting Office
  1988 *Foreign Investment: Growing Japanese Presence in the U.S. Auto Industry.* NSIAD-88-111. Washington, D.C.: U.S. Government Printing Office.
Vendrell-Alda, J.L.M.
  1978 *Comparing Foreign Subsidiaries and Domestic Firms: A Research Methodology Applied to Efficiency in Argentine Industry.* New York: Garland.

FIGURE B-1 Continued

OTHER IMPORTANT TOPICS

Caves, R.E.
    1982 *Multinational Enterprise and Economic Analysis: Chapter 8.* New York: Cambridge University Press.
Grubert, H., T. Goodspeed, and D. Swenson
    1991 *Explaining the Low Taxable Income of Foreign-Controlled Companies in the United States.* Washington, D.C.
Hartman, D.
    1984 Tax policy and foreign direct investment in the United States. *National Tax Journal* 37(4):475-488.
Slemrod, J.
    1990 Tax effects on foreign direct investment in the United States. In A. Razin and J. Slemrod, eds., *Taxation in the Global Economy.* Chicago: University of Chicago Press.
Wheeler, J.E.
    1988 An academic look at transfer pricing in a global economy. *Tax Notes* 40(1)87-96.

NOTE: We thank Guy V.G. Stevens of the staff of the Federal Reserve Board for his assistance in preparing this table.

FIGURE B-2 Selected Published Studies Using TIC Data

Cooper, I.A., and Kaplanis, E.
    1991 What Explains the Home Bias in Portfolio Investment? Unpublished paper, London Business School.
French, K., and Poterba, J. M.
    1989 Are Japanese Stock Prices Too High? Working paper, University of Chicago.
    1991 Investor diversification and international equity markets. *American Economic Review* 81(May):222-226.
Howell, M., and Cozzini, A.
    1990 *International Equity Flows.* International Equity Research, Salomon Brothers.
Tesar, L.L., and I.M. Werner
    1992 Home Bias and the Globalization of Securities Markets. Working paper, University of California at Santa Barbara and Stanford University.

NOTE: We thank Linda L. Tesar of the University of California, Santa Barbara, and Ingrid M. Werner of Stanford University for contributing information for use in this table.

References and Bibliography

Ambler, C.A., and T.L. Mesenbourgh
  1992 *EDI–Reporting Standard for the Future.* Washington, D.C.: U.S. Department of Commerce.
Angeloni, C., C. Cottarelli, and A. Levy
  1992 Cross-border Deposits and Monetary Aggregates in the Transition. (March) Temi di Discussione No. 163, Banca d'Italia.
Bank for International Settlements
  1986 *Recent Innovations in International Banking.* Basle, Switzerland: Bank for International Settlements.
  1988 *Guide to the BIS Statistics on International Banking.* Basle, Switzerland: Bank for International Settlements.
  1989 *International Interest Linkages and Monetary Policy.* Basle, Switzerland: Bank for International Settlements.
  1992a *International Banking and Financial Market Developments.* Basle, Switzerland: Bank for International Settlements.
  1992b *Recent Developments in International Interbank Relations.* Basle, Switzerland: Bank for International Settlements.
  1994a *International Banking and Financial Market Developments.* Basle, Switzerland: Bank for International Settlements.
  1994b *Macroeconomic and Monetary Policy Issues Raised by the Growth of Derivatives Markets.* Basle, Switzerland: Bank for International Settlements.
  1994c *Public Disclosure of Market and Credit Risks by Financial Intermediaries.* Basle, Switzerland: Bank for International Settlements.

See also works listed in Figures 2-2 (pp. 50-51), B-1 (pp. 182-185), and B-2 (p. 185).

1995   *Issues of Measurement Related to Market Size and Macroprudential Risks in Derivatives Markets.* Basle, Switzerland: Bank for International Settlements.

Bank of England
1990   *Bank of England Quarterly Bulletin* 30(August):352-361. London: The Bank of England.

Basle Committee on Payment and Settlement Systems
1992   *Delivery Versus Payment in Securities Settlement Systems.* (September) Basle, Switzerland: Basle Committee on Payment and Settlement Systems.

Bergsten, C.F., T. Horst, and T.H. Moran
1978   *American Multinationals and American Interests.* Washington, D.C.: The Brookings Institution.

Bierman, Jr., H., L.T. Johnson, and D.S. Peterson
1991   *Hedge Accounting: An Exploratory Study of the Underlying Issues.* Research Report. Norwalk, Conn.: Financial Accounting Foundation.

Bloomstron, M., R.E. Lipsey, and K. Kulchycky
1988   U.S. and Swedish direct investment exports. In R.E. Baldwin, ed., *Trade Policy Issues and Empirical Analysis.* Chicago: University of Chicago Press.

Branscomb, L.M.
1991   The changing global economy. *The Bridge* (Spring):21-33. Washington, D.C.: National Academy of Engineering.

Bryant, R.C.
1980   *Money and Monetary Policy in Interdependent Nations.* Washington, D.C.: The Brookings Institution.

1983   Money and monetary policy. *The Brookings Review* (Spring) 1(3):6-12.

1987   *International Financial Intermediation.* Washington, D.C.: The Brookings Institution.

Bureau of Economic Analysis
1990   *The Balance of Payments of the United States: Concepts, Data Sources and Estimating Procedures.* Washington, D.C.: U.S. Department of Commerce.

1991   U.S. international transactions, fourth quarter and year 1990. *Survey of Current Business* 71(3):34-68. Washington, D.C.: U.S. Department of Commerce.

1992a   *Survey of Current Business* 72(6).

1992b   *Survey of Current Business* 72(9).

1992c   U.S. international transactions, fourth quarter and year 1991. *Survey of Current Business* 72(3):51-74. Washington, D.C.: U.S. Department of Commerce.

1993a   *Survey of Current Business* 73(6).

1993b   U.S. International Transactions, Fourth Quarter and Year 1992. Press release, BEA 93-09, March 16.

1994a   *Survey of Current Business* 74(6).

1994b   *Survey of Current Business* 74(7).

1994c   *U.S. Direct Investment Abroad: Operations of U.S. Parent Companies and Their Foreign Affiliates, Preliminary 1992 Estimates.* Washington, D.C.: U.S. Department of Commerce.

Bureau of Economic Analysis and Bureau of the Census

1992   *Foreign Direct Investment in the United States: Establishment Data for 1987.* Washington, D.C.: Economics and Statistics Administration, U.S. Department of Commerce.

1994   *Foreign Direct Investment in the United States: Establishment Data for Manufacturing, 1991.* Washington, D.C.: U.S. Department of Commerce

Bureau of Labor Statistics

1992   Employment and Wages in Foreign-owned Businesses in the United States. Press release, Washington, D.C.

1993   New Research on Occupations in Foreign-owned Manufacturing Establishments in the United States. Press release, Washington, D.C.

Carson, C.S., and J. Honsa

1990   The United Nations system of national accounts: An introduction. *Survey of Current Business* 70(6):20-30.

Caves, R.E.

1982   *Multinational Enterprise and Economic Analysis.* New York: Cambridge University Press.

Caves, R.E., J.A. Frankel, and R.W. Jones

1990   *World Trade and Payments: An Introduction.* Glenview, Ill.: Scott, Foresman and Company.

Cayton, M.

1992   The TIC Bank-Reported Data: Basic Features and Comparisons with Other Balance of Payments Components. Draft paper prepared for U.S. Department of the Treasury.

Cooper, R.N.

1986   Economic interdependence and the coordination of economic policies. Pp. 1195-1234 in R.W. Jones and P.B. Kenen, eds., *Handbook of International Economics.* New York: Elsevier.

Copeland, M.A.

1941   Economic research in the federal government. *American Economic Review* (September):526.

Corbo, V., and O. Havrylyshyn

1982   Production Technology Differences Between Canadian-owned and Foreign-owned Firms Using Translog-Production Functions. NBER Working Paper No. 981. National Bureau of Economic Research, Cambridge, Mass.

Courtney, W.H., and D.M. Leipziger

1975   Multinational corporations in LDC's: The choice of technology. *Oxford Bulletin of Economic Statistics* 37(4):297-304.

Data Interchange Standards Association, Inc.

1991   *An Introduction to Electronic Data Interchange: American*

National Standards Institute's Accredited Standards Committee X12. Washington, D.C.: Washington Publishing Company.

Eason, R.J.
  1991 Balance of Payments Statistics in the United Kingdom, A Review of Collection and Compilation. (July) Project 17, The Chancellor's Initiative. Chancellor of the Exchequer, London, England.

Eisner, R., and P.J. Pieper
  1990 The world's greatest debtor nation? Pp. 9-32 in *The North American Review of Economics and Finance* 1(1). Cedar Falls, IA.

Encarnation, D.J., and L.T. Wells
  1986 Evaluating foreign investment. In T.H. Moran, ed., *Investing in Development: New Roles for Private Capital?* New Brunswick, N.J.: Transactions Books.

Federal Reserve Bank of New York
  1987-1988 *Quarterly Review* 12(4):6-13.
  1992a *Quarterly Review* 17(1).
  1992b Summary of Results of U.S. Foreign Exchange Market Turnover Survey Conducted in April, 1992, by the Federal Reserve Bank of New York.
  1994 Public Disclosure of Risks Related to Market Activity, New York.

Federal Reserve Board of Governors
  1990 The Federal Reserve in the payments system. *Federal Reserve Bulletin* 76(5):293-298.
  1991 *Federal Reserve Bulletin* 77 (July).
  1992 *Federal Reserve Bulletin* 78 (October).
  1993 *Federal Reserve Bulletin* 79 (January).
  1994 *Federal Reserve Bulletin* 80 (July).

Federal Reserve Board of Governors, Federal Deposit Insurance Corporation, and Office of the Comptroller of the Currency
  1993 *Derivative Product Activities of Commercial Banks.* A joint study conducted in response to questions posed by Senator Riegle on derivative products, January 27, 1993. Washington, D.C.: Federal Reserve Board of Governors.

Feigenberg, A., M. Arvandi, and S. Sundaram
  1993 Hedging Prepayment Risk for Financial Institutions. (March) Salomon Brothers, Inc., New York.

Financial Accounting Standards Board
  1990a Disclosure of Information about Financial Instruments with Off-Balance-Sheet Risk and Financial Instruments with Concentrations of Credit Risk. Statement of Financial Accounting Standards No. 105. (March). Stamford, Conn.
  1990b Discussion memorandum: An analysis of issues related to distinguishing between liability and equity instruments and ac-

counting for instruments with characteristics of both. *Financial Accounting Series* No. 094. Stamford, Conn.

1991a Disclosure about Fair Value of Financial Instruments. Statement of Financial Accounting Standards No. 107. (December). Stamford, Conn.

1991b Discussion memorandum: An analysis of issues related to recognition and measurement of financial instruments. *Financial Accounting Series* No. 109A. Stamford, Conn.

1991c Highlight: FASB's plan for international activities. *Financial Accounting Series* No. 106:6. Stamford, Conn.

1992 Offsetting of Amounts Related to Certain Contracts. Financial Accounting Standards Board Interpretation No. 39. (March). Stamford, Conn.

1994 Disclosure about Derivative Financial Instruments and Fair Value of Financial Instruments. Statement of Financial Accounting Standards No. 119. (October). Stamford, Conn.

Frankel, J.A.
1988 International capital flows and domestic economic policies. In M. Feldstein, ed., *The United States in the World Economy.* Chicago: University of Chicago Press.

Froot, K.A., and J.C. Stein
1989 Exchange Rates and Foreign Direct Investment: An Imperfect Capital Markets Approach. NBER Working Paper No. 2914. National Bureau of Economic Research, Cambridge, Mass.

Gilbert, R.A.
1992 Implications of netting arrangements for bank risk in foreign exchange transactions. *Federal Reserve Bank of St. Louis Quarterly Review* 74(1):3-30.

Graham, E.M., and P.R. Krugman
1991 *Foreign Direct Investment in the United States.* Second edition. Washington, D.C.: Institute for International Economics.

Greenwich Associates
1993 *Big Job Gets Bigger.* Greenwich, Conn.: Greenwich Associates.

Group of Thirty
1989 *Clearance and Settlement Systems in the World's Securities Markets.* New York: Group of Thirty.

1990a *Clearance and Settlement Systems, Status Reports. Spring 1990.* London: Group of Thirty.

1990b *Clearance and Settlement Systems, Status Reports. Year-End 1990.* London: Group of Thirty.

1990c *Conference on Clearance and Settlement Systems.* Presentations to the Group of Thirty, London, March 14. London: Group of Thirty

1993 *Derivatives: Practices and Principles.* Global Study Group. Washington, D.C.: Group of Thirty.

Grubert, H., T. Goodspeed, and D. Wenson
1991   Explaining the Low Taxable Income of Foreign-Controlled Companies in the United States. (November) Unpublished paper, Tax Policy Group in the Office of International Taxation, U.S. Department of the Treasury.

Grubert, H., and J. Mutti
1991   Financial flows versus capital spending: Alternative measures of U.S.-Canadian investment and trade in the analysis of taxes. In P. Hooper and J.D. Richardson, eds., *International Economic Transactions*. Chicago: University of Chicago Press.

Habermann, H., and P. Weiss
1992   Electronic Data Interchange in the United States Statistical System. Paper presented to the Conference on New Techniques and Technologies for Statistics in Bonn, February 24-26.

Hartman, D.
1984   Tax policy and foreign direct investment in the United States. *National Tax Journal* 37(4):475-488.

Helkie, W., and L. Stekler
1987   *Modeling Investment Income and Other Services in the U.S. International Transactions Accounts*. International Finance Discussion Paper No. 319. Washington, D.C.: Federal Reserve Board of Governors.

Hickok, S., and J. Hung
1992   Explaining the persistence of the U.S. trade deficit in the late 1980s. *Federal Reserve Bank of New York Quarterly Review* 16(4):29-46.

Hufbauer, G.C.
1975   The multinational corporation and direct investment. In P.B. Kenen, ed., *International Trade and Finance: Frontiers for Research*. New York: Cambridge University Press.

Institute of International Finance
1994   *A Preliminary Framework for Public Disclosure of Derivatives Activities and Related Credit Exposures*. Washington, D.C.: Institute of International Finance

International Monetary Fund
1987   *Final Report of the Working Party on the Statistical Discrepancy in World Current Account Balances*. Washington, D.C.: International Monetary Fund.
1992a   *Determinants and Systemic Consequences of International Capital Flows*. Washington, D.C.: International Monetary Fund.
1992b   *Report on the Measurement of International Capital Flows*. Washington, D.C.: International Monetary Fund.
1993a   *Balance of Payments Manual*. Fifth Edition. Washington, D.C.: International Monetary Fund.
1993b   *Balance of Payments Statistics Yearbook*. Fifth Edition. Washington, D.C.: International Monetary Fund.

Jones, S.L.
1992 Treasury Data on U.S. International Portfolio Investment Collection Methods and Uses. Paper presented to the Panel on International Capital Transactions, Washington, D.C., April 23, 1992.

J.P. Morgan
1991 Swaps: versatility at controlled risk. *World Financial Markets* (April).

Kester, A.Y., ed.
1992 *Behind the Numbers: U.S. Trade in the World Economy.* Panel on Foreign Trade Statistics, Committee on National Statistics, National Research Council. Washington, D.C.: National Academy Press.

Kindel, S.
1992 The esperanto of documents. *Financial World* 161(14):64-65.

Kindleberger, C.P., and D.B. Audretsch
1983 *The Multinational Corporation in the 1980s.* Cambridge, Mass.: MIT Press.

Kliesen, K.L., and J.A. Tatom
1992 The recent credit crunch: The neglected dimensions. *The Federal Reserve Bank of St. Louis Quarterly Review* 74(5):18-36.

KPMG Peat Marwick, Policy Economics Group
1992 *Review of Internal Revenue Service Statistics on Foreign-Controlled Domestic Corporations in 1983 through 1988.* Paper prepared for the Organization for International Investment. Washington, D.C.: KPMG Peat Marwick.

Krueger, R.C.
1992 Financial Innovations and National Accounts. Paper presented at the 22nd General Conference of the International Association for Research in Income and Wealth. (August) Flims, Switzerland.

Lall, S., and P. Streeten
1977 *Foreign Investment, Transnationals and Developing Countries.* London: Macmillan.

Landefeld, J.S., and A.M. Lawson
1991 Valuation of the U.S. net international investment position. *Survey of Current Business* 71(5):40-49.

Landefeld, J.S., A.M. Lawson, and D.B. Weinberg
1992 Rates of return on direct investment. *Survey of Current Business* 72(9):79-86.

Lary, H.B., and Associates
1943/ *The United States in the World Economy.* Originally pub-
1975 lished by the U.S. Department of Commerce. Westport, Conn.: Greenwood Press.

Lebaube, P.
  1992　EDI and Statistics: A Challenge for Statisticians. Strategy and progress report. EUROSTAT/A1/NT92-32. Luxembourg.
Levy, H., and P.A. Samuelson
  1992　The capital asset pricing model with diverse holding periods. *Management Science* 38(11):1529-1542.
Lewis, C.
  1937　*America's Stake in International Investments.* Washington, D.C.: The Brookings Institution.
Lim, D.
  1977　Do foreign companies pay higher wages than their local counterparts in Malaysian manufacturing? *Journal of Development Economics* 4(1):55-66.
Lintner, J.
  1965　Security price, risk, and maximum gains from diversification. *Journal of Finance* 20(5):587-616.
  1972　Equilibrium in a Random Walk and Lognormal Security Market. Discussion Paper No. 235, July 1972. Harvard Institute of Economic Research, Harvard University, Cambridge, Mass.
Lipsey, R.E.
  1985　Comment. In A. Erdilek, ed., *MNC's as Mutual Invaders: Intra-Industry Direct Foreign Investment.* London and Sydney: Croom Helm.
Lipsey, R.E., and I.B. Kravis
  1987　The competitiveness and comparative advantage of U.S. multinationals, 1957-1984. *Banca Nazionale del Lavoro Quarterly Review* 40(161):147-165.
Lipsey, R.E., I.B. Kravis, and R.A. Roldan
  1982　Do multinational firms adapt factor proportions to relative factor prices? In A.O. Krueger, ed., *Trade and Employment in Developing Countries: Factor Supplies and Substitution.* Chicago: University of Chicago Press.
Lipsey, R.E., and M.Y. Weiss
  1981　Foreign production and exports in manufacturing industries. *The Review of Economics and Statistics* 63(4):488-494.
  1984　Foreign production and exports of individual firms. *The Review of Economics and Statistics* 66(2):304-308.
Lowe, J.H., and R.J. Mataloni, Jr.
  1991　U.S. direct investment abroad: 1989 benchmark survey results. *Survey of Current Business* 71(10):29-55.
Markowitz, H.M.
  1952　Portfolio selection. *Journal of Finance* 6(1):77-91.
Mataloni, R.J., Jr.
  1990a　Capital expenditures by majority-owned foreign affiliates of U.S. companies, 1991. *Survey of Current Business* 70(9):30-36.
  1990b　U.S. multinational companies: Operations in 1988. *Survey of Current Business* 70(6):31-44.

1991   Capital expenditures by majority-owned foreign affiliates of U.S. companies, latest plans for 1991. *Survey of Current Business* 71(3):26-33.

Merton, R.C.
1973   An intertemporal capital asset pricing. *Econometrica* 41(5):867-887.

Morley, S.A., and G.W. Smith
1977   The choice of technology: Multinational firms in Brazil. *Economic Development and Cultural Change* 25(2):239-264.

Musgrave, J.C.
1981   Fixed capital stock in the United States: Revised estimates. *Survey of Current Business* 61(2):57-68.

Musgrave, P.B.
1975   Direct Investment Abroad and the Multinationals: Effects on the United States Economy. Subcommittee on Multinational Corporations, Committee on Foreign Relations, U.S. Senate. Washington, D.C.

Nance, D.R., C.W. Smith, Jr., and C.W. Smithson
1993   On the determinants of corporate hedging. *Journal of Finance* 48(March):267-284.

National Advisory Council on International Monetary and Financial Policies
1990   *International Finance: Annual Report of the Chairman of the National Advisory Council on International Monetary and Financial Policies to the President and to the Congress for Fiscal Year 1990.* Washington, D.C.: National Advisory Council on International Monetary and Financial Policies.

National Association of Business Economists
1991   Business economics. *The Journal of the National Association of Business Economists. Directory Issue.* (March) Cleveland: National Association of Business Economists.

National Institute for Research Advancement
1991   Prospective international capital ownership patterns across the Pacific at the turn of the century. *Research Output* 4(1).

O'Brien, R.
1992   *Global Financial Integration: The End of Geography.* New York: Council on Foreign Relations Press.

Ogata, S., R.N. Cooper, and H. Schulmann
1989   *International Financial Integration: The Policy Challenges. A Task Force Report to the Trilateral Commission.* New York: The Trilateral Commission.

Pickford, S.
1989   *Government Economic Statistics: A Scrutiny Report.* London: Her Majesty's Stationery Office.

Post, M.E.
1992   The evolution of the U.S. commercial paper market since 1980. *Federal Reserve Bulletin* 78(12):879-891.

Rawls, S.W., III, and C.W. Smithson
    1989   The evolution of risk management products. *Journal of Applied Corporate Finance* 1(Winter):18-26.

Ray, E.J.
    1989   The determinants of foreign direct investment in the United States: 1979-1985. In R. Feenstra, ed., *Trade Policies for International Competitiveness.* Chicago: University of Chicago Press.

Reuber, G.L.
    1973   *Private Foreign Investment in Development.* Oxford: Clarendon Press.

Roemer, M., and J.J. Stern
    1975   *The Appraisal of Development Projects.* New York: Praeger.

Samuelson, P.A.
    1969   Lifetime portfolio selection by dynamic stochastic programming. *Review of Economics and Statistics* 51:239-246.

Scarlata, J.G.
    1992   Institutional developments in the globalization of securities and futures markets. *Federal Reserve Bank of St. Louis Review* 74(1):17-30.

Seiler, R.
    1992   The Statistical Recording of Capital Transactions in the Context of Germany's Balance of Payments Statistics. Paper presented to the Panel on International Capital Transactions, Washington, D.C., April 23.

Sharpe, W.F.
    1964   Capital asset prices: A theory of market equilibriums under conditions of risk. *Journal of Finance* 19(September):425-442.

Slemrod, J.
    1990   Tax effects on foreign direct investment in the United States. In A. Razin and J. Slemrod, eds., *Taxation in the Global Economy.* Chicago: University of Chicago Press.

Smith, C.W., Jr., C.W. Smithson, and L.M. Wakeman
    1986   The evolving market for swaps. *Midland Corporate Finance Journal* 3(4):20-32.
    1988   The market for interest rate swaps. *Financial Management* 17(4):34-44.

Smithson, C.W., and D.H. Chew, Jr.
    1992   The uses of hybrid debt in managing corporate risk. *Journal of Applied Corporate Finance* 4(4):79-89.

Standard & Poor's Corporation
    1992   *Register of Corporations, Directors and Executives.* Vol. 1. New York: Standard & Poor's Corporation.

Stekler, L.E.
    1991   The statistical discrepancy in the U.S. international transactions accounts: Sources and suggested remedies. *International*

Finance Discussion Papers. (July) Board of Governors of the Federal Reserve System.

Stekler, L.E., and G.V.G. Stevens
1991 The adequacy of direct investment data. In P. Hooper and J.D. Richardson, eds., *International Economic Transactions: Issues in Measuremnt and Empirical Research.* National Bureau of Economic Research Studies in Income and Wealth Series. Chicago: University of Chicago Press.

Stekler, L.E., and E.M. Truman
1992 The Adequacy of the Data on U.S. International Financial Transactions: A Federal Reserve Perspective. Paper presented to the Panel on International Capital Transactions.

Stevens, G.V.G.
1969 Fixed investment expenditures of foreign manufacturing affiliates of U.S. firms: theoretical models and empirical evidence. *Yale Economic Essays* 9(1):137-198.

1972 Capital mobility and the international firm. In F. Machlup, W. Salant, and L. Tarshis, eds., *The International Mobility and Movement of Capital.* New York: National Bureau of Economic Research.

1974 The determinants of investment. In J.H. Dunning, ed., *Economic Analysis and the Multinational Enterprise.* London: George Allen & Unwin.

Stevens, G.V.G., and R.E. Lipsey
1992 Interactions between domestic and foreign investment. *Journal of International Money and Finance* 11(1):40-62.

Stone-Tice, H., and L.J. Moczar
1986 Foreign transactions in the national income and product accounts: An overview. *Survey of Current Business* 66(11):23-36.

Summers, B.J.
1991 Clearing and payment systems: The role of the central bank. *Federal Reserve Bulletin* 77(2):81-91.

Tavlas, G.S., and Y. Ozeki
1991 The Japanese Yen as an International Currency. Unpublished working paper. International Monetary Fund.

Terrell, Henry S.
1993 U.S. branches and agencies of foreign banks: A new look. *Federal Reserve Bulletin* 79(10):913-928.

Toto, G., and G. Monahan, eds.
1991 *Securities Industry Association 1991 Fact Book.* New York: Securities Industry Association.

Twentieth Century Fund
1991 *Partners in Prosperity.* A report of the Task Force on the International Coordination of National Economic Policies. New York: Priority Press.

Ulan, M., and W.G. Dewald
    1989   *The U.S. Net International Investment Position: The Numbers Are Misstated and Misunderstood.* Washington, D.C.: U.S. Department of State.
United Nations, International Monetary Fund, the World Bank, the Organization of Economic Cooperation and Development, and the Statistics Office of the European Communities
    1993   *System of National Accounts 1993.* New York: United Nations.
U.S. Office of Management and Budget
    1993   *Statistical Programs of the United States Government, Fiscal Year 1993.* Washington, D.C.: U.S. Government Printing Office.
    1994   *Statistical Programs of the United States Government, Fiscal Year 1994.* Washington, D.C.: U.S. Government Printing Office.
U.S. Office of Technology Assessment
    1990   *Trading Around the Clock: Global Securities Markets and Information Technology.* Background paper, OTA-BP-CIT-66. Washington, D.C.: U.S. Government Printing Office.
U.S. Department of the Treasury
    1989   *Report on Foreign Portfolio Investment in the United States as of December 31, 1984.* Office of the Assistant Secretary for International Affairs. Washington, D.C.: U.S. Department of the Treasury.
    1992a   *Outbound Portfolio Investment Survey Interim Report.* Unpublished paper, Office of the Assistant Secretary for Economic Policy. (April) U.S. Department of the Treasury.
Vendrell-Alda, J.L.M.
    1978   *Comparing Foreign Subsidiaries and Domestic Firms: A Research Methodology Applied to Efficiency in Argentine Industry.* New York: Garland.
Vukmanic, F.G., M.R. Czinkota, and D.A. Ricks
    1985   National and international data problems and solutions in the empirical analysis of intra-industry direct foreign investment. In S. Erdilek, ed., *MNC's as Mutual Invaders: Intra-Industry Direct Foreign Investment.* London and Sydney: Croom Helm.
Wheeler, J.E.
    1988   An academic look at transfer pricing in a global economy. *Tax Notes* 40(1):87-96.
Whichard, O.G.
    1981   Trends in the U.S. direct investment position abroad, 1950-79. *Survey of Current Business* 61(2):39-56.
    1989   U.S. multinational companies: Operations in 1987. *Survey of Current Business* 69(6):27-39.

Whichard, O.G., and M.A. Shea
  1985   1982 benchmark survey of U.S. direct investment abroad. *Survey of Current Business* 65(12):37-57.
Willett, T.D., and Wihlborg, C.G.
  1990   International capital flows, the dollar, and U.S. financial policies. In W.S. Haraf and T.D. Willett, eds., *Monetary Policy for a Volatile Global Economy*. Washington, D.C.: The AEI Press.
Yoshikuni, S.
  1992   Compilation of Balance of Payments Data in Japan—With Special Emphasis on the Capital Account. Paper presented to the Panel on International Capital Transactions.
Young, R.A.
  1930   *Handbook of American Underwriting of Foreign Securities*. Washington, D.C.: U.S. Department of Commerce.

Biographical Sketches of Panel Members and Staff

SAM Y. CROSS (*Chair*) is executive in residence at the School of International and Public Affairs at Columbia University. He formerly served as executive vice president of the Federal Reserve Bank of New York, manager for foreign operations of the System Open Market Account for the Federal Reserve System, and U.S. executive director of the International Monetary Fund. He also served in the U.S. Department of the Treasury as special assistant and as Deputy Assistant Secretary for International Monetary and Investment Affairs. He has a B.S. and an M.S. from the University of Tennessee.

STEPHEN H. AXILROD is vice chair of Nikko Securities International, Inc. He previously served as staff director and secretary for the Federal Open Market Committee of the Federal Reserve System and staff director for monetary and financial policy at the Federal Reserve Board. He has also served as U.S. representative on a number of committees of the Organization of Economic Cooperation and Development and the Bank for International Settlements on the subject of international and domestic monetary policy and in advisory positions with the Central Bank of Oman, the Korean Economic Institute, and the Investment Committee of the Japan Society. He has been a regular columnist in the *Japan Economic Journal* and *The American Banker*. He received an A.B. from Harvard University and an M.A. from the University of Chicago.

RICHARD N. COOPER is the Maurits C. Boas professor of international economics at Harvard University. He previously served as Under Secretary for Economic Affairs and Deputy Assistant Secretary for International Monetary Affairs in the U.S. Department of State and as senior staff economist for the Council of Economic Advisers. He was also provost and professor of international economics at Yale University and chair of the Federal Reserve Bank of Boston. He has served as chair of the advisory committee and director of the Institute for International Economics. He serves on the board of directors of a number of corporations and is a member of the Trilateral Commission and the Council on Foreign Relations. He has published over 300 articles and books. He received an A.B. from Oberlin College, an M.Sc. (Econ.) from the London School of Economics, and a Ph.D. from Harvard University.

DAVID T. DEVLIN is a vice president and deputy senior adviser for international operations of Citibank. Previously, he served as chief of operations in setting up the Institute of International Finance in Washington, which monitors economic developments in some 50 countries for major international banks. Prior to joining Citibank, he was associate director for international economics at the Bureau of Economic Analysis of the U.S. Department of Commerce and chief of the Balance of Payments Division of the Federal Reserve Bank of New York. He has a Ph.D. in economics from Columbia University.

RIMMER DE VRIES is a managing director and senior economic adviser at Morgan Guaranty Trust Co. Previously, he was an economist at the Federal Reserve Bank of New York. He served as a member of the Competitiveness Commission during the Reagan administration and a member of the Balance of Payments Commission during the Ford administration. He is a member of the Council on Foreign Relations and a member of the Advisory Committee of the Institute of International Economics. He received an A.B. from the Netherlands School of Economics and an M.A. and a Ph.D. from Ohio State University.

JEFFREY A. FRANKEL is a professor of economics at the University of California, Berkeley, and director of the university's Center for International and Development Economics Research. He is also a research associate and director for international finance and macroeconomics at the National Bureau of Economic Research. He is currently a senior fellow at the Institute for International Economics. He was formerly senior staff economist at the Council of Economic Advisers; a visiting professor at Harvard University; and a visiting scholar at the International Monetary Fund, the Federal Reserve Board, and the Federal Reserve Bank of San Francisco. He is the author of numerous books and articles. He has a Ph.D. from the Massachusetts Institute of Technology.

ROBERT F. GEMMILL is an independent economic consultant. He has served on a number of international missions, providing technical assistance and advice to central banks and other institutions. Formerly, he was staff advisor and associate director of the Division of International Finance of the Federal Reserve Board. He has worked on banking issues for several committees of the Bank for International Settlements. He received a Ph.D. from Harvard University.

EDWARD I. GEORGE is a professor of statistics in the Department of Management Science and Information Systems at the University of Texas at Austin. Previously, he was an associate professor of statistics in the Graduate School of Business at the University of Chicago. He is a member of the American Statistical Association, the Institute of Mathematical Statistics, and the Royal Statistical Society. He is currently an associate editor of the *Journal of the American Statistical Association*. He holds an A.B. in mathematics from Cornell University, an M.S. in applied mathematics and statistics from the State University of New York at Stony Brook, and a Ph.D. in statistics from Stanford University.

JOHN G. HEIMANN is chair of the Global Financial Institutions Group at Merrill Lynch and Co. and a member of the Office of the Chairman. Previously, he was deputy chair of A.G. Becker Paribas, Inc., Paribas International; senior vice president and director of E.M. Warburg, Pincus, and Co., Inc.; and vice president of Smith Barney and Co. He has also held positions as U.S. Comptroller of the Currency, New York State Commissioner of Housing and Community Renewal, and New York State Superintendent of Banks. He is a director of Merrill Lynch National Financial Bank, a member and the treasurer of the Group of Thirty, and senior advisor to the Board of River Bank America, New York. He has a B.A. in economics from Syracuse University.

PETER B. KENEN is a professor of economics and international finance at Princeton University. Previously, he taught at Columbia University. He is the author of numerous books and articles, including *The International Economy* and *The EMU After Masstricht*. He is a member of the advisory committee of the Institute for International Economics, the steering committee of the Group of Thirty, the executive committee of the Bretton Woods Committee, and the Council on Foreign Relations. He received an A.B. from Columbia University and an M.A. and a Ph.D. from Harvard University.

ANNE Y. KESTER, who served as study director of the panel and an earlier Panel on Foreign Trade Statistics, is currently affiliated with the International Monetary Fund. Previously, she was assistant director of the U.S. General Accounting Office and a research associate at the Graduate School of Business Administration at Harvard University. She has also held positions as a senior management consultant at a Harvard-affiliated consulting firm and as an economic consultant to several federal agencies, research institutions, and various corporations. She received an M.A. in public policy and administration and a Ph.D. in economics from the University of Wisconsin-Madison.

LAWRENCE R. KLEIN is Benjamin Franklin professor of economics, emeritus, at the University of Pennsylvania. He is a member of the National Academy of Sciences and a Nobel Laureate for Economics. He has served as director, W.P. Carey & Co, New York; consultant, United Nations; cochair, Economists Against the Arms Race; member, advisory panel, Congressional Budget Office; and a visiting professor at Ritsumeikan University in Kyoto and Reitaku University in Tokyo, Japan. He has also been a columnist for *Il Messagero*, Rome; *Shinano Mainichi Shimbun*, Japan; and *Seoul Kyungje Shinmun*, Republic of Korea. He received a B.A. from the University of California, Berkeley, and a Ph.D. from the Massachusetts Institute of Technology.

SAMUEL PIZER is a long-time consultant to the International Monetary Fund, having served at various times as the director of the technical staff and member of the Working Party on the Discrepancy in the World Current Account, consultant to the managing director, and consultant to the Working Party on the Measurement of International Capital Flows. Previously, he was senior adviser and senior economist for the Division of International

Finance at the Federal Reserve Board, and he worked at the U.S. Department of Commerce and served as assistant chief of the Balance of Payments Division. He has a B.A. and an M.A. from George Washington University.

ROBERT L. SAMMONS is an independent consultant, principally to U.S. government agencies, including the Departments of the Treasury, State, and Commerce and the Agency for International Development, but also to the International Monetary Fund and the Center for Strategic and International Studies. Formerly, he was director of the Monetary Division of the Department of Economics and Statistics of the Organization for Economic Cooperation and Development, associate director of the Division of International Finance of the Board of Governors of the Federal Reserve System, statistical consultant to the Puerto Rico Planning Board, and chief of the Balance-of-Payments Division at the U.S. Department of Commerce. He holds an A.B. and an M.A. from George Washington University and an M.A. in public administration from Harvard University.

COURTENAY M. SLATER is president of Slater Hall, Inc., a data preparation and analysis firm. Before founding Slater Hall, Inc., she served as chief economist for the U.S. Department of Commerce, senior economist with the Joint Economic Committee of Congress, and senior economist with the Council of Economic Advisers. She is a fellow of the American Statistical Association and has served as chair of the Council of Professional Associations on Federal Statistics. She has also served on the Committee on National Statistics of the National Research Council. She holds a B.A. from Oberlin College and a Ph.D. in economics from American University.

ROBERT SOLOMON is a guest scholar at the Brookings Institution. He previously served as director of the Division of International Finance at the Federal Reserve Board and senior staff economist of the Council of Economic Advisers. He is a member of the Council on Foreign Relations and the editor of *The International Economic Letter*. He received a B.A. from the University of Michigan and an M.A. and a Ph.D. from Harvard University.

J. MICHAEL STEELE is C.F. Koo professor of statistics at the Wharton School of the University of Pennsylvania. Previously, he was a professor at Stanford University and Princeton University.

He is a fellow of the American Statistical Association and the Institute of Mathematical Statistics. He has served on several panels at the National Research Council and on the advisory committee of the American Statistical Association to the Bureau of the Census. He was the founding editor of the *Annals of Applied Probability*. He received a Ph.D. from Stanford University.

NANCY H. TEETERS is a former governor of the Federal Reserve Board and former vice president of economics and chief economist at the IBM Corporation. Earlier, she served as assistant director and chief economist of the Committee on Budget of the U.S. House of Representatives, senior specialist at the Congressional Research Service of the Library of Congress, economist at the U.S. Bureau of the Budget, staff of the Council of Economic Advisers, and staff economist for the Government Financial Section of the Federal Reserve System Board of Governors. She has also been an instructor at the University of Michigan and the University of Maryland. Currently, she serves on corporate boards for Prudential Mutual Funds and Inland Steel Industries and is a member of the Council on Foreign Relations. She received an A.B. from Oberlin College and an M.A. from the University of Michigan.

LAWRENCE A. THIBODEAU is a partner at Price Waterhouse and directs the statistical practice within the Dispute Analysis and Corporate Recovery Group. He is a member of the American Association for the Advancement of Science and the American Statistical Association. He previously served as associate professional lecturer in statistics at George Washington University, director of the Statistical and Quantitative Services Division at Applied Management Sciences, and assistant professor at Harvard University. He received a Ph.D. in statistics from the University of Minnesota.

H. DAVID WILLEY is an advisor to Morgan Stanley & Co., Inc. Formerly, he served as vice president of the Federal Reserve Bank of New York and director of the Research and Policy Division of the Office of Foreign Direct Investment in the U.S. Department of Commerce. He has also served as a slate analyst at ESSO International, Inc., and as a foreign service officer and analyst for the U.S. government. He received a B.A. from Colgate University, an M.A. from the Fletcher School of Law and Diplomacy, and a Ph.D. from Columbia University.

Index

A

Accounting systems
  and derivatives, 121, 123-124, 127, 129-131
  regulatory versus generally accepted, 101, 109, 113, 129-131, 171, 175, 177
  of U.S. government agencies, 72, 93-95
Accuracy of data, 21, 73, 74, 75, 89, 179
  government transactions, 94, 95
  securities transactions, 84, 168-170
Acquisitions and mergers, 25, 29, 59
Adequacy of data, *see* Data gaps and needs
Agency for International Development (AID), 70, 72
American National Standards Institution (ANSI), 144, 148
Annual Statistical Digest, 133
Assets, *see* Bank deposits; Capital flows and mobility; Claims and liabilities; International investment position; Loans and lending activity; Off-balance-sheet transactions; Securitization of assets; Valuation of assets

B

Automated systems
  accounting, 101, 109, 136-137, 171, 174
  filing and record-keeping, 109, 136-137, 144-145, 165, 166, 174
  trading execution, 26-27

B forms, 8, 64, 67, 68, 70, 89, 96-98, 113, 170-172, 174
Bahamas, U.S. banks in, 91
Balance-of-payments accounts, 3, 7, 8, 38, 43-49, 50-51
  electronic data transfers, 15-16, 144-149
  errors and omissions, 46, 158, 160, 161, 179
  Germany, 160-161
  Japan, 158, 161, 162
  nonbank transactions in, 90-91
  statistical discrepancies in, 8, 9, 39, 42, 45-46, 49, 52, 161
  U.K., 153-154, 161-162
  see also Capital accounts; Current accounts; External debt
Balance of Payments Manual, 10, 58, 89-90, 127, 128, 134